THE POWER OF THE SOCRATIC CLASSROOM

Students.
Questions.
Dialogue.
Learning.

CHARLES AMES FISCHER

The Power of the Socratic Classroom
Students. Questions. Dialogue. Learning.
by Charles Ames Fischer

Published by

ISBN: 978-1-940107-02-8 (Paper)
ISBN: 978-1-940107-03-5 (eBook)
LCCN: 2018907765

Editing: Peggie Ireland, Barb Wilson
Indexing: John Maling
Book Design: Nick Zelinger, NZGraphics.com
Consulting: Judith Briles, the Book Shepherd

Education | Curriculum & Instruction | Education Administration

First Edition

Published in the United States of America

To Louise and Neil Stilphen and Sparhawk School
for making this incredible journey possible.

To all of my amazing K-12 students and families
for making this book possible.

Contents

Foreword

Charles Fischer's *The Power of the Socratic Classroom* is an unprecedented resource for classroom educators interested in developing a serious Socratic environment in their classrooms.

In some respects, leading a Socratic dialogue in a classroom is extremely simple. Eva Brann, a revered tutor at St. John's College, where all classes are variations on Socratic Seminars, states:

> ... once we have explained that a seminar has two leaders, that it begins with a question, that students must have the assigned text in mind and the book on the table, that address is formal and conversation responsive, that all should participate and support their opinions with argument—when that has been said, all has been said. There is no further method. The rest develops as living conversation.
> ~Brann, "Statement on Educational Policy," 1991

But Brann is teaching at a college at which all students have deliberately chosen to attend. All courses are Socratic (either Socratic Seminars or "tutorials," which are largely Socratic in format). In order to create "living conversation" in a school classroom, it is helpful to have a large repertoire of techniques and strategies in order to create classroom cultures in which living intellectual conversations become the norm.

Many people, including many educators, assume that serious intellectual dialogue is really only possible in some classrooms, perhaps with gifted students, or in an AP Literature course. What some of us have discovered, however, is that with enough artistry, experience, and persistence, almost any group of students anywhere can learn how to engage in serious intellectual dialogue—even classrooms that seem initially hostile or indifferent. But the key clause is "with enough artistry, experience, and persistence."

Experienced Socratic practitioners gradually develop a very large repertoire of strategies for engaging very diverse arrays of students. What does a teacher do if a class is silent? What if the students are constantly talking over each other? What if some students are dominating the discussion all the time? What if students don't listen to each other's statements? What should be done if students are not focused on the text at hand? Fischer provides not merely answers to these questions, but an entire analysis of how one creates a consistent Socratic classroom in which these less-than-ideal behaviors gradually take place less frequently and higher quality intellectual dialogue begins to take place more consistently.

Moreover, Fischer has adapted this approach to the constraints of K-12 school teaching. How does one fit Socratic dialogue into the curriculum and evaluation constraints and classroom sizes typical of schools?

Finally, some teachers might look at the lengthy set of techniques, tools, and explanations provided herein and wonder, "Why bother?" Why not take the path of least resistance and teach in a more traditional fashion?

The simple answer to this question is the joy of engaging students in authentic intellectual dialogue. Those of us who have developed the skills needed to create Socratic environments even in the most challenging classrooms do so because it is extremely rewarding. Many educators chose this profession because they love learning, and they love working with young people. Developing a classroom Socratic practice allows educators themselves to learn endlessly by exploring the ideas of their students. Doing so creates a form of community in the classroom over time that is socially and emotionally rewarding to students and educators alike.

I'm grateful that Fischer has provided such a comprehensive resource for those who would like to continue learning and developing community in their classrooms. Our schools need this now more than ever.

Michael Strong
Author, *The Habit of Thought: From Socratic Seminars to Socratic Practice*
Founder, The Academy of Thought and Industry

Preface

Never doubt that a small group of thoughtful, committed citizens can change the world. Indeed, it is the only thing that ever has.
~ Margaret Mead

The Power of the Socratic Classroom was written from my tremendous passion for helping students and teachers develop thinking skills through the most powerful method I have ever seen: Socratic Seminar. As we move into the future, these thinking skills become increasingly important as we try to prepare students for life-changing products that haven't yet been invented and jobs that don't yet exist.

Chapters 1 and 2 introduce and explain why Socratic Seminars are an essential part of a 21st-century education. Chapter 3 explains the basic components and is a great place for a beginning teacher to start. Chapters 4 to 10 then go into considerable detail about the components of Socratic Seminar using my 20 years of experience: Pre-Seminar (chapter 4), The Text (chapter 5), Questions (chapter 6), The Students (chapter 7), The Facilitator (chapter 8), and Post-Seminar (chapter 9). Chapter 10 focuses on the three aspects of evaluation: tracking, assessment, and grading. Chapter 11 focuses on active listening, something rarely taught in school even though students listen a significant portion of any school day. Chapter 12 puts all the pieces together with a sample seminar plan. Chapter 13 then answers some frequently asked questions.

Enjoy!

Charles Fischer 2018

Why Socratic Seminar?

Education is not preparation for life; education is life itself.
~ John Dewey

---

*Since I started Socratic Seminar at the beginning of this year,
I think of everything I see, read, hear, and feel differently than
I did before. I generate questions and mentally "annotate"
everything in life, semiconsciously. For example, driving around
downtown today, I recall asking myself questions such as,
"Why are traffic lights red, yellow, and green, for the colors have
no apparent relation to each other (if it were, say, red, yellow
and blue, I would understand because they are primary colors,
but why red, yellow and green)?" and "Is it a coincidence that
most 'Yard Sale' signs are bright pink?" and just now, I asked
myself if it is significant that most of the questions I can
remember from earlier today are color-oriented.*

~ RP (grade 6)

WE ARE IN an age of information. Look around and you will see people on their phones checking sports scores and stats while watching a game. People waiting for busses can access an entire library of books on a single tablet. Type in a Google search for *critical thinking* and in under a second, millions of results are at your fingertips (even more for *creative thinking*). When we include Wi-Fi and satellite signals, text messages, bluetooth, cell phone calls, radio waves and more, then we are literally living in an ocean of digital signals and information.

In this Information Age, thinking skills are definitely growing in importance. Before the advent of the internet, information was a valuable resource, especially if it was collected together into a single, well-educated person. Now, however, more information than anyone could use in several lifetimes is freely available—and not just at the public library. Now even ten-year-olds carry smart devices and can access the internet with a voice command.

What is now much more important for contemporary students is what they are able to do with all of this information. For example:

- Can they find reliable sources?

- Can they organize information into more complex forms?

- Can they synthesize multiple perspectives to create informed opinions?

- Can they reframe issues in order to generate new and innovative ideas?

- Will these new ideas have any value?

- Can they create innovative solutions to our current ecological or social problems?

- Can they work collaboratively with people from different cultures to think through unforeseen future problems and create practical solutions?

For students to be successful with these challenges, they need to be taught concrete skills and have time to practice those skills in a safe or brave environment. Students need to be challenged in a collaborative "laboratory of learning" where they can courageously take risks and offer their most innovative ideas, confident that their peers have the creative space to elaborate and improve upon those ideas. Collaborating in powerful ways, these students go beyond traditional information and patterns to ask previously unasked questions. In short, these students could use a Socratic classroom.

Socratic Seminar is a structured classroom practice and philosophy that promotes critical and creative thinking, intellectual curiosity, collaboration, and scholarly habits of mind.

For years, education leaders have been talking and writing about the thinking skills that students will need in this Information Age. Whether these are Dr. Tony Wagner's seven skills for the future (the first is critical thinking and problem-solving) or the fourteen "Best Practices" from Zemelman, Daniels, and Hyde, or the focus on creativity from Sir Ken Robinson, Socratic Seminar is always a strong match for students to practice and hone the entire range of 21st-century thinking skills.

A recent example appeared in a December 20, 2017 *Washington Post* article by Valerie Strauss entitled "The surprising thing Google learned about its employees—and what it means for today's students." Strauss writes:

> The seven top characteristics of success at Google are all soft skills: being a good coach; communicating and listening well; possessing insights into others (including others different values and points of view); having empathy toward and being supportive of one's colleagues; being a good critical thinker and problem solver; and being able to make connections across complex ideas.

All of these skills are modeled for students or directly practiced by them during Socratic Seminar. Of note, being a good coach can and should be modeled by an effective teacher, who essentially demonstrates and encourages the other characteristics in order to achieve the best group results. The last characteristic is essentially the goal of a good seminar, where students make connections across complex ideas. Even in such a STEM environment such as Google, Strauss notes: "Those traits sound more like what one gains as an English or theater major than as a programmer." Obviously, if we want our students to succeed into the unknown future, they will need to practice these skills in Socratic classrooms.

> **Participants in Socratic Seminar engage in *dialogue*, which differs from both *debate* and *discussion*.**

Socratic Seminar Is Dialogue

Socratic Seminar is a structured classroom practice and philosophy that promotes critical and creative thinking, intellectual curiosity, collaboration, and scholarly habits of mind. The main goal of Socratic Seminar is to build deep conceptual understandings of texts and ideas, where the word "text" is used loosely to refer to a piece of writing, visual art, music, or movement. In seminars, the teacher shifts his or her role to that of facilitator or questioner, so that the students can move from passively receiving knowledge to actively constructing meaning and understanding. They build on others' ideas, cite the text, ask questions and voice their own opinions. With consistent practice, the students become self-sufficient but together they can tackle even the most challenging texts.

> **The goal of a Socratic Seminar is to engage the entire group to explore truth, to pull away from the battle of opinions and rise up above the fog, and see what a text is really trying to say.**

Participants in Socratic Seminar engage in *dialogue*, which differs from both *discussion* and *debate*. Examining the roots of the words themselves is revealing. *Discuss* and *discussion* both come from roots meaning "to dash to pieces or agitate" (think of the word concussion). Debate comes from the notion of "fighting, quarreling or even beating." *Dialogue*, however, has its roots in the ideas of "speaking across" and "to collect and gather." Of the three, *dialogue* is clearly the most cooperative and collaborative.

Discussions can look and feel very similar to dialogues, but there are important differences that are not easily noticeable. A main difference is that discussions typically have a desired outcome and are characterized by the teacher or other power figure being the gatekeeper or endorser of ideas. Watch a classroom discussion, and many times, the teacher speaks nearly every other time—known sometimes as the Initiation, Response, Evaluation (IRE) model. The goal of a discussion is often to broaden a topic, exchange opinions, review previous concepts, or partly engage students by soliciting their ideas. Discussions are great for reviewing for tests, eliciting opinions, sharing, hearing other viewpoints, and creating interest.

Debates, characterized by two oppositional sides, create competitive environments. Each side attempts to win by proving their views and disproving the views of the opposition. The goal of a good debater is often to manipulate others into agreement. Debates can be combative and sometimes feel as though both sides just want to tear the other down instead of building up understandings. Debates are primarily useful for critical thinking, data analysis, expanding research skills, synthesizing information, and improving public speaking skills. In a debate we might ask to hear the *other side*, but in Socratic Seminar we want to ask about *all sides*—and even generate new sides.

> ***Dialogue is shared exploration towards greater understanding, connection, or possibility.***
>
> **~ Tom Atlee**

Dialogue is characterized by a powerful cooperative atmosphere, where all participants work together to form better, stronger, shared understandings. Listen to a dialogue and the goal is clearly to deepen a topic, extend understandings, and create and test new ideas. Watch a Socratic Seminar and the teacher may even appear to be an ordinary, equal participant. Even if a participant emerges from Socratic Seminar with the same opinion as when he or she entered, it will be strengthened and enlarged through the inquiry process. This is not just opinion-swapping.

Socratic Seminars *require* proof. They *demand* evidence. They *call* for logic. The goal of a Socratic Seminar is to engage the entire group to explore truth, to pull away from the battle of opinions and rise up above the fog, and see what a text is really trying to say; to see what is behind the standard words that one might read; to elevate as a group. One way I think of differentiating a seminar from a discussion: A discussion is the sum of its parts, whereas a Socratic Seminar is the whole—the whole being greater than the sum of its parts.

The best way I know how to communicate these subtle differences to participants is to create a visual experience. Give each member of the seminar group two puzzle pieces or two Lego blocks. These blocks represent their opinions and ideas. To demonstrate a discussion, have the students show each other the pieces or blocks, have them swap a few, and perhaps have them link some together. For debate, they could cluster themselves together to argue the pros of their particular pieces and the cons of others. Notice at the end that they haven't built much together. To demonstrate a Socratic Seminar, have the participants share their pieces together. Give them cooperative time to build a Lego tower or to connect the puzzle pieces. Notice at the end the participants will have achieved what was not possible as a collective of individuals.

To summarize: A Socratic Seminar is an organic effort where the authority and the power is held by the entire group. It is not dominated by the teacher or any individuals. A seminar demonstrates that which a group can achieve beyond the individual. When observing a Socratic Seminar, there should be a strong *espirit de corps*—tangible cooperation, not competition. There should be a sense that students are challenging each other, not to be competitive, not to be egotistical, not to impress their peers, but in order to climb the ladder of understanding together as a group.

Harold Saunders, author of *A Public Peace Process*, put it this way:

> Dialogue is a process of genuine interaction through which human beings listen to each other deeply enough to be changed by what they learn. Each makes a serious effort to take others' concerns into her or his own picture, even when disagreement persists. No participant gives up her or his identity, but each recognizes enough of the other's valid human claims that he or she will act differently toward the other.

Brief History in the Socratic Timeline

The term Socratic Seminar derives its name from the ancient Greek philosopher Socrates, whom we know primarily through Plato's *Dialogues*. However, the seminar format described in this book should not be confused with the general questioning techniques known collectively as "Socratic Method" that are used in many contexts, ranging from law schools, to philosophy courses, to book clubs—mainly because not everyone can agree on what exactly the "Socratic Method" is or how it is supposed to be implemented.

> **Socratic Seminar facilitators must always be in service to the needs of their students, to help them see, appreciate, and elaborate upon *their own* ideas.**

For example, the first thing that most people associate with Socrates is that he was the "guy who asked lots of questions." This simplified connection is problematic because sometimes people only associate the general "Socratic Method" with asking questions. Many teachers claim that they are Socratic simply because they ask a lot of questions, yet they lack the specific norms, structures, and procedures associated with Socratic Seminar.

Asking questions is certainly important in Socratic Seminar, but there are two other concepts associated with Socrates that are as important: his idea that he was an intellectual midwife and his claim that he didn't know anything. Without these two other fundamental pieces, teachers are not facilitating Socratic Seminars to their fullest potential. As a quick example of the first, teachers who ask *leading* questions—questions with the answer implied in them—are not going to midwife independent thinking in their students. The same is true of a teacher who "knows everything" and purposefully funnels a class discussion into a pre-conceived agenda.

Socrates claimed that he didn't know anything. He did not walk around as a know-it-all dispensing information. He "didn't know anything," so his students couldn't passively receive knowledge from him, for example, in the form of an informative lecture. Perhaps this is why he referred to himself as a midwife. He intended to help his students develop *their* ideas and would have been, I suspect, more interested in the process and development of ideas that have value.

Socratic Seminar facilitators must always be in service to the needs of their students, to help them see, appreciate, and elaborate upon *their own* ideas. The bottom line: *Are the questions serving the students' interests or the teacher's?* So in addition to asking questions, a Socratic Seminar facilitator must transition away from the role of know-it-all with an agenda and instead focus on the process and development of students' ideas.

According to Michael Strong, author of *The Habit of Thought*, the term "Socratic Seminar" was first used by Scott Buchanan in 1937 and likely evolved from the "Great Books" movement associated with Alexander Meiklejohn at Amherst College, John Erskine at Columbia University and others at the University of Virginia. Socratic Seminar then developed as a more specific teaching strategy through organizations such as St. John's College, The University of Chicago, The Great Books Foundation, the National Paideia Center and others. Practitioners like Strong and Matt Copeland, author of *Socratic Circles*, trace the popularity of Socratic Seminar to Mortimer Adler's *Paideia Proposal.*

Today, Socratic Seminars have various names based on variations of procedure, philosophy and implementation, but many of them would look and feel similar in the classroom: Socratic Circles, Touchstones® Discussions, Paideia Seminars, Shared Inquiry™ Discussions, Spider Web Discussions™, Socrates Cafés, and Harkness Method, to name the most prevalent.

> In Socratic Seminar, I have learned that everything has a deeper meaning than what you see. Socratic Seminar has really opened locked doors for me, doors that lead into worlds of thoughts, consideration and symbolic meaning ... doors I never knew I had. ~ IB (grade 7)

Student Benefits

Some part of the curriculum of every school must give students opportunities to wrestle with big ideas and issues in deep and meaningful ways. When students engage in such classes, they develop the critical thinking skills of analysis to cleave through bias and appreciate differing viewpoints. They develop the creative thinking skills to generate new ideas that have value. Through close reading, or text archaeology, the students build thinking skills applicable to all of their other subjects and studies. Socratic Seminar is the perfect classroom technique or tool for doing all of these, no matter what age or subject area.

Like most techniques, Socratic Seminar is designed for specific purposes, namely developing academic and social skills. Because seminars involve genuine conversations where students do most of the talking, the list includes better active listening skills, developing courage, clearer speaking skills and more complete interpersonal skills. Because of the depth of inquiry and the number of viewpoints involved, students also develop stronger critical and creative thinking skills, gain practice with close reading strategies, and become more open to other viewpoints. As a constructivist approach where students develop their own understandings, learning how to learn is perhaps the most important benefit of all.

> **When students are engaged in their own learning, when they are creating their own meanings and making connections to their own lives, they will *enjoy* learning.**

There are many skills that students practice and develop in such a collaborative environment. Howard Zeiderman from the Touchstones Discussion Project, for example, adds: admitting when you are wrong, learning from and teaching others, and becoming aware of how others see you. Michael Strong, author of *The Habit of Thought*, adds: taking ideas seriously, sensitivity and politeness, integrity and honesty, willingness to accept criticism, and responsibility and initiative. Matt Copeland includes several others: critical reflection, improved writing skills, conflict resolution, love of reading, and community-building. Alexis Wiggins, author of *The Best Class You Never Taught*, also includes developing empathy, better homework completion, and improved self-assessment.

Socratic Seminars produce active instead of passive learning. Many students are passive learners who expect to be spoon-fed. They are content to sit back and let someone else do the thinking work. In a typical class discussion, for example, there are always those students who are willing to drift through forty-five minutes without participating. Unless specifically called upon, those students will not engage their minds. When seminar facilitators transition to the more seemingly *passive* role of facilitator, the students will be forced into more *active* roles. Some seminar facilitators take this idea seriously by sitting outside of the dialogue circle and not participating, literally forcing the students to take ownership of the process.

> **Numerous students over the years have told me that Socratic Seminar was their favorite class activity.**

At some point in a seminar, it is common to hear a couple of students say, "My brain hurts!" This is because they are engaging their minds in heavy thinking work, and many of them are just not used to it. Working the brain, though, is a lot like exercising a muscle—it's hard at first, and then it gets easier. This active engagement will cause students to internalize information and relate to it on a strong, personal level. Because students will constantly be required to substantiate their ideas, they will constantly be searching their prior knowledge and experiences to connect the past to the present. In other words, they will be creating meaning.

When students are engaged in their own learning, when they are creating their own meanings and making connections to their own lives, they will *enjoy* learning—and often school as a whole. As Michael Strong writes: "At present, students experience school as a situation in which they try to incorporate someone else's ideas into their existing understanding by means of memory. This is hard and tedious, and for some students, implicitly humiliating work. As individuals construct their own understanding, instead of accepting the understandings provided by authorities, they find themselves in dialogue with all texts, all ideas, all experience, all of reality. This is empowering, exciting, invigorating work."

We sat in a circle at the edge of the field with our books open to the wind. The smell of freshly cut grass floated on the June air like a smile. The hiking trails to parts unknown were forgotten. The canoes and paddleboats sat unused by the waterfront. The playground balls and Frisbees, the tetherball court, and even the arcade were lonely and quiet. We had worked hard to raise money to come to this campground for a week, but it 'would have to wait, for my students had chosen to continue our Socratic Seminar.

Numerous students over the years have told me that Socratic Seminar was their favorite class activity. One year a group even got together and *wanted* more Socratic Seminars, so we started a weekly after-school Philosophy Club. They *wanted* two more hours of grueling thought work. When I took my first middle school class camping for a week, they actually chose Socratic Seminar as one of the activities that they scheduled. We continued reading, analyzing, and dialoguing about George Orwell's *Animal Farm* even though we were at a campground with dozens of amazing outdoor activities surrounding us!

Seminars promote acceptance of and respect for others and their viewpoints. When students see that different conclusions can be drawn and substantiated from the same text, when they see that there's not even agreement about what a word means, they see that the world is not simply black and white, right and wrong. In a safe, cooperative environment, they'll begin to see that context and upbringing, purpose and intent are all important parts of establishing a viewpoint. Equipped with the tools of inquiry and analysis, they'll appreciate that things are not as simple as they first appear.

Many students do not have a lot of opportunities to truly wrestle with great ideas, to engage in meaningful thought experiments through productive struggle. Socratic Seminars require participants to ask questions, to hold ideas up to the light of truth and see what is revealed. Developing curiosity and wonder *as a habit* will enable them to investigate nearly anything, and may even help level the educational playing field. Daisy Yuhas, author of the article "Piqued: The Case for Curiosity," notes recent studies are suggesting that highly curious students learn better and that students from lower socioeconomic backgrounds with a strong thirst for knowledge are performing as well as those from affluent homes.

> I learned how to annotate and look past words on a page to find an inner, widened meaning of silent poetry that secretly lurks within every student's soul. Advice I would give to future students is to widen their horizons, think outside the box, and act as different or weird as possible when creating questions and annotations.
> ~ AP (grade 6)

Summing Up

1. Students need "soft skills" for the unknown future.
2. Socratic Seminar is dialogue, not discussion or debate.
3. Socrates asked questions, was an "intellectual midwife" and claimed he didn't know anything.
4. Student benefits of a Socratic classroom include:
   - Active and engaged learning.
   - Practicing critical and creative thinking.
   - Close reading and annotation skills.
   - Developing curiosity and wonder.
   - Admitting when you're wrong.

- Learning from and teaching others.
- Awareness of how others see you.
- Taking ideas seriously.
- Sensitivity and politeness.
- Integrity and honesty.
- Willingness to accept criticism.
- Responsibility and initiative.
- Critical reflection.
- Improved writing skills.
- Conflict resolution skills.
- Love of reading.
- Community-building and belonging.
- Developing empathy.
- Better homework completion.
- Developing courage.
- Improved self-assessment.

Your Next Steps

- Learn more about Dr. Tony Wagner and the seven skills students need for their future.

- Watch Sir Ken Robinson's amazing TED Talks.

- Compare and contrast discussion, dialogue, and debate.

- Investigate places in your curriculum where you could use Socratic Seminar.

- Consider using Socratic Seminar for advisory periods, staff meetings, professional development, think tanks, and for social justice conversations.

- Explore the many variations of Socratic Seminar: Socratic Circles, Touchstones Discussions, Paideia Seminars, Shared Inquiry, Socrates Cafés, Spider Web Discussions, and Harkness Method.

- Reflect on how you and your school actually teach "soft skills." Is there a curriculum? Is there a scope and sequence?

- Read Plato's accounts of Socrates. Why do you think we still read about Socrates thousands of years later? What was important about what he said or did?

- What are the differences between communicating through social media and face-to-face interactions?

2

Best Practices

Dialogue is a conversation in which people think together in relationship. Thinking together implies that you no longer take your own position as final. You relax your grip on certainty and listen to the possibilities that result from being in a relationship with others—possibilities that might not otherwise have occurred.

~ Bill Isaacs

Facilitator Benefits

In a Socratic classroom, a teacher transitions to the role of facilitator, questioner, observer, and especially learner. Therefore, teachers enjoy many of the same benefits as the students. In fact, if all goes well, teachers learn more from a good seminar than the students. By listening and observing, tracking and making notes, teachers will get to know and understand their students better, will get to hear new and exciting insights from shy students, and they can then offer praise and encouragement to certain students who might otherwise never get any.

As facilitators, teachers can learn how to release responsibility by listening and allowing the students to do most of the talking. They will observe and learn from the students, see the dynamics that are occurring, and track and code progress. They can diagnostically watch shy students, troubled students, and opinion bullies. They can craft questions and create goals to help challenge them as individuals. This observation time will become an incredible resource—especially for writing report card comments or narratives.

Many teachers and researchers talk about reflective practice, and how important it is, but the reality is that teachers are extremely busy. A teacher's "free time" is often a matter of correcting papers and tests, wolfing down lunch, attending to duties, making copies, and preparing for the next class period. There is often little or no time to reflect on pedagogy, not to mention on a detailed basis for each student. That vital reflection time can be built into the school day during seminar.

Adopting the role of facilitator will provide some of the best teacher professional development in the form of "action research." For beginning facilitators, the learning is often through trial-and-error. By trying a question out on their first-period class, and if it flops, trying a different question, those teachers eventually will understand which questions work universally and why.

In my early days of facilitating, I tried out numerous ideas and found out the hard way what tends to work and what doesn't. For example, I once wanted my students to get better at asking questions. I told the group that they were going to be graded exclusively on their questions. Well, I got what I asked for: numerous questions. One student managed to annotate 57 questions in pre-seminar. Although the students asked numerous questions during seminar, they neglected to follow through with any of them before asking more questions that were unrelated to previous ones. The conversation was stilted and lacked coherence and depth.

The action research can also take a more structured form. For example, through observation and tracking, a teacher may recognize that three students are exceptionally good at citing the text. The action research question becomes: *How are they able to do that and how can I get the rest of the class doing that?* From there, a series of questions may lead the teacher to a solution: How many times did those students read the text? *How* did they read it? How did they annotate? If they did annotate, how did they recognize the sentence or section was important? Through such mini-action research projects, possible during Socratic Seminar, teachers can significantly improve their craft.

> I have matched up the benefits and outcomes of seminar with numerous taxonomies, core principles, and belief statements, and with very few exceptions, Socratic Seminar will meet all or most of the criteria.

A huge benefit for facilitators is that teaching becomes more exciting and enjoyable. The students will generate new and exciting ideas that inject enthusiasm and life into the curriculum. Instead of repeatedly teaching the same material period after period, the students will constantly surprise you with amazing interpretations. Christopher Phillips, author of *Socrates Café*, described the excitement of Socratic questioning in this way: "By becoming more skilled in the art of questioning, you will discover new ways to ask the questions that have vexed and perplexed you the most. In turn, you will discover new and more fruitful answers. And these new answers in turn will generate a whole new host of questions. And the cycle keeps repeating itself—not in a vicious circle, but in an ever-ascending and ever-expanding spiral that gives you a continually new and replenishing outlook on life."

For many teachers, Socratic Seminars start as a classroom activity, but often develop to become the backbone of an entire approach to teaching. In other words, they develop a Socratic Classroom.

Best Practices

Socratic Seminars work well with nearly every local, state, or federal educational standard, including the Common Core State Standards. This is simply because communication, which is at the heart of almost every subject, has four components: reading, writing, listening, and speaking. When students engage in Socratic Seminar about a written text, they will practice and employ close reading skills, engage in speaking and listening skills, and on many occasions, they will also embark on writing projects.

Here are the seven overarching outcomes for students from the Common Core State Standards for college and career readiness in reading, writing, speaking, listening, and language.

- They demonstrate independence.
- They build strong content knowledge.
- They respond to the varying demands of audience, task, purpose, and discipline.
- They comprehend as well as critique.
- They value evidence.
- They come to understand other perspectives and cultures.
- They use technology and digital media strategically and capably.

The first six are commonly and consistently practiced in a Socratic Classroom. Seminar could also be a great tool for "strategically and capably" investigating the uses of media and technology, including how both affect the way we think. According to Marshall McLuhan, for example, "the medium is the message"—an idea that places emphasis on the method of communication in addition to the actual content. Teachers could set up seminar experiences where students compare and contrast dialoguing in various ways: in person, through discussion forums, instant messaging, texting, video conferencing and more.

Socratic Seminar may seem to promise too much to be believable. However, there are three-common sense principles based on simple numbers that make all of these outcomes plausible. For example, in many classrooms, teachers do *at least* 80% of the talking (by some estimates up to 97%), which leaves 20% to be divided amongst all of the students. In Socratic Seminar, the reverse is true. Facilitators typically only speak 5% of the time, maybe less. This leaves 95% divided amongst the students.

Those numbers in reverse also apply to the amount of time a facilitator can use to reflect on the needs of the students. If a teacher spends 80% of a class period talking, and additional time eliciting answers from students, then only a small percentage of time remains to reflect on the class. In seminar, the facilitator can instead spend significant time tracking conversations and collecting data.

Besides the benefits for students and teachers, seminars match up very well with many educational paradigms considered "best practices." Obviously, there is not agreement amongst educators about how education should be organized and implemented. Some advocate for core knowledge or essential content, while others focus much more on process. However, no matter what system you may believe is the most beneficial to students, Socratic Seminars will help bring out the best of its potential.

When matching the benefits and outcomes of seminar to numerous taxonomies, core principles, and belief statements, with very few exceptions, Socratic Seminar will meet most or all of the criteria. A very clear example of this can be seen from Zemelman, Daniels, and Hyde's *Best Practice: Bringing Standards to Life in America's Classrooms*. In this text, the authors synthesized fourteen "interlocking principles, assumptions, or theories" from the conclusions of numerous national curriculum projects. Whether you agree about their "best practices" or not is certainly not the point here. What is important is that these components were drawn from numerous schools across many disciplines and represent a wide array of legitimate concerns and ideas. Despite the variety, Socratic Seminar directly addresses twelve of the fourteen and can potentially address the remaining two. That's the power of Socratic Seminar.

Straight-A Syndrome and Failing Geniuses: Reexamining "Good" Students

Teachers who facilitate several seminars with the same group often note an interesting phenomenon: Many of the straight-A students are remarkably quiet, whereas many of the students at-risk for failing contribute the most. In addition, when "good" students contribute, their ideas are stale and clichéd, but the "bad" students offer amazing insights and fresh ideas.

What's going on?

Schools often create a learning environment where a "good" student is defined as someone who follows all of the rules and expectations and a "bad" student is someone who cannot or will not. For the "good" student, this means: listening, taking notes, studying for tests, memorizing information, and reciting back what the teacher wants. In short, it's doing what you're told. Or, perhaps simply: "Obey." By the way, Shepard Fairey's work is great for Socratic Seminar.

Component	Explanation	Socratic Seminar
Student-Centered	Schooling should focus on investigating students' own questions.	Almost Always
Authentic	Real, rich, complex ideas are at the heart of the curriculum.	Almost Always
Holistic	Whole ideas, events and materials should be presented in purposeful contexts.	Often[1]
Experiential	Learning should involve active, hands-on experiences.	Possibly[2]
Challenging	Students learn best when faced with genuine challenges, choices and responsibility.	Almost Always
Cognitive	Students should engage with higher order thinking skills and self-monitoring.	Almost Always
Developmental	Activities should fit the developmental level of the students.	Almost Always
Constructivist	Students' work in school should be building knowledge through inquiry.	Almost Always
Expressive	Students must employ the whole range of communicative media.	Almost Always
Reflective	Students should set goals for themselves, monitor their progress, and take responsibility for growth.	Almost Always
Interactive	Powerful learning happens when there is lively conversation, discussion and debate.	Almost Always
Sociable	Learning happens most efficiently in a safe atmosphere of friendliness and mutual support.	Almost Always
Collaborative	Children should be learning with and from one another in groups.	Almost Always
Democratic	Students should have options in school and learn how to make good choices.	Almost Always

[1.] Socratic Seminars are often used to explore large, universal themes, although they can also be used to deeply investigate small details.

[2.] Although Socratic Seminars do not often involve kinesthetic, hands-on experiences, the students are actively involved in constructing their own understandings. This aspect has its own category under "Constructivist." However, character-based seminars, which involve role-playing, can be experiential. Also, Socratic Seminars could be conducted incorporating dance, movements or other kinesthetic activities.

Source: Components from *Best Practice* (Fourth Edition): *Bringing Standards to Life in America's Classrooms* by Steven Zemelman, Harvey Daniels, and Arthur Hyde.

Teachers who facilitate several seminars with the same group of students often note an interesting phenomenon: Many of the straight-A students are remarkably quiet, whereas many of the students at-risk for failing contribute the most.

Some straight-A students take this compliance to an alarming level where they are virtually unable to generate original thoughts or opinions of their own. These students do not have a lot of practice with critical and creative thinking because they spend most of their time doing what they're told and getting rewarded with high grades for it.

At the other end of the spectrum are the bright students who refuse to play the "school game" and are at risk of failing. Sometimes these students are rebelling against authority, but many of them are disengaged because to them regurgitating information is incredibly boring. Even worse, the "amazing" ideas and contemplations in their current classes were their routine thoughts from previous years. For such students, school is an uninspiring place of repetitive tedium. Some of the smartest and most interesting people I knew in high school hovered on failure and nearly dropped out of school.

Socratic Seminar benefits the students in both of these extremes. Students with straight-A syndrome are often quiet in seminar because they're not sure what to do or how to behave without being passive recipients. They can find ways to participate, though. Because they are often very rule-conscious, some of them will become excellent guides for the structure of seminars. They will make sure procedures are followed, rules are obeyed, and expectations are met. Because they often have a good store of information, they can quickly learn to contribute by citing examples and making connections to prior knowledge. Eventually, they can be challenged to take risks with their own ideas.

The failing geniuses likely learned a long time ago that their coolest ideas will get them labeled as weird and nerdy, which is why they stopped sharing. In a supportive environment, though, their innovative and amazing ideas are valued and appreciated. They even have the time to fully explain themselves and how their outlier ideas are relevant. In safe Socratic Seminars, these students will hardly stop talking, especially older students who have years of insights and marvels stashed away for such occasions.

Socratic Seminar can help redefine and expand what a "good" student is. Rather than the narrow definition of *Obey*, an expanded definition allows many more students to be successful. In a Socratic classroom, "good" students are those who contribute meaningfully to a community process, whether they do so procedurally, intellectually, socially, or any other way that helps build teamwork and understanding.

> **Teachers must practice asking better questions, especially follow-up questions, if they are going to model being expert critical and creative thinkers.**

Summing Up Best Practices

For students:

- Develop a variety of academic and social skills.
- Practice engaging with depth instead of breadth.
- Increase the joy of learning.
- Refine language and create new ideas.
- Promote acceptance and understanding of others and their ideas.
- The definition of "good student" is redefined and broadened.
- Take ownership of learning.
- Develop intellectual curiosity.
- Develop empathy and listening skills.

For teachers/facilitators:

- Excellent personal professional development.
- Change learning into an active process.
- Increase reflective practice and listening skills.
- Challenge all students by learning to ask better questions.
- Increase enjoyment in teaching.
- Know students as individuals better.
- "Best practices" throughout the curriculum.

- Develop wonder and curiosity.
- Become better at asking questions.

Thinking About Inquiry and Inquiry About Thinking

Let's take a closer look at that last benefit for teachers: "Become better at asking questions." Questions are the key to deeper, more critical and creative thinking, but only if they are deep enough or "thick" enough, and only if students have sufficient time to explore them. Teachers must practice asking better questions, especially follow-up questions, if they are going to model being skilled critical and creative thinkers. Author Larry Lewin writes: "Among the many higher-level thinking skills our students need is the skill of generating thoughtful questions. The ability to routinely generate mental questions while reading, listening, or viewing something not only boosts attention and alertness, but also strengthens comprehension. When you ask yourself questions about incoming information, you are paying attention, self-monitoring, and actively constructing knowledge." However, asking better questions, like everything, takes practice—for students and teachers.

Students and teachers already ask questions, though, right? What's the problem? The issue is that many of the questions being asked in schools are not challenging and do not demand a lot of thinking. Lewin writes: "Yes, students already ask us questions. But it has been my experience as both a classroom teacher for 24 years and a staff developer in schools for more than a decade that the questions kids ask typically either seek clarification on procedural matters (Which numbers are we supposed to do?); attempt to cut a deal (Can we write two paragraphs instead of three?); or try to detour the group from the lesson (What time does this period end?)."

> The advice I would give would be to ask questions. Asking questions really helps you understand the text.
> ~ KR (grade 6)

As an example, I once had the great experience of going into a school as a consultant and recording every question I overheard in the classrooms, the cafeteria, the playground and the hallways. Over 80% of the questions I noted asked for basic facts or opinions, or were phrased as either/or, yes/no questions that required little thinking to answer.

The main solution, of course, is to practice asking questions ... and then to practice asking better questions. There are plenty of strategies for manufacturing better questions, like using specific verbs or sentence stems. There are also different types or levels of questions that can be formulated using Bloom's Taxonomy, Webb's Depth of Knowledge Levels, or Gardner's Multiple Intelligences.

Even with such question-generating tools, students and teachers must still practice thinking about and asking better questions. As an example, here's a great activity derived from Postman and Weingartner. Jot down a list of thirty questions—any questions. These can be stream-of-consciousness or school-related, simple or essential questions. Here are mine:

1. What does the letter 'r' mean?
2. Why is 7 considered a special number?
3. What are perfect numbers?
4. What is the difference between a sun and a star?
5. What direction is the wind blowing right now?
6. Would parallel lines ever meet in curved space?
7. How many types of trees are there?
8. How many phyla do scientists currently recognize?
9. Where is Senegal?
10. How did I choose my clothes this morning?
11. What is synesthesia?
12. What is your favorite flavor of ice cream?
13. What does "beyond the pale" mean?
14. What in the text makes you think that?
15. What approach would you use for this problem?
16. How would you classify that experiment?
17. How much does love weigh?
18. How were words invented?

19. Is reincarnation real?
20. What is ten plus eight?
21. Which one is better: a tree or a coffee mug?
22. How do you know what you know?
23. What does "meaning" mean?
24. When is a person considered old?
25. What was the best year for pop music?
26. When does watching a sport become tedious?
27. Why is a dozen equal to twelve?
28. Who discovered Mars?
29. Aren't blue pens better than green pens?
30. Why are stop signs red?

Just to demonstrate the power of asking questions and exploring ideas, I once asked myself the first question and discovered the letter 'r' can be more than just a letter or sound. For example, according to Joseph Rael and Lindsay Sutton in *Tracks of Dancing Light*, the letter "r" has the meaning "radiance, radiating light, abundance." The whole alphabet may contain hidden meanings …

Did you pause in your reading to write your list? Did you skip reading the list? What choice did you make? Did you actually write your list of thirty? What does that say about your practice?

Make your list.

Now take some time to examine your questions. What types of questions did you generate? How could you categorize your questions? What questions about your questions do you have? Which question words (who, what, where, when, how, why) did you use the most often, least often?

Write ten questions about your questions. Here's my example:

1. Which questions should be rephrased? Why?
2. Which, if any, would make good essential questions?
3. Which ones require follow-up questions and/or research?
4. Which questions are unanswerable?
5. How many questions have a specific "right" answer?
6. Which questions ask for an opinion?

7. Which questions have answers that are likely to change over time?
8. Which questions require making predictions?
9. Which questions can be answered with certainty? How can I be certain?
10. How many questions are phrased in the negative?

If you aren't question-fatigued, here are a final few. How long did this activity take? How difficult was it? How would your students do with something like this? (Modified for their age and experience). What made this activity difficult or easy? How hard or easy would it be to create another list? Another list? And still another?

Activities like this can really help with building curiosity and wonder, which is much more important than many teachers suspect. In her article entitled "The Case for Curiosity," Susan Engel writes, "... research shows unequivocally that when people are curious about something, they learn more, and better." What are you curious about?

Your Next Steps

- Choose a page of text or an object and have the students write five to twelve questions. Ask them the same follow-up questions. Have the students write questions about their questions. Get them to dig deeper.

- Students can practice crafting questions with question-based activities, such as *Teaching Critical Reading with Questioning Strategies* by Larry Lewin.

- Postman and Weingartner suggested creating an entire curriculum of questions.

- Have students write questions about the questions at the end of the chapters of textbooks.

- Have students include one question they have for each homework or test. Use these questions as a formative assessment. You can gauge understanding by monitoring the types of questions they ask.

- Have the students categorize the questions at the end of each chapter or unit *ahead of time.* Before a chapter or unit, have the students examine the questions they will be asked. They can then use them as an anticipation guide.

- Have students count the number of questions they hear in a class period or an entire day. Have them track data about the questions. What time of day did they hear the most questions? Where did they hear the most? Who in their lives asks the most questions?

- Investigate The Right Question Institute.

- Reflect on what a "good student" is for you. Make a list of the qualities you would like to see in your students. How will you help them practice these qualities?

- Research and explore the concept of "Beginner's Mind."

3

Socratic Seminar Basics

The Socratic method, then, is the art of teaching not philosophy but philosophizing, the art not of teaching about philosophers but of making philosophers of the students.

~ Leonard Nelson

Seven Socratic Seminar Components

A well planned Socratic Seminar or dialogue has seven components that should be considered:

1. Purpose, Getting Started, and Timings (this chapter)
2. Pre-Seminar (chapter 4)
3. The Text (chapter 5)
4. Questions (chapter 6)
5. The Students (chapter 7)
6. The Facilitator (chapter 8)
7. Post-Seminar and Evaluation (chapters 9 and 10)

Purpose

An important part of establishing the purpose of Socratic Seminar is deciding how it is connected to the curriculum. Although curriculum frameworks include benchmarks and standards for critical and creative thinking, interpersonal skills and close reading, the reality is that measuring them is extremely difficult. Many state standards, therefore, focus on content transmission, since content can be more easily measured. The result is that Socratic Seminars must often be used to deliver content or at least supplement curricular content.

Michael Strong, however, suggests five main models that range in frequency from using seminars once in a while to forming an entire Socratic Seminar course of study. Two of my own additional models, *Seminar to Promote Blogging* and *Combining Seminars with Debates*, are presented where my experience says they belong in the continuum.

Seminar Purpose	Frequency
1. Seminar for Supplemental Skills	Occasional seminars
2. *Seminar to Promote Blogging*	
3. Seminar as Conceptual Scaffold	Several at beginning of unit
4. Seminar for Synthesis	One or two at end of unit
5. Seminar for Deep Concept Development	Numerous seminars throughout
6. *Combining Seminars with Debates*	
7. Seminar as a Course of Study	Most classes are seminar format

Seminar for Supplemental Skills

In the supplement model, seminar is used to add critical and creative thinking and reading skills to a curriculum, essentially helping students develop prerequisite abilities for other course work. As Strong writes: "The natural inclination of many teachers is to view seminars as a thinking-skills supplement to their teaching practice. Thus, they may hold a seminar occasionally, perhaps once a week or once a month, as a means of adding more critical thinking to their teaching repertoire."

There are still benefits to this model. Because seminars are skills-based, texts are easy to select, since any text that can promote thinking could be used. Using this model, teachers and students will still be able to practice and develop their skills—if the seminars are frequent enough (at least once every two weeks and preferably once per week). This frequency could be easily accomplished in a coordinated way if, for example, the students had one seminar a month in each of their main subject area classes.

Seminar to Promote Blogging

A specific use of the seminar for supplemental skills is to use Socratic Seminar as a means to drive thoughtful blogging. In this variation, the students can be introduced to an extremely difficult, extremely complex text during Socratic Seminar and then continue blogging about it outside of class. Once the students exhaust their ideas and questions about the text (this could be weeks later), they can start another Socratic Seminar to jump-start a new round of blogs. Using text pairings or multiple texts can keep the online discussions lively and useful.

Blogging does present some challenges, so read more in Chapters 9 and 10.

Seminar as Conceptual Scaffold

In this model, Socratic Seminar is used to explore the major themes, essential questions or big ideas *before* standard content begins. Seminars are used to frontload or anchor a thematic or conceptual scaffold for the subsequent curricular content to build upon. Strong writes: "For example, a conventional geometry class may begin with four weeks of seminar geometry, using Euclid's *Elements*. In this case, students would be thinking about proof, rigor, abstraction, truth, reality, making their own judgments about the nature of mathematics, the relationship of mathematics to the physical world, their standard of rigor, and of reality ... At the same time students are getting a deep understanding of the concept "geometric proof," which will serve them well for the remainder of the year as they work through textbook geometry ... The time spent on the seminars will not be sacrificed from a content-coverage perspective because the deep conceptual knowledge the students will have gained ultimately allows the class to cover content more quickly."

The main benefit of this model is that it will help students subsequently piece together disparate bits of knowledge into a more cohesive understanding. Grant Wiggins and Jay McTighe, authors of *Understanding by Design*, write: "A big idea may be thought of as a linchpin. The linchpin is the device that keeps the wheel in place on an axle. Thus, a linchpin is one that is essential for understanding. Without grasping the idea and using it to 'hold together' related knowledge, we are left with bits and pieces of inert facts that cannot take us anywhere ... For instance, without grasping the distinction between the letter and the spirit of the law, a student cannot be said to understand the U.S. constitutional and legal system—even if that student is highly knowledgeable and articulate about many facts of constitutional history. Without a focus on the big ideas that have lasting value, students are too easily left with forgettable fragments of knowledge."

However, in this model, text selection and crafting questions are both extremely important. Strong warns: "Where there is some doubt about either one's ability to pick appropriate texts or the adequacy of the students' skills, there is a risk that the time spent in seminar will not result in a subsequent compensation in terms of faster content coverage. For teachers interested in the other benefits of seminar, this risk may be minor; for those facing strict constraints, the risk may be excessive." In other words, a well-chosen text can pave the way for faster and more comprehensive content learning, but a poorly chosen text may essentially be a waste of time (at least in terms of later learning content). Keep in mind that the students are still developing thinking skills in the process.

Seminar for Synthesis

A popular version employs Socratic Seminar at the culmination of a unit of study. In this model, seminars are used primarily for students to synthesize information and for teachers to check for the conceptual understandings the students have. This model is often used just before a final project, test or written paper so that the students can further develop their ideas through dialoguing with their peers. Unlike most other Socratic Seminar applications, students in this model are often encouraged to make notes, collect references or citations, and otherwise accumulate and record more information in order to strengthen their viewpoints. This model is even occasionally used for performance-based final exams.

Seminar for Deep Concept Development

In the concept development application, teachers focus on conceptual understandings, rather than specific facts or details of content. Socratic Seminar is, therefore, primarily used to explore *concepts as curriculum*.

In this model, Strong writes: "Seminar may become the dominant classroom activity, three or four days a week, while presentation of knowledge becomes the weekly supplement."

The benefit of this model is that the students would get the regular practice they need in order to make progress with many seminar skills. This model only requires one teacher of a single subject to provide the students with enough seminars. (Although for reasons of *skills transference*, having all of the seminars in a single subject may not be ideal.) If your frameworks and standards are written as concepts or questions instead of discrete facts, this model may be fairly easy to implement. In addition, many are general enough that they can be addressed simply by choosing an appropriate text. However, in situations with real or perceived need for coverage of material, this may not be possible.

Combining Seminars with Debates

Another model is to combine Socratic Seminars with research and debates. In the fullest use of this model, the students initially explore a proposition through reading, writing, and research. The teacher then uses Socratic Seminar to explore a text or idea *for* a certain position, then a second seminar with a text against that position. After both seminars, students then write a position paper attempting to synthesize and explain which side they favor. Afterward, the teacher can place each student on the opposite position's debate team, where they must argue against their own position. After these stages, the teacher assigns a final position paper along with a reflection about the entire process.

1. Initial introduction: reading, journaling, researching, etc.
2. Socratic Seminar for a proposition
3. Socratic Seminar against the proposition
4. Position paper, journaling or blogging
5. Debate (opposite team)
6. Final position paper
7. Reflection

Seminar as a Course of Study

Another possibility is to use Socratic Seminar as a complete course, either as an elective, an after-school offering, or as a required skills class. This allows teachers to focus on the critical and creative thinking, interpersonal, and close reading skills that the students need in order to be successful.

In this model the seminars become the curriculum. Critical and creative thinking, interpersonal, active listening and close reading skills (and others) become the focus of learning. According to Strong, this model "allows for the full use of the 'emerging curriculum' concept, according to which the next textual selection is determined by the conversational needs of the group. Thus, curriculum emerges based on the direction the students take the class. English classes generally have this freedom, because language skills are central to their content mission."

I used this model for many years at the middle school level with two Socratic Seminars a week. I definitely enjoyed the freedom of text selection and used a wide variety so that the students could practice approaching any text or problem in thoughtful and meaningful ways. Students became so confident and their thinking habits so strong that they coined the word *Socraticize*. When handed nearly any text, no matter how difficult, the tudents asked, "Should we *Socraticize* this?" and they'd get to work annotating and generating questions.

> **Teachers will find that the students have amazing ideas,**
> **that certain students suddenly become remarkably engaged,**
> **and that the room is full of excitement, energy, and enthusiasm.**

Unknown Purpose

If you're not sure what your purpose is, but you know you want to try Socratic Seminars, then feel free to use them as isolated classes. This will allow you to try them without worrying about how they connect to the curriculum, where they should be placed in a scope and sequence, or even how to assess the students. Your time and energy can be geared toward transitioning toward various roles as a facilitator—such as questioner, clarifier, and coach—observing, listening, and reflecting to make the most out of the conversation. In other words, you have the opportunity to better practice being a "guide on the side," rather than a "sage on the stage."

A Word of Caution

A successful first seminar can create a great deal of intellectual excitement for everyone. The students will like the fact that they are being encouraged to share their ideas. They will be even more impressed when their ideas are taken seriously and that they are actually able to steer the conversation in ways that interest them. Teachers will find that the students have amazing ideas, that certain students suddenly become remarkably engaged, and that the room is full of excitement, energy, and enthusiasm.

A really bad first seminar, however, can be disastrous. Opening up the floor to student dialogue may lead to someone getting offended or hurt. The conversation may be dull and unenlightening. The students may wander away from the text with long, unrelated anecdotes. A few students may get into a heated argument that excludes the rest of the class. Teachers may feel confused and powerless.

In general, introduce Socratic Seminar to your students only after establishing good rapport with them. There should already be an established set of norms or agreements for the classroom, including how to speak respectfully and what respect actually means (which could be an early seminar topic). A few weeks of establishing general norms and agreements should suffice, and then add the more specific procedures for a seminar.

Getting Started

Socratic Seminars are more complicated than the following list suggests, but for those who would like to get started right away (without reading the rest of this book, for example), here's basically what to do:

1. Consider how the students will be assessed or graded (if at all).

2. Encourage the students by telling them that seminars have high standards, but that you have confidence in them that they can

achieve those standards. I like to tell my students that these seminars will be their hardest classes.

3. Students form a circle (if under 22 students) or concentric circles (inner circle for participants, outer circle for observers) for larger classes.

4. Students should have already done a close reading or viewing of the text. It is suggested to have the students read every text twice. The first read is often read aloud by the teacher (modeling good reading) and the second is often an additional silent reading or paired reading. Students annotate the text. Two great resources for close reading are Kylene Beers and Robert Probst's *Notice and Note: Strategies for Close Reading* (2013) and *Reading Nonfiction: Notice and Note Stances, Signposts, and Strategies* (2015).

5. If the participants are unfamiliar with the procedures and norms of a Socratic Seminar, explain to them that they will be having a special dialogue where they must cooperate together to form a greater understanding of the text.

6. Explain that you will be shifting to the role of facilitator, by *only* asking questions, or by sitting outside of the circle.

7. Help set group and individual goals: "I will speak at least once" or "We need more silence."

8. Set a good amount of time for the seminar, leaving time to debrief at the end.

9. In the role of facilitator, ask an opening question that has "multiple right answers" justifiable in the text. This question should not have an agenda attached to it.

10. The students dialogue and do not raise their hands. Instead, they must learn how to take turns by reading nonverbal cues, actively listening, and staying focused on the group. This will likely be sloppy at first. Use turn-taking devices, such as talking sticks, and specific procedures only if necessary.

11. Students must (learn to): speak to the group, cite evidence, build ideas, ask questions, make connections, and contribute new lines of thought based on the opening question.

12. In the role of sentinel, maintain the safety of the seminar by holding the students accountable to the norms of the classroom and the seminar. For example, by insisting that participants disagree with ideas and not people.

13. DO NOT affirm or challenge ideas (except by asking questions), verbally or nonverbally (even from the back of the room). Do not rescue the students and do not have the last word.

14. Make notes for reflective practice and improvement. These are usually "dialogue maps" and/or tally marks about how and how often each student contributes.

15. Near the end of the seminar, consider asking a "closing question." This question helps students think about how the text relates to the present day or their personal lives.

16. Finish the seminar and congratulate the students. Celebrate the little successes.

17. Debrief the seminar by reflecting on what went well and what could use improvement for the next time. Consider exit tickets, journaling and other reflective practices.

18. Have the students set both personal and group goals for improvement next time.

19. Plan mini-lessons to help students improve in areas such as: close reading and annotating, active listening, taking turns, understanding nonverbal cues, asking meaningful questions, and recognizing logical fallacies.

20. As the students get better, plan on strategies for the *gradual release of responsibility.* Model for them what you want them to do, and then have them take over.

21. Always be on the lookout for good texts.

Large Groups (more than 22)

Many facilitators have discovered that the ideal number of students for seminar is generally 13-18. With fewer than this range, there are often not enough opinions and ideas; more than this range and students begin to lose precious speaking time. All things being equal, I find that 16 participants is an ideal number, with 22 being the high-end range where I wouldn't change any of my seminar procedures.

Facilitating a larger number of students (more than 22) can be difficult, but there are a number of solutions. With fairly large groups in the 23-27 range, I prefer to select up to five students to participate outside of the dialogue as "sociologists." These students collect data on the process, creating dialogue maps, noting participation, making notes, tallying logical fallacies, and anything else that may help set individual and group goals. I rotate these students so that everyone has a turn as observers, but the majority of students would always be a part of the conversation.

For even larger groups (more than 28), the most common solution is to create two concentric circles, an inner and an outer circle, where only the inner circle participants dialogue about the text, while the outer circle observes the process. After a set amount of time, the two groups switch places. In these setups, it is typical to pair the students up so that they each take turns in the inner and outer circle and help each other become better participants and reflective thinkers. This does mean that students have half the speaking time, though everyone will still benefit from both dialogues.

Another solution is to have two separate seminars, though this will usually necessitate having a second teacher, an experienced former student, a parent volunteer, etc. I have tried facilitating back and forth between two simultaneous seminars, and I find that I cannot truly listen to either conversation or properly help either group improve. However, I would certainly consider this solution with a group of experienced students.

One common variation is the fishbowl discussion, where only a small number of inner circle participants are allowed to talk about the text. An outer circle participant can exchange places with someone in the inner circle if he or she wants to speak. This is done either by signaling an inner circle participant and swapping places, or by using a "hot seat." The hot seats are empty chairs in the inner circle that outer circle participants may use to enter the conversation. This model often breaks down quite easily because of the movement involved and the eagerness with which some students seek a hot seat. Although various strategies can still make this version work, nothing truly compares to a full seminar where student talk time is maximized.

In all cases, the main tasks for outer circle participants are to actively listen, make notes, and then reflect on the process in order to improve the quality of the conversation. Matt Copeland writes: "Rather than focusing on the content of the inner circle's dialogue, the outer circle focuses on the inner circle's behavior and process, reflecting on their experiences, assessing the quality of their dialogue, and establishing goals for future performance."

> **Because seminars can be mentally exhausting, students and teachers will most likely need to build mental stamina.**

Timings: Scheduling and Frequency

There are many recommendations for how often to have Socratic Seminars, but the simple answer is to have them as often as possible. Howard Zeiderman suggests at least once a week for the Touchstones program. The National Paideia Center recommends "that teachers dedicate 15-20% of classroom time to seminar discussion in order that students will row in their ability to think conceptually." My own experience has shown that students must engage in seminar at least once every two weeks to maintain continuity.

For many teachers this will at first mean stealing time out of the schedule to try a Socratic Seminar here or there, building up to a goal of having seminar once every two weeks or so with all students. With practice, planning, and effective text selection, Socratic Seminar can become an integrated and regular part of any curriculum.

Because seminars can be mentally exhausting, students and teachers will most likely need to build mental stamina. In the beginning, start with shorter seminars in greater frequency, maybe 10-20 minutes for young students and 20-40 minutes for older participants. Mortimer Adler (1984) recommends: "At the lower level, where the classroom teacher engages in all three kinds of teaching, seminar-like discussions should occur much more frequently than at the upper level, perhaps every day, though only for relatively brief spans—at most a half hour or so for the very young, and a little more for those who are older."

As students gain experience, the seminar sessions should be longer. In fact, they will most likely get longer on their own as students excitedly engage with their own interests and inquiries. As this happens, longer sessions become better, since students can go deeper into the material. Adler (1984) recommends, for example: "At the upper level, seminars should occur less frequently, once a week or at most twice a week, depending on the character and length of the book to be read in advance. They should never run less than ninety minutes and should usually run for two hours." Michael Strong suggests developing seminars starting in the earliest possible grades, with K-3 students meeting up to 30 minutes a session for 1-5 sessions a week. For grades 4-6, he suggests three to five, 60-minute seminars a week; grades 7-9 three to five seminars a week each 2-4 hours; and grades 10+, as many as is appropriate. This seems like a lot, but the program he outlines is essentially the Seminar as a Course of Study model.

Be cautious about using Socratic Seminars intermittently without building toward goals. Because students need practice at working together and developing the necessary skills for successful seminars, only occasional practice (less than every few weeks) can be counter-productive. As Strong indicates: "If the conditions for improvement do not exist, it is much better not to practice seminar at all than to drag students through meaningless, unproductive class periods." In my experience this is because intermittent practice will likely keep the group in the *storming* stage of group development. See chapter 7 for more.

Block scheduling is the most favorable for facilitating seminars, especially when the students are still learning to work together. Many conversations about a stimulating text can easily carry on for 2-3 hours, sometimes more. After 9/11, I used *The Pledge of Allegiance* in middle school and our conversation carried on constructively for three 90-minute periods over the course of three weeks. For years I tracked the best *Eureka!* moments (when students had a truly amazing breakthrough) and discovered that many of them occurred around the 70-minute mark. Ideas take time to come to fruition.

Timings can be boiled down to two basic principles: *The older the students are, the longer the seminars should be. The more experience the students have, the longer the seminars should be.*

Example Timings

Second Grade (35 minutes) One Circle, Year-end, Text was partially prepared in pre-seminar:

8 minutes	Review norms, reminders from last time, etc.
4 minutes	Teacher reads short text aloud (for second time).
2 minutes	Teacher asks opening question. Students do turn-and-talk.
18 minutes	Sustained dialogue.
3 minutes	Debrief. What went well? What needs improvement?

Sixth Grade (60 minutes) One Circle, Mid-Year, Text was not prepared or annotated in pre-seminar:

14 minutes	The teacher reads the text aloud; students annotate. Then students read silently with a specific type of annotation in mind.
4 minutes	Review expectations, set goals, reminders from last time, etc.
2 minutes	Teacher asks opening question. Students do turn-and-talk.
30 minutes	Sustained dialogue.
7 minutes	Debrief and exit ticket. What went well? What needs improvement?

Ninth Grade (90 minutes) Two Circles, Beginning of Year, Text was thoroughly prepared and annotated in pre-seminar:

7 minutes	Review expectations, set goals, establish jobs. Students share a question from their entrance tickets.

4 minutes	Teacher and students share and select opening question.
2 minutes	Teacher asks opening question. Students do turn-and-talk.
28 minutes	Sustained inner circle dialogue.
5 minutes	Feedback from outer circle.
1 minute	Students switch.
28 minutes	Sustained inner circle dialogue.
5 minutes	Feedback from outer circle.
7 minutes	Debrief and exit ticket. What went well? What needs improvement? Goal setting for individuals and group.

> I would say (to future students), don't be afraid to talk. Also, don't be afraid to change your mind and opinion on topics. Write as much as you can when you annotate, don't just skim over the text, really look over it and try to understand it. If you can't, just ask a question. ~ SM (grade 8)

Physical and Mental Preparation

The most important aspect of preparation is to arrange the space so students are in a circle (or two concentric circles) where the participants can all see each other. Depending on the classroom arrangement, this sometimes means a long rectangle or a strange polygon, but make sure all students can see each other. Consider assigning seats ahead of time so that students know exactly where to go and what their initial role might be, depending on if they are in the inner or outer circle.

The first responsibility for students is to be physically and mentally prepared for the seminar, which is often a function of the pre-seminar component (next chapter). Of course, the first thing is for students to arrive to class on time with all required materials. If there was homework, then students MUST have it done in order to participate, otherwise they will not be able to effectively dialogue. Students may also need highlighters, rulers, protractors, colored pencils or markers, dictionaries, and any other necessary tools. Using an entrance ticket in or immediate task will get them mentally engaged right away.

To help students prepare mentally, change your classroom routine for Socratic Seminar (a standard change is that students do not raise their hands). Sometimes just forming a circle with the desks or chairs and breaking out of rows is enough. Some teachers like to have the students sit on the floor, or change the lighting by turning off the fluorescent lights and using soft light lamps instead. Others put up specific posters, use name tents, or even change clothes (put on a thinking cap or take off a tie) to mark the occasion.

Thinking through the various senses can generate other suggestions. Spatially, you could put out a small rug to add some new color or invite students to sit in a circle on the floor. You could use tablecloths or put out a few fancy library desk lamps. If your school allows it, you could burn incense or use essential oils. Smells make great triggers for memory, so try it out.

I have had a lot of success with readiness music. Pick an appropriate song to play only on Socratic Seminar days and create a routine for the students to be settled and prepared by the time the song ends. This means circling up, getting the text, sharpening pencils, and putting backpacks out of sight—maybe in about four minutes. Played before every Socratic Seminar, the students will habituate to mentally preparing to work.

> **If the students are *really* going to generate a lot of ideas, if they are going to be truly creative and critical, there must always be safety and trust within the seminar classroom.**

You can even create a special routine for entering the classroom. When I practiced martial arts, we had a set of movements we had to do in order to enter the dojo. It was a mark to ourselves and to others that we were entering a special place of training, dedication, and purpose. More than thirty years later, not only do I remember the exact movements, but I also can still connect to the feelings of entering the dojo. The same, of course, could be true of the classroom. Wouldn't it be amazing to have the students remember twenty years later what it was like to enter your classroom?

Have several different dictionaries available if possible (or tablets or computers with websites ready to go). Some students are afraid to talk, or ask questions, but they will often volunteer to read from a dictionary. First on my list for middle school or higher would be the amazing two-volume slipcase compact edition of the Oxford English Dictionary. Not only does it go into word origins and histories, but it also provides the actual sentences where the words first appeared in print. Plus, it comes with a magnifying glass, which is often a bonus with students. If you can't get the O.E.D., then go for the next biggest, most impressive dictionary possible—it's like having a magical tome, and many students will gravitate to it. Other specialty dictionaries can serve as counterpoint to the main dictionary. I have used *Brewer's Dictionary of Phrase and Fable* a lot, along with various naming dictionaries. With multiple dictionaries, students will see that there are various definitions, and that they're reading from *a* dictionary, not *the* dictionary.

Safety and Belonging: "Here is a safe place to give effort."

If the students are *really* going to generate a lot of ideas, if they are going to be truly creative and critical, there must always be safety and trust within the Socratic Seminar. Students must feel open and free to speak their minds, must be willing to take risks and say what they really think, even if it seems unrelated or insubstantial at the time. There should never be any "stupid ideas" in a Socratic classroom. Redefine such concepts as "currently unconnected or unsubstantiated," because you never know when one seemingly irrelevant or outlandish idea is exactly what the conversation needs. As a teacher, your role as Sentinel must be to protect the integrity of the seminar.

In his article "Enhancing Classroom Conversation for All Students," author and teacher William Goldsmith writes:

Holding students accountable for partaking in class discussions really does make children feel safe if you teach them why we have discussions. Think back to a time you were asked a question in public and didn't know the answer. How did you feel? More than likely, your feeling depended on the environment. We have to shift students' understanding of questions (which prompt discussions) from an opportunity to be right or wrong to an opportunity to explain their thinking. A number of times, I have asked students to explain their thinking only to have them quickly change their answer because they wanted to be sure their response was correct. Discussions aren't simply about right or wrong answers. Discussions are about learning from each other, expanding on what we know, reasoning through problems, and justifying or explaining our thinking.

Of course, this can lead to complications with facilitating. When would a highly inventive idea be too disconnected or irrelevant? How much reasoning time should an idea take, and when is it simply too far off track? When should a facilitator intervene in a conversation lost in creative tangents? What is a good balance between creative thinking and critical thinking? When are there too many ideas and not enough follow-throughs?

These are not easy questions to answer, but err on the side of open-ended, open-minded conversation. The students will get better at staying focused and relevant as they practice engaging in genuine conversations during Socratic Seminar. But they will never be truly creative or critical if they feel their ideas are treated as dumb, worthless, or irrelevant.

In addition, students must feel like they belong to the group, especially if they are initially quiet and reserved outsiders. There are many ways to build community, including simple actions, such as giving all of the students a special nametag or name tent. Numerous teambuilding exercises help to break the ice and having students practice empathic listening activities can help build trust.

Students should also feel as though they belong to the seminar group. This sense of belonging starts at the beginning of the year by building rapport and creating basic classroom norms, but should extend more specifically to the seminar group. Further camaraderie and a sense of belonging might be easier to achieve than teachers suspect. Daniel Coyle, author of *The Culture Code*, notes one study from a team of psychologists that "discovered that one particular form of feedback boosted student effort and performance so immensely that they deemed it 'magical feedback.' Students who received it chose to revise their papers far more often than students who did not, and their performance improved significantly." This feedback was a simple phrase: *I'm giving you these comments because I have very high expectations and I know that you can reach them.*

Coyle continues: "None of these words contain any information on how to improve. Yet they are powerful because they deliver a burst of belonging cues. Actually, when you look more closely at the sentence, it contains three separate cues.
1. You are part of this group.
2. This group is special; we have high standards here.
3. I believe you can reach those standards. These signals provide a clear message that lights up the unconscious brain: *Here is a safe place to give effort.*"

> If you don't understand something, don't give up right away, for that is something everybody should learn in life.
> ~ JK (grade 6)

Hard Work Atmosphere

It's worth stressing before the chapter ends that the atmosphere of a Socratic Seminar should not be one of random playfulness, informal idea swapping, casual conversation, or just having a good time. Students who misunderstand the basic premises of seminar often enjoy the apparent relaxed recess from the normal class period, and it can often be seen in their postures. Sometimes they even go home and say, "We just talked in class today."

Socratic Seminar should instead be formal and intense, thoughtful and deep. This is reasoned talk. Students can achieve the good feeling of a job well done through hard work, collaboration, and honest reflection. Coyle notes: "One misconception about highly successful cultures is that they are happy, lighthearted places. This is mostly not the case. They are energized and engaged, but at their core their members are oriented less around achieving happiness than around solving hard problems together. This task involves many moments of high-candor feedback, uncomfortable truth-telling, when they confront the gap between where the group is, and where it ought to be."

Catch the Way of It

Although Socratic Seminars typically involve forming a circle (or concentric circles) in a standard classroom setting, they can take a variety of forms. For example, a science teacher may set up a seminar-like experience by creating a crime scene investigation lab where the students work together in small groups to investigate clues, ask questions, and develop theories about what happened. A physical education teacher could set up "thinking stations" where students run, skip, and hop in order to answer various multiple choice questions. For example, the students could run in place if they think the answer is **A**, they could skip around cones if they think it is **B**, and so on.

One favorite example of a seminar-like classroom is for music teachers. Erik Johnson, in his article "Developing Listening Skills through Peer Interaction," describes a seminar-like approach for music ensemble rehearsals. He starts by mentioning that traditional power structures in the classroom are usually one direction, from the teacher to students and that ensemble rehearsals are similarly one way, from conductor to musicians. He writes:

> Recognizing the need to have everyone engaged and learning, a conductor will often ask the trumpets to listen to what is being said to the clarinets in hope that some transfer of information will happen without providing any direct instruction. The problem with this type

of participant structure is again that the instruction is primarily in one direction. The student, even when attentively listening to the clarinets, is left with relatively little power to develop a deeper understanding of the important concepts being addressed. On a practical note, it is often intimidating for students to ask questions in this traditional participant structure, where information flows primarily from the expert teacher to the novice student—and this is particularly true when the student is not in the group or section being specifically addressed.

Johnson sets up three levels of listening for his rehearsals that can "help students and teachers isolate ensemble skills into practical and manageable segments." This way students can interact with each other on multiple levels without being stuck in the role of passive listeners. The students decide how to talk and rehearse with each other across these levels depending on the needs of the rehearsal:

> Level 1 – Collaboration between two musicians playing the same part.
>
> Level 2 – Collaboration within a section of instruments.
>
> Level 3 – Collaboration within the entire ensemble.

Johnson finds that "Giving students the opportunity to share their knowledge and ideas with their peers is a great way to enliven and generate enthusiasm for musical collaboration." He continues:

> Having rehearsed this way, I can testify to the success of this approach. The students typically interact on a very sophisticated level, which often provides invaluable information to me as the teacher about their understanding. In my experience, it does not take long for students to start asking to see the score so they can visually confirm a collaboration that needs to take place.

Summing Up

1. Socratic Seminar has several components to carefully consider.

2. There are various models on how to incorporate Socratic Seminar, ranging from Seminar for Supplemental Skills to Seminar as a Course of Study.

3. Large groups may require different norms or procedures.

4. Socratic Seminars work on the principle of gradual release of responsibility.

5. Catch the way of a Socratic Classroom. Socratic Seminar principles can be applied to a variety of classrooms, including music ensemble rehearsals.

Your Next Steps

- Consider using thinking caps on seminar days. The hats could be tied into jobs or functions. See Edward de Bono's *Six Thinking Hats* for ideas.

- Plan your seminar procedures ahead of time in as much detail as possible. Check out Wong and Wong (1998) *The First Days of School: How to Be an Effective Teacher.*

- Try using Socratic Seminar in a variety of ways throughout the curriculum, for example in the beginning, middle, and end of a unit. Ask the students which model was the most helpful for them.

- Watch other teachers to learn various facilitation techniques. Many facilitator actions and non-actions are very subtle. Debrief afterward and ask why certain decisions were made.

- For a great personal challenge: Facilitate a seminar outside of your comfort zone. This will help you become a learner along with the students and should allow you to naturally model wonder and curiosity. Math teachers could try a poem, English teachers could try a geometric proof, and history teachers could facilitate a chemistry text.

- Because Socratic Seminars involve speaking and listening skills, they could be used as a model for staff meetings, student government meetings, and more.

- Socratic Seminar could be used in advisory periods and homeroom to explore interpersonal issues and potential solutions.

- Consider Mortimer Adler's idea to have the entire school participate in weekly Socratic Seminars at the same time. This includes ALL faculty and staff members.

- Research articles like Science Net Links' "Belonging to a Group."

4

Pre-Seminar

You can teach a student a lesson for a day; but if you can teach him to learn by creating curiosity, he will continue the learning process as long as he lives.

~ Clay P. Bedford

THE PRE-SEMINAR STAGE can be likened to warm-ups that athletes do prior to sporting events. Just as jogging, stretching, and going through certain routines help athletes, pre-seminar activities help students mentally and physically prepare for seminars. There are many strategies that can be effective, but the goals are always similar.

This stage of seminar assists students in using strategies and finding avenues into the text. For the most part, this stage involves annotating and "preparing a text" ahead of time: looking up vocabulary words, journaling, organizing information, putting symbols in the margins, generating questions, reading background material, and blogging.

For written materials, which make up the majority of seminar texts, this component is essentially pre-reading: establishing the specific purpose of the assignment, to making notes while reading or listening, to using the headings of a text to create an outline. It is not within the scope of this book to go into details of specific strategies, such as preview maps and graphic organizers, the KWL, or the SQ3R, since much has been written about them elsewhere. However, I do want to share specific Socratic Seminar ideas.

The Main Goals for Pre-seminar

- Generating initial interest in the text or subject (often accomplished by having the students generate their own questions).
- Activating prior knowledge.
- Focusing curiosity and investigation.
- Identifying bias and viewpoint.
- Organizing or reorganizing information.
- Maximizing potential items, themes, issues, or ideas to discuss.
- Clarifying expectations and procedures.
- Increasing comprehension.
- Setting personal or group goals.
- Increasing student interest and investment.

Kinesthetic Warm-up Activities

There are a number of effective activities that can be used, from simple in-the-seat movements, to using the entire classroom, outdoors, or a gym in order to get the students physically moving. These activities can be particularly good in the morning to wake students up and after recess or physical education to build cohesion and focus.

There are a lot of great ideas at Ashley Bible's blog *Building Book Love*, but my favorite is probably the Socratic soccer ball. For this warm-up, purchase a soccer ball or beach ball and then write the suggested questions on it to help get students ready for the actual seminar. Toss it (safely) around the room and students can take turns answering questions and building on responses.

Another idea is to post butcher paper around the room or make spaces available on whiteboards. Have markers available and instructions for the students to get up, move around the room and put their annotations on the community spaces or papers. One paper or space could be for questions, one for vocabulary words, one for important names, dates, and/or phrases, and still another for significant thoughts or ideas. One space could have graphic organizers or association maps. Another couple of poster boards could be for sentence frames or phrases with which the students agree and disagree. An extra space can be left blank in order to encourage new ideas.

> **I have found over the years that many disagreements and conflicts have their roots in different assumptive understandings of definitions.**

Another idea is to create physical points in the room that the students can move to based on their personal viewpoints. For example: Strongly Agree, Agree, Undecided, Disagree, and Strongly Disagree. Pull a sentence or phrase out of the text and ask the students to move to the part of the room that aligns with their view. Another continuum could be: Very Important, Important, Undecided, Unimportant, and Irrelevant. Once in those areas, the students can turn-and-talk to briefly share their thoughts and explain themselves.

As an example, take a classroom where the teacher is using chapter 2 of the *Tao Te Ching* for seminar. She explains that she will read two sentences from the text and they are to think about it for 30 seconds and then, after she rings a bell, they are to move to the appropriate location in the room. When they are ready, she reads the first one: *When people see some things as beautiful, other things become ugly.* After 30 seconds, she rings the bell and the students move in the room. She gives them one minute to share in their small groups and then she asks a single person from each group to volunteer his or her personal opinion. "Jessica, why do you Strongly Agree? Eric, why are you Undecided?" When they are done she reads the next sentence that she wants them to further contemplate: *Being and non-being create each other.* After 30 seconds, she rings the bell again and they shuffle around the room, redistributing themselves.

The Importance of Definitions

I have found over the years that many disagreements and conflicts have their roots in different assumptive understandings of definitions. I have often seen people argue for ten or twenty minutes only to realize that they actually agreed in principle, but disagreed somewhere about foundational differences in definition.

Some of these arguments are worthwhile since the students will gain a deeper appreciation of words through exploring nuances. However, many of these arguments are long and drawn out, use precious seminar time and are typically only useful for a few students. It is much better to establish the definitions of key words in the pre-seminar stage. This way a shared under-standing can immediately be achieved and the actual seminar conversation can move on to the bigger ideas and issues.

Mini-Lessons

Mini-lessons can target skills or information that students need before, during, or after the seminars. Mini-lessons that focus on pre-seminar skills tend to focus on pre-reading or preparatory practices that help students comprehend, decode, or interpret the text. Some mini-lessons focus on skills needed during the seminar itself, such as listening or taking turns. Other mini-lessons focus on post-seminar skills, such as reflecting, synthesizing, or transferring ideas.

Mini-Lessons for Pre-Seminar Skills

- Pre-reading strategies.
- Close reading.
- How to listen to music.
- Whole brain reading.
- Annotating.
- Types of questions.
- Generating questions.
- Creative and critical thinking.

- Opening questions.
- How to arrive to seminar.
- How to use a class blog or forum.
- How to share in pairs and small groups.
- How to use various resources like dictionaries.

Mini-Lessons for Seminar Skills

- Active listening.
- Barriers to active listening.
- How to take turns.
- How to interject politely.
- SSLANT.
- Logical inconsistencies or fallacies.
- Barriers to critical thinking.
- Reading aloud.
- Citing the text.
- Building on thoughts and ideas.
- Disagreeing with ideas, not people.
- Making notes.
- Ways to participate.
- How to ask for clarification.
- How to listen to one's inner voice or intuition.

Mini-Lessons for Post-Seminar Skills

- Debriefing a seminar.
- How to synthesize information.
- How to use notes to write papers.
- How to self-assess.
- Giving warm and cool feedback to others.
- How to understand a rubric.
- Going beyond like and dislike.
- Making connections to other texts.
- Setting individual and group goals.

Close Reading and Annotating

The most prevalent pre-seminar activity is to have students close read and annotate a text. This usually involves reading or listening at least twice, marking the text and/or making notes, and jotting down thoughts and questions. For written texts, this means making notes and drawing symbols in the margins, underlining and highlighting passages, writing questions, noticing and noting patterns, etc. Other types of texts can be dealt with similarly, but may require different systems, such as using sticky notes, employing graphic organizers, selecting emojis, etc.

> I have learned that the more annotations you write down, the more the text is understandable.
> ~ MY (grade 7)

There are many different close reading and annotating strategies that range from generally just "jot down what you're thinking" to specific strategies and systems. Adler and Van Doran, for example, in *How to Read a Book*, outline about two dozen specific ideas for marking a text.

My favorite resource for literature is Kylene Beers and Robert Probst's *Notice and Note: Strategies for Close Reading*, and for nonfiction I really like their *Reading Nonfiction: Notice and Note Stances, Signposts, and Strategies*. Both have specific signposts with accompanying lessons that could probably be used as low as third grade. Their book *Disrupting Thinking: Why How We Read Matters* provides strategies that could likely be useful starting in kindergarten.

> **When possible, have students write directly in their books or on their handouts, but otherwise they can craft their annotations on sticky notes, compile them in notebooks, or use dry-erase markers over plastic sleeves.**

Sample Ideas for Annotations

- Write one closed and one open-ended question that you have on page 2.
- Circle the two most confusing paragraphs.
- Number the stanzas.
- Underline your favorite sentence.
- Put a W in the margin where the author's ideas seem weak.
- Put an M in the margin if you feel the author is trying to manipulate you.
- Put an E in the margin where the author seems to be exaggerating.
- Write page numbers of other pages for recurring ideas or themes.
- On a sticky note, write the definition of a word that seems important.
- Write two questions on each page. Then rank the most important three.
- Note a personal connection at the bottom of the page.
- Put a box around any of the words that are on our word wall.
- Draw an emoji where the main character is feeling an important emotion.
- Mark where the author appears uninformed or misinformed.
- Draw a vertical line in the margin to mark long passages. Add other notes or symbols as well.
- Use numbers to organize sequences and lists.
- Arrange this information into a graphic organizer.

Sometimes teachers get overwhelmed with the close reading process because they feel inclined or obligated to constantly ask comprehension questions or otherwise check for understanding. They may stress about levels of questions, depth of knowledge and other complexities. Such considerations are certainly useful, but are also time-consuming and usually not necessary during pre-seminar.

A simple, very effective pre-seminar close reading activity is called the Directed Reading-Thinking Activity (DRTA). Formulated by Russell Stauffer, the DRTA as envisioned by Lee Gunderson is simple but highly effective. Provide the students with a text, but make sure they can only read it (or see it or listen to it) in small sections at a time, so that they are constantly making predictions. Reveal the title first, and then a few lines or paragraphs and another few lines or paragraphs, and after each section, have the students make a prediction. Ask mainly three questions (save others for later):

- What do you think this story is about?
- What do you think will happen next?
- What made you think so? (How would you revise or change your prediction?)

When possible, have students write directly in their books or on their handouts. Otherwise they can craft their annotations on sticky notes, compile them in notebooks, or use dry erase markers over plastic sleeves. Websites like *Padlet.com* allow for digital sticky notes that can be shared and viewed by entire classes. Overall, questions are often the best annotations because of their ability to promote wonder, curiosity, interest, and dialogue.

For some students, annotating is remarkably easy and they will go on to generate all kinds of connections and interesting ideas. It's fun for some students because they get to write what they think and know, and not what a textbook or other source wants them to think. For many students, though, annotating is quite challenging and won't produce much. Reading is already a complicated process, especially with a difficult text. Adding another level of thought process onto the reading, by requiring students to generate annotations, makes the task even more difficult.

Part of the issue is in asking the students to *write* the annotations. As many teachers are aware, the act of writing stalls many students since thoughts get lost somewhere between the mind and the hand. Another issue is simply that some students don't have a lot of thoughts crossing their mind. They often haven't had a lot of practice with critical or creative thinking. They may still be concrete thinkers who have not yet moved to abstract thinking.

> **It is often much easier to respond to a question than it is to a statement, and many shy students find it easier to participate by asking a question than sharing an opinion.**

Explain to the students that they should write down what is going on in their minds as they read or listen. If they don't understand something, then they should generate a question. Sounds easy, right? Well, for many students, it's not. But they can practice, especially with a structure. As an example, Tony Stead writes about a time when he worked with a group of fourth and fifth graders. They had become confident (in using the RAN, a strategy similar to the KWL), but they "became stuck when it came to raising wonderings. For the most part they were content to just confirm and negate prior knowledge and gather new information ... They were used to answering questions, not raising them."

To help structure the process, the students all thought deeply about one particular fact and shared their questions regarding that one fact. Then the students formed hypotheses on possible answers to those questions. Stead continues: "It wasn't long before the students in the grade 4 and 5 classrooms were not just collecting facts when they heard informational literacy, but raising questions and making connections with what they were hearing."

The students will get better with modeling from an experienced teacher. When reading and preparing a text, make sure to speak aloud your own wonderings and ideas. Pause and have the students annotate your thoughts to start practicing. Periodically, have the students think-pair-share or think-draw-share so that they can also jot down thoughts and questions from each other. Remember, they need to practice, even if the annotations aren't their own yet.

Generating Questions

Because seminars are meant to be engaging conversations, questions are absolutely vital. It is often much easier to respond to a question than it is to a statement, and many shy students find it easier to participate by asking a question than sharing an opinion. When the students prepare a text, always have them generate questions. This process will also create more interest in the topic or text because the students will tap into their own curiosity. In the beginning, push for quantity so that students can practice asking questions, and later focus on the quality of those questions. The quantity helps students develop fluid thinking habits and the quality helps them better engage with the material.

When I'm first working with a group of middle school students, I often assign them one page of text and ask them to write twelve questions. For many students this will be a difficult challenge, simply because they do not have adequate practice asking questions. Later, I will transition toward quality by teaching them about specific types of questions and eventually ask them to bring in 1-3 questions that could qualify as opening questions.

> **With practice, the students can develop habits to investigate the world around them with greater awe and wonder.**

I once went in to a sixth and seventh grade classroom to work with the students around some pre-seminar activities. They were reading *Jonathan Livingston Seagull* by Richard Bach. I put them in small groups and assigned each group one page of text. Their task was to generate twelve questions about that page. They struggled even in groups of three or four, and no group managed to get twelve written in a timely manner.

These were bright students with no shortage of talking and excitement, but many of them had never in their school lives been asked to generate questions. They didn't know where to look or how to form the wording for the questions. Several groups stopped after a few questions and declared that they didn't have any more (just when it started getting hard). Essentially, they didn't know where to focus their curiosity.

This is where I usually intervene and ask one of the groups what the word *the* means. After blank stares and blinking, most students struggle to define it. They know what it is (sort of), but they can't put it into words. The word *the* is probably on every page of most books and yet, perhaps because it so familiar, students pass over it as not interesting or important. I am not trying to be overly clever. The point is to quickly show that there are questions all around us, yet our awareness of them is minimal. If a question can be asked about such a common word, then they can be generated about anything ... with habits of mind—and that is what we are aspiring to with Socratic Seminar.

With this exercise, the twelve questions themselves were not what concerned me; it was a means to practice the habit of generating questions. With practice, the students can develop habits to investigate the world around them with greater awe and wonder. After that, twelve questions on one page of text becomes easy—even twelve questions about a single word. Take the word *question*. Here are twelve questions about it:

- What is the etymology of the word?
- Do all words starting with a "q" have a "u" that follows?
- Does it have to do with the idea of undertaking a quest?
- Does the suffix "-ion" mean anything?
- What could ions have to do with the word?
- Why do languages often inflect questions?
- What is the origin of the question mark?
- The vowel "a" is the only one missing in the word. Is that significant somehow?
- How many types of questions are there?
- Do all languages have the concept of questions?
- Is it significant that there are eight letters in the word?
- It can be a verb or noun. How many words can do this? What do they have in common?

Students can do challenges like this as practice for annotating. Start with large ideas, such as listing questions about ice hockey, and then make it harder by narrowing the topic. For example, have the students list twelve questions about the offense, twelve about defense, then twelve about shooting the puck. See the chapter on questions for more.

Over-Highlighting and Under-Annotating

When students are first taught close reading and annotating, they have a tendency to over-highlight. In my experience, it is not unusual for students to highlight or underline an entire block of text, sometimes an entire page or more. When asked why they marked everything, they often respond with something like, "Well, it was all important." This issue is one of not differentiating what is truly important. After all, if everything is important, then nothing was really important. After discussing the problem further, these students were also not distinguishing between *interesting* and *important.* To them, interesting meant important and deserved the same highlighting.

With more focus, students are better able to differentiate between interesting and truly important. Ask students questions like: "Of the things you found significant, what were the three most important?" and "What are the three most important sentences on this page? Why are they more important than the others?" Eventually, students are able to determine what was very, very important and they began to highlight fewer sentences and passages through closer reading.

Novice students also tend to under-annotate, even with specific instructions. They have a tendency to underline whole paragraphs without an accompanying symbol in the margin to indicate what they were thinking or wondering. The most common example of this is the lone question mark in the margin without an actual question. I often tell my students that a question mark is the mark of a question, and that they should write out the full question in the margin. A simple solution for this is to stop periodically during pre-seminar for students to check their annotations in pairs or small groups.

Tickets In

Students can be given a variety of tasks to prepare them for effective and efficient participation in seminar. The main purpose of a ticket in, or entrance ticket, is to help students participate and collaborate better in order to investigate the text more efficiently. It's common for students to bring in additional background research, class notes, and other materials. One ticket framework is the 3-2-1 model. Simply create three short tasks for students. For example:

Setting Goals (Personal and Group)

Another pre-seminar activity is to have the students set goals, either personal, group, or both. For shy students, this can be as simple as participating

Ticket In

Name:

List the page numbers of your three best annotations:

List two things you found interesting from the text:

Craft one potential opening question:

once, and for others it may be asking a question or quoting the text. Goals can also be based on the quality of participation, such as supporting a claim effectively, building on what others say, asking clarifying questions, and more. Use name tents or index cards so that participants can stay reminded of their goals.

In order to constantly improve, seminar groups should have goals as well. During post-seminar, students can debrief and create goals for better cohesion. These can include: using wait time after each speaker, citing the text better, not repeating, not engaging in side conversations, balancing participation, and anything else that will help the group improve their teamwork.

A great tool for creating both group and personal goals is Arthur Costa and Bena Kallicks's *16 Habits of Mind*. These can be used in many ways, from a basic checklist to increase awareness; as mini-lessons; as an assessment and feedback tool; or even as a tool for grading.

> For next trimester, I would like to become an even better listener, and to generate higher quality ideas that can lead our conversation to a great understanding of a text.
> ~ EF (grade 6)

Obviously, a great deal could be said about each of these, as Costa and Kallick elaborate in their books and trainings, but for the current purpose of setting goals, students could choose one of these as an area of focus for a time. As individuals or in small groups, they could research more about each of the habits to bring to seminar. For example, out of everything that Costa and Kallick could have created, why did *Finding Humor* make the list? What is so important about humor as a habit of mind?

During dialogue, the list can be used to help guide the conversation. Which of the sixteen habits would help us right now? How can we use Applying Past Knowledge to New Situations right now? These could also be used for debriefing: How well did we Persist today? On a scale of 1 to 10, how well did we Strive for Accuracy? Fist of five vote: How well did we use Questioning and Posing Problems?

Costa and Kallick's 16 Habits

1. Persisting
2. Managing Impulsivity
3. Listening with Understanding and Empathy
4. Thinking Flexibly
5. Thinking About Our Thinking (Metacognititon)
6. Striving for Accuracy
7. Questioning and Posing Problems
8. Applying Past Knowledge to New Situations
9. Thinking and Communicating with Clarity and Precision
10. Gathering Data Through All Senses
11. Creating, Imagining, and Innovating
12. Responding with Wonderment and Awe
13. Taking Responsible Risks
14. Finding Humor
15. Thinking Interdependently
16. Remaining Open to Continuous Learning

> **Students must practice sharing, just as they need to practice any other skill. Don't assume that they can turn-and-talk to each other effectively about a text.**

Sharing in Pairs or Small Groups

There are two important reasons for including a sharing stage—like a think-pair-share—before the formal Socratic Seminar. The first is that many students are too shy to share in a larger group, but they will share in smaller settings, especially with friends. This can provide them with important practice in formulating ideas and speaking to others. As Maria Nichols, author of *Comprehension through Conversation*, writes: "In small group, children often develop confidence by taking risks they would not take in whole group situations. As children take risks and realize that, with the support of the teacher and others in the group, they are able to communicate their thinking and construct meaning, they begin to speak more often." The second is that students who haven't yet made connections to the text can hear ideas and questions from others. This will give them additional material that they might need in order to effectively contribute.

Students must practice sharing, just as they need to practice any skill. Don't assume they can turn-and-talk to each other effectively about a text. Set a time limit for the sharing so that there is a sense of urgency and importance. Thirty seconds to a minute is usually enough for pairs, and maybe a minute to two minutes for small groups—any longer and students will probably wander. Consider choosing a few pairs or groups to share their collective thoughts with the entire class, so that this added pressure will help keep them focused.

Lastly, keep in mind that sharing in pairs or small groups can happen at any time, not just in the pre-seminar stage. My single favorite strategy for rebooting a stalled conversation is to use a turn-and-talk right after a new question. In these spontaneous or pre-planned sharing times, Nichols writes: "Children have an opportunity to process, try out, and strengthen their thinking with their peers, then come together and use their partner talk to build a whole group conversation."

> **It is tempting to think that students can look at a text effectively, since the image is right there in front of them and all they have to do is look at it. The reality, though, is that we do not all see the same things, and literally don't even see the whole picture.**

Visual Texts and Inattentional Blindness

Students do not have a lot of experience with asking questions and even less with thinking about things like paintings, photographs, maps, statues, or even the general visual world around them. But just as we have to teach close reading to students, we must also teach them "close looking."

It is tempting to think that students can look at a text effectively, since the image is right there in front of them. The reality, though, is that we do not all see the same things, and literally don't see the whole picture. Rita Carter, author of *Exploring Consciousness*, writes about the concept of inattentional blindness: "... an observer typically focuses on four or five small parts of a scene, and continues to scrutinize only these details even when they go on looking at the same thing for some time. Yet their subjective impression is that they have observed the whole image. The fact that they haven't studied the whole scene only becomes apparent when they try to recall it and find they can't."

The most effective method that I have found for visual texts is a simple exercise that can be done in pairs, small groups, or by an entire class. Remember that the main idea of pre-seminar is to provide the students with material to talk about during the full dialogue.

Hand out the visual or project it on a screen and have the students take turns saying something that they notice—and notice only. There are no interpretations, inferences, or opinions at this point, since those are for the seminar. Allow students to pass if eventually they don't see anything new. Also, you may want to have the shy students start first, so that they can be successful. Keep going until the group slows down and then you can finish "popcorn style" by having the students call out any last observations.

The following example is from the back of a one-dollar bill (please get one out and have a look as you read). The strikethrough words are things many students might say, but encourage them to stay with the pure objectivity of basic observations. Inferences, opinions, and ideas are for sharing during the seminar itself. This example assumes the students are each looking at a different dollar bill.

Pre-seminar for Back of Dollar Bill:

Jess	It's ~~not colorful and only~~ green and off-white in color.
Devante	It says 'The United States of America' at the top.
Nia	It says 'In God We Trust' above a large 'ONE.'
Mara	There are two circles, one on the left and one right. I like the symmetry.
Mike	The left circle has a pyramid with an eye at the top. ~~That's too steep to be an Egyptian pyramid.~~
Erik	It says 'Annuit Coeptis' above the pyramid.
Maxim	There are Roman numerals at the base of the pyramid.
Keisha	It says 'Novus Ordo Seclorum' on a banner under the pyramid.
Justin	Under that it says 'The Great Seal.'
Aniya	In the circle on the right there's a bald eagle, ~~which is a symbol of freedom.~~
Desiree	It's got a ribbon in its mouth that reads 'E Pluribus Unum.'
Patrick	There's a design above its head with ... 13 stars. ~~That's a reference to the thirteen original colonies.~~
Emil	There's a block or shield on the eagle's chest. It has vertical and horizontal lines on it.
Lucas	There are seven white vertical lines on it and six striped lines. They have ... three smaller lines each.
Mia	In the eagle's left, no right, claw is a branch.
Sofia	In the other, it's grasping ... 13 arrows.
Essina	Whoa, the branch has 13 berries!
Thomas	... and 13 leaves.
Arya	The eagle is facing the branch not the arrows, ~~which means that it first embraces peace.~~

Dayton	*Underneath it says 'Of The United States.'*
Coty	*To the left of the eagle's circle there's the number 111.*
Kyle	*Mine has the number 40.*
Frieda	*Mine has 144 there.*
Aidan	*The background has a lot of lines on it that crisscross.*
Noah	*The stars in the design above the eagle are arranged from top to bottom 1-4-3-4-1.*
Caleb	*There are ~~really cool~~ swirly patterns around the circles.*
Caris	*The eagle has nine tail feathers.*
Idris	*The top of the pyramid on the left is not connected to the rest.*
Ava	*It says 'One' and has the number '1' in all four corners.*

One note regarding what Aniya said. Does she actually *know* that's a bald eagle? Can she actually differentiate an eagle from a hawk or a falcon? Is she assuming that because it's a bird of prey in the context of the U.S. that it must be a bald eagle? Does she actually *know* it's a symbol?

This visual pre-seminar activity can be extended into a See-Think-Wonder routine. After the initial objective observations, ask the students what they think about certain elements of the visual text. Afterward, students can generate questions about what they wonder. Add a think-pair-share or a think-draw-share for further engagement. Here are some questions: *Why is our money green? Why a pyramid? Why put an eye at the top of the pyramid? Why the repetition of the number thirteen? Why does this piece of paper (linen) represent money? How does it have value? Why have symbols on money?*

Once the students have scrutinized the text and "closely seen" it, they can then move into the formal conversation part of the seminar.

> **The biggest enemy of thinking is complexity,**
> **for that leads to confusion.**
> **~ Edward de Bono**

Pre-Seminar Jobs

The idea of preparing a text for seminar without focusing on something specific often overwhelms students. They might stare at the page, unable to find a starting place in the text. As Edward de Bono (1985) writes: "The biggest enemy of thinking is complexity, for that leads to confusion." Overwhelmed students generally only have a few reactions: they quit; they wait for someone else to do the work; or they return to old habits whether those work or not. Very few overwhelmed students take risks and try something new—in this case, contributing something or practicing a skill for seminar.

One way to help is giving students specific jobs, individually, in small groups, or as a class. This will allow them to focus on a single aspect of the text, both for annotating and/or for participating in the seminar itself. With the *gradual release of responsibility* idea in mind, you will be able to introduce and assign individualized jobs, and the students will be able to focus on more specific aspects of the text (product-based jobs) or the seminar (process-based jobs) or both.

Sample Pre-Seminar Jobs	
Vocabulary Finder	Researcher
Question Maker	Sequencer
Discussion Leader	Bias Detector
Symbol Decoder	Mapmaker
Illustrator	Survey Maker
Real World Connector	Character Trait Collector
Summarizer	Choreographer

There are numerous jobs that students could do at the pre-seminar stage. It is not within the scope of this book to explicate many of them, since there are already numerous resources available, such as *Literature Circles: Voice and Choice in the Student-Centered Classroom* by Harvey Daniels. This book outlines several jobs for literature circles (easily adapted for seminars) that each have accompanying planning sheets for students. Examples include: Illustrator, responsible for drawing an important snapshot from the text; Summarizer, responsible for conveying main points or highlights; Discussion Leader, responsible for directing the conversation, and many more.

There are a few important things to remember about seminar jobs. The first is that the students should rotate having various jobs, so that they all can practice important skills. In sports, coaches use drills to practice specific skills, but then try to put them all together in scrimmages and games. The same situation exists for Socratic Seminar. The students may practice specific skills, but eventually they need opportunities to put everything together. Some students may already be good at certain tasks, so it would be a good idea to do some kind of skills assessment ahead of time. This way students could test out of certain areas and practice the specific skills they need as individuals.

The second thing to keep in mind is *gradual release of responsibility*. With all of these skills, students should eventually be expected to do them on their own. Obviously, teachers are likely to have to model some or all of these skills, but they can release responsibility with the "I do," "we do," "you do" model or something similar.

Pre-seminar jobs should generally stay in the pre-seminar until such a time as the information becomes relevant to the conversation. The students can share their findings with a partner or in small groups, but then set their pre-seminar jobs aside when the formal conversation part of the seminar begins. The jobs should not become the seminar.

> **Alone we can do so little; together we can do so much.**
> ~ Helen Keller

Tao Te Ching Chapter 2

When the world knows beauty as beauty, ugliness arises

When it knows good as good, evil arises

Thus being and non-being produce each other

Difficult and easy bring about each other

Long and short reveal each other

High and low support each other

Music and voice harmonize each other

Front and back follow each other

Therefore the sages:

Manage the work of detached actions

Conduct the teaching of no words

They work with myriad things but do not control

They create but do not possess

They act but do not presume

They succeed but do not dwell on success

It is because they do not dwell on success

That it never goes away

~ Lao Tzu

Without setting the jobs aside, the pre-seminar tasks may overly structure the dialogue, leading to stilted conversations and disconnected ideas. For example, a student responsible for bringing the opening question for chapter 2 of the *Tao Te Ching* may start the seminar with a question about how the expression "opposites attract" applies to the text. Instead of responding to the question, a student responsible for vocabulary (who settled for "sages") follows with a non-sequitur by defining the word. A third student adds historical information about Lao Tzu. Another student tells a story about supply and demand to explain the line: *High and low support each other.*

In this case, the students are not really listening to each other and working together, but are instead just doing their jobs. They may have been doing what they were asked to do, but they are not having a quality conversation.

If everyone *only* did his or her job during seminar, then there wouldn't even be a conversation.

So, help the students understand that these jobs are mainly used in the pre-seminar stage for generating *potential* ideas and talking points for dialogue. It might be frustrating for them at first if the research or idea they prepared isn't ever used, but once they understand that Socratic Seminar is a community effort, they will appreciate that sometimes their jobs will produce a relevant and useful idea and sometimes they won't.

> **Anchor papers help clarify not only how the teacher perceives the grading scale for the assignment, but they also help students understand what they need to do in order to improve.**

Grading Annotations

Because annotations form the foundation of pre-seminar, teachers must have effective ways to assess and grade the students. I have tried many things over the years and nothing is as powerful as using anchor papers. Even after being thoroughly taught about something as complex as annotating, students can easily lose sight of exactly what quality work is (and is not). The line between what constitutes an A and a C grade can be remarkably unclear to many students.

Anchor papers clarify not only how the teacher perceives the grading scale for the assignment, but they also help students understand what to do in order to improve. After teaching my students how to annotate and giving them a few seminars to practice, I create several fictitious anchor papers that roughly range in my grading scale from A to F and then copy them onto colored paper. See the examples in the appendices.

Then I have the students examine the five papers in small groups to assign each one a grade or rank. They should look for what is there and also what is missing. I walk around and facilitate conversations about their decisions. For example, a group might assign one of the papers an A (or exceeds expectations). Since an A would qualify for honor roll in most schools, I might say something like, "This got an A? Okay. If a student got all A's, he or she would qualify for honor roll. Is this honor roll effort?"

Most students are shy about giving papers a failing grade, perhaps because they have innate fears about failing themselves. Whatever the reason, I have found that students will often give extremely weak papers a passing grade simply because the fictitious student "did something" or "at least tried." However, I will challenge them: "So, this got a D-minus? Hmmm. If a student got all D-minuses, he or she would pass every class with this amount of effort. Is that okay?" Usually, they answer with something like: "No way! They have to do better!"

After grading the papers in small groups, I have the students justify their answers as a whole class. This allows them to see what other groups appreciated about certain papers, and what they thought could be improved. The grades for the papers are usually close to what mine would be, but once in a while there will be a paper that gets an outlier grade. This may seem like a problem, but I actually like when this happens because we can talk about and clarify expectations.

Once the students understand the grades that each anchor paper would receive, I like to make copies and affix the examples to folders that are posted near the door. From this point on, the students can grade themselves on their annotations by placing their papers in the folder with the anchor paper that most closely resembles theirs. This gives them a constant visual reminder of what their goals are for their annotations, provides an opportunity for a bit of self-assessment, and takes a lot of the surprises out of the grading process.

Having the students self-select the appropriate folder also helps gather information about the students. Some students, for example, will downgrade their work by almost always putting their papers in the B or C folder simply because they "could always do better." In this case, their concept of the A grade is something like "perfect" instead of "very good," which is worthy of a conversation. Quite a few students also feel strange about giving themselves high grades because they equate the process to bragging.

Other students inflate their grades because they feel they worked hard enough or perhaps because they have misguided ideas about expectations. I had a student once who always put her paper in the B folder no matter what she did. After seeing a wide variety of quality from her, I began to wonder why she kept choosing the same folder. I finally asked her and she said, "I've been told I'm a B student so I put my papers there." So I had to work with her about seeing beyond other peoples' expectations and seeing her efforts and work for what they truly were.

Creating and using anchor papers takes a class or two, but is well worth the time. The value in this process is that students become clearer, not only about expectations for annotations, but also how certain grades can be achieved.

Summing Up

1. Pre-seminar can be likened to the warm-ups that athletes do before sporting events.
2. Mini-lessons can help students focus on specific skills for pre-seminar, seminar, or post-seminar.
3. Annotating is for generating ideas, crafting questions, and increasing interest.
4. Because of "inattentional blindness," visual texts must be specially examined ahead of time.
5. Students can be assigned pre-seminar jobs, but those jobs should not become the seminar.
6. Generating questions is vital to the inquiry process.
7. Use anchor papers for grading annotations.

Your Next Steps

- Research "pre-reading" and "close reading" for additional text preparation ideas.

- For students struggling with literacy or language, the pre-seminar could include any combination of read-aloud, audio books, interactive iBooks, movie versions (with or without closed captioning), translations and more.

- As needed, consider visual ways to prepare for seminars. Students could draw graphs or maps, could use Thinking Maps, graphic organizers, or any other means to visually organize information.

- Research and use any number of "thinking routines" and protocols to get students focused and ready. A great resource is Project Zero's *Visible Thinking* website.

- Research the concept of "Pre-listening" to help you and your students better prepare for any type of discussion, lecture, or Socratic Seminar.

- Consider hanging the seminar text in the classroom a few weeks ahead of time, so that students can keep looking at and familiarizing themselves with it through repeated contact.

- Pre-made discussion balls to toss around are sometimes known as "Throw & Tell" or "Toss 'n Talk-About" balls.

5

The Text

There are two ways to slide easily through life; to believe every-thing or to doubt everything. Both ways save us from thinking.

~ Alfred Korzybski

THE "TEXT" OR artifact for a Socratic Seminar can be anything that will promote a complex thinking process—typically a well-chosen poem, a short piece of fiction, an excerpt from a novel, a work of art, a deep question or quotation, a geometric proof, a movie clip, a song, etc. In less formal settings, a seminar could even be about how a hole appeared in a fence or the "story" that is told from tracks in a sandbox.

Choosing a text is complicated and may even be the hardest part of planning for a Socratic Seminar. A poorly chosen text can flop even with an adept facilitator, a solid opening question and experienced students, whereas a well-chosen text can stimulate conversation even in the most unenthusiastic or inexperienced classrooms. However, even well chosen texts may not work for every group or teacher.

As an example, I once had some middle school students who were struggling to understand spelling and grammar conventions. It was my theory that they were struggling to learn because they didn't have a value for them. I decided to use a text with unconventional spelling and grammar as a way to explore the territory. In this case it was *"a glazed mind layed in a urinal"* by E. E. Cummings (though any non-conventional text, like *Flowers for Algernon* by Daniel Keyes, would probably have worked).

I hoped that we could have conversations around: *Whose responsibility is it to make a text clear? Is it the author's, the reader's or both? What are conventions for? Why would we want to use them?* I didn't have an agenda to push, but I was interested to listen to them about where they were coming from and what their ideas were.

The first class period appreciated Cummings' unconventional spelling and grammar and recognized that there was a technique somehow operating. The students discussed how difficult it was to determine Cummings' point and how much work they had to do in order to create even basic understandings. I learned a lot from them and was excited for more insights from the second class.

With the next class, something was immediately different. The students were working furiously during pre-seminar, and after what I considered a significant amount of time, they still weren't done annotating. What I discovered was that they were busy fixing grammar and spelling. Some of them had even started rewriting the poem in conventional language. Our subsequent conversation was shallow and students were fixated on how "stupid" the text was because of all the supposed mistakes.

Even after years of facilitating, I still make mistakes choosing texts. There is no magic formula for what will work, but a mistake is often a better teacher than success, so I don't mind. Trial and error is still my main strategy for picking a text and I'm not sure that will ever change. I have, however, gotten more consistent and learned some important lessons.

Most importantly, the text should have no obvious right or wrong answer or concept, such as a moral. This is so that the dialogue will be genuine inquiry and investigation, rather than an exercise in arriving at the "right" answer. If the text has a moral, such as one of Aesop's fables, or an overly conclusive summary, remove that part of the text so that the students can draw their own morals and conclusions. Be careful about sharing the actual moral, since the students will evaluate themselves on their accuracy.

> I would tell [future students] that not every situation has a designated right and wrong answer, to respect each other's ideas, and to try to help each other arrive at an explanation, rather than proving each other wrong.
> ~RW (grade 8)

Additional Thoughts on Text Selection

- In the beginning, the text should be relatively short—typically only a few paragraphs at first so that the conversation can stay focused. When using a novel or other long text, use seminars to focus in on specific sections.

- The text should be complex enough to require close reading and annotating.

- The text should be difficult for the participants to comprehend as individuals so that everyone is needed in order to create meaning.

- The text should have widespread "big idea" appeal for most or all participants.

- The text should have interpretive issues, ambiguities, contradictions, and/or multiple justifiable interpretations.

- At the beginning of a unit, use a text to introduce and explore essential questions, big ideas, or themes.

- In the middle of a unit, use a text to deepen ideas, unravel difficult spots, and investigate complex issues.

- At the end of a unit, use a text to gauge student understandings, to make connections to themes or objectives, and to synthesize and expand information.

Text Complexity

In the Common Core State Standards, there is a three-part model of text complexity. The first is *Qualitative measures of text complexity,* which includes the meaning and purpose of the text, structure, levels of meaning, language conventionality and clarity, and knowledge demands. The second is *Quantitative dimensions of text complexity*, which are those that are more measurable, such as word length, sentence length, and text cohesion. The third is *Reader and task considerations*, which include things like reader motivation, the purpose of the text, and the actual questions posed of the text. All three are important considerations.

In general, better Socratic Seminar texts, pairings, and sets will:

- have multiple interpretations or levels of meaning.
- be implicit rather than explicit.
- be unconventional more often than conventional.
- be unusually structured or presented.
- be figurative, ironic, allegorical, or symbolic.
- present multiple viewpoints or experiences.

Further Considerations

According to Strong, the ideal text is "one in which students know the meaning of each word individually, but have no understanding of the paragraph as a whole. Meaning is constructed by the group clause by clause, sentence by sentence, or paragraph by paragraph, based on the group's determination of how finely the text must be broken down in order to reach comprehension." If there are challenging vocabulary words in the text, then the students should define them in pre-seminar; otherwise the text will likely only generate a discussion about connotations and denotations.

A well-chosen text *before* an upcoming unit can act as a framework for the larger ideas. Texts after the main lesson(s) can help students further engage with the material in new ways. For example, in a unit on Homer's *The Odyssey*, a supplemental Socratic Seminar based on the question *Do you believe in fate?* may help students engage with the ideas of free will versus predeterminism, which are important for understanding the ancient Greek world. A seminar conducted after Cream's song lyrics *Tales of Brave Ulysses* or C. P. Cavafy's poem *Ithaka* can help students make new connections.

Be cautious of texts that bring up extremely controversial, heated subjects, such as the death penalty, since these will often depart into debates where students deviate from the text and almost always return and stick to their preconceived ideas and opinions. Generally speaking, use such texts and topics in debate class.

Howard Zeiderman also suggests choosing non-contemporary texts. One of the dangers with contemporary texts is that students might become locked into thinking about them only in terms of like and dislike, rather then attempting to actually understand them. He writes, "If the text were entirely familiar and contemporary, it would only reinforce the opinions of some participants and run counter to the opinions of others. The result would be argument and debate rather than discussion. A degree of unfamiliarity, which is found in non-contemporary works, is therefore necessary." Although I do not agree that non-contemporary texts are *necessary,* the idea is still important to consider. In my experience, students have rarely practiced thinking deeply, even about such things as their favorite songs that they hear everyday.

Types of "Texts"

A "text" for Socratic Seminar is any artifact or piece that will be the focal point for inquiry and dialogue. Nearly anything with complexity, ambiguity, implicit meaning, and/or levels of thought should work well. Short stories, poems, and song lyrics are often particularly provocative, since many tend to be very dense and abstract. Excerpts from philosophical and scientific writings can also be good seminar texts, since they, too, are often dense with big ideas and complexities. Dialogues about whether advertisements are misleading can be remarkably insightful.

Visual arts, such as paintings, photographs, optical illusions, and film clips often work well because of the inherent interpretive complexities. Artists such as Salvador Dali, Leonora Carrington, M. C. Escher, Abelardo Morell, Remedios Varo, Kurt Wenner, Kay Sage, Shepard Fairey, Erik Johansson, and Michael Parkes all have great pieces for seminar. Street artists always intrigue me, often because they have hidden messages behind their art that students can discover and uncover during seminar. Some street artist suggestions: Banksy, Above, Roa, Laguna, SpY, Hyuro, and Mentalgassi.

Dali's *Persistence of Memory* and episodes of the television shows *Night Gallery* and *The Twilight Zone* have been some of my students' favorite pieces of all time. Chapters from the *Tao Te Ching* are extremely reliable for middle and high school students. Numerous short stories by Ray Bradbury and Philip K. Dick have made excellent seminar texts for me.

Fables, folktales, and poems are great for younger elementary students, though remember to consider taking off any strong conclusions or morals so that students can do their own thinking. Aesop's fables are very popular, and many other good moral stories can be found all over the web. Robert Louis Stevenson, Shel Silverstein, A. A. Milne, Judith Viorst, and Paul Fleischman have some great poems for younger students.

I have had a lot of success using Dr. Seuss with middle and high school students. They tend to underestimate the complexities in stories such as *Yertle the Turtle* and *The Lorax* ... until they realize that the stories contain universal themes that they probably missed when they were younger. A turtle was just a turtle; a tree was just a tree. As they revisit the text in seminar, these may take on new meanings. A turtle may become a symbol of oppressed people. A tree may symbolize the human mind.

Interesting conversations often emerge about whether Dr. Seuss put those "additional meanings" in the text to begin with or not. Are we simply bringing new understanding to the text? If so, what does that say about the reading process? Such lines of questioning can make for many wonderful Socratic Seminars, especially for middle school students who are beginning to see and appreciate allegory and symbolism for the first time.

Text Examples

Poetry	"anyone lived in a pretty how town" by E. E. Cummings
	"I'm Nobody! Who Are You?" by Emily Dickinson
Short Story	*An Ominous Baby* by Stephen Crane
	Through the Tunnel by Doris Lessing
Short Text	*Tao Te Ching* chapter 2
Picture Book	*The Sneetches* by Dr. Seuss
	Weslandia by Paul Fleischman
Movie Clip	*Indiana Jones and the Raiders of the Lost Ark*
	Pleasantville
Painting	*Persistence of Memory* by Dali
Excerpt from novel	Opening paragraph to *A Tale of Two Cities*

Text Examples (continued)

Question	"What is boredom?" "Do you believe in Fate?"
Quotation	"First they came …" by Martin Niemoller
Song + Lyrics	"Daughter" by Pearl Jam "The Sounds of Silence" by Paul Simon
Song + Lyrics + Visual	"This Must Be the Place (Naive Melody)" by Talking Heads and contemporary art from *What the Songs Look Like*
Classical Music	"The Planets" by Gustav Holst
Math Proof	Euclid's *Book of the Elements*
Chart or Graph	Immigration in the 19th Century
Performance	Jérome Murat's *The Statue with Two Heads*
Primary Resource	Columbus's Journal
Political Cartoon	"Join or Die" by Benjamin Franklin
Map	"The Spread of Islam"
TV Show	*Star Trek: Voyager* episode 191: "Living Witness"
Paradox	"This sentence is false." (True or false?)
Event	Hole in a fence — "What happened here?"
Diagram	Abraham Maslow's Hierarchy of Needs

It's arguably easier to facilitate conversations *outside* of your expertise, since you actually would have genuine questions.

Conversations on visual arts, music, sports, or other areas besides written texts may at first seem more difficult to facilitate, but they aren't. They may appear to be harder since some students and teachers may not be familiar with the basic tools of analysis in some disciplines like music or art: color theory, shape and proportion, harmony and dissonance, major and minor keys, music theory and much more. For example, where do you start with a painting? How do you determine the meaning of music?

However, teachers and students should realize that the life of a seminar is always in the questions—and anyone can ask those. By focusing on asking questions, art teachers can easily facilitate seminars about math, English teachers on music, and math teachers on poetry. In fact, any teacher can facilitate a seminar on just about anything. There still may be times where the conversation steers too far away from a teacher's academic comfort zone, but that shouldn't scare anyone away from inquiry. It's arguably easier to facilitate conversations *outside* of your expertise, since you would actually have genuine questions.

Choose Printed Text Over Digital

A key decision is whether to have students use digital or printed texts. Given the choice, a lot of teachers may want to choose digital media in order to save paper or copies, because of using a flipped classroom model, or maybe because of recently purchased technology. Ask the students, and many of them say they prefer to read on digital devices. The digital version of a text seems to have many advantages: it's harder to misplace or lose, it's portable across multiple devices, it can be digitally manipulated, and notes and highlights can be saved and shared. Printed texts remain a reliable standard that students can highlight, make notes in the margins, and doodle in the extra spaces, but are they boring or outdated?

Given the choice, should Socratic Seminar facilitators choose digital or print?

In an October 15, 2017 article for *Business Insider*, Patricia Alexander and Lauren Singer write about their findings regarding the differences. Essentially, they found that for texts longer than a page, students were better able to comprehend information in print. More importantly for seminar facilitators, they also found that for specific questions going beyond general concepts such as the main idea of the text that "comprehension was significantly better when participants read printed texts." My own observations support the use of printed texts as well, largely because I have found that my students are more focused and academically inclined when they read and wrestle with a printed text.

So, especially for Socratic Seminar, print texts appear to be the best choice.

Text Pairings

Combining two (or more) texts together for a seminar can create excellent complexity and great dialogue. These pairings can be chosen because of the similarities or their differences. Similar texts often help to focus discussion on different perspectives and viewpoints on universal themes. For example, pairing *The Giver* by Lois Lowry with the short story "The Ones Who Walk Away from Omelas" by Ursula K. Le Guin may help students explore morality and the nature of happiness.

Choosing two texts that contradict each other can lead to powerful critical and creative thinking as well, since the right pairings will show multiple viewpoints of the same time period, event, or issue. For example, juxtaposing two artists such as Norman Rockwell and Lewis Hine can show students that there are differing viewpoints and experiences of the same time period. Contradictory informational or persuasive texts are obvious choices since they often both seem factual and correct. For example, if your curriculum presents a certain historical character in a heroic light, then choosing a text that vilifies that person will put the students in the twilight of uncertainty.

Books like Greenberg's *Heart to Heart: New Poems Inspired by Twentieth-Century American Art* pair poetry and art together in complex ways. *The Chronicles of Harris Burdick* by Chris Van Allsburg is a great collection of inspired stories based on the author's mysterious illustrations. *The New York Times*' The Learning Network, in collaboration with the Poetry Foundation, offers "Poetry Pairings" that make for excellent seminar texts.

One fun source for linguistic pairings is Montague Brown's *The One-Minute Philosopher.* The book is set up to explore dozens of conceptual word pairs, such as admiration/envy, confidence/pride, error/fault, friendship/fellowship, justice/law, reason/logic, and wonder/bewilderment. These pairings make excellent texts because students can explore the polarity of the pairings, as well as the overlapping gray area between those ideas. In addition, the further reading section suggests specific pairings of classical texts that explore the issues further.

A fantastic resource entitled *Suggestions for Pairing Contemporary Music and Canonical Literature* can be found at *CornDancer.com* and websites like Pinterest and Teachers Pay Teachers have vast resources. Other websites for pairings and text sets:

- *CommonLit.org*
- *NewsELA.com*
- *ListenWise.com*
- *ReadWorks.org*

For added complexity, combine several types of media into a seminar text set, or dossier. The students then must weigh evidence and examine levels of validity from various sources. For example, a text set about dress code might include: a national newspaper article or blog advocating for dress code, a scientific paper against, a school newspaper article against, and a thought-provoking photo of a team all wearing their uniforms.

One of my favorite sources for language arts, music, and art is the book *What the Songs Look Like: Contemporary Artists Interpret Talking Heads' Songs* by Talking Heads and Frank Olinsky. This book combines the song lyrics with pieces of contemporary art. By incorporating the music as well, the lyrics, and the visuals create a three-part complex text set.

Quotations

Famous sayings and short quotations can be tricky for seminar. On one hand, they can work well since they are often about universal big ideas or issues. However, many sayings and quotations are very short. With inexperienced groups this is often not enough material, so participants are forced to move *beyond the lines* of the text in order to make meaning. This often leads to a large amount of speculation and personal anecdotes, which often do not promote critical thinking and close reading.

If you really want to use a quotation, consider collecting several together and then using them as a set. For example, take these five quotes from legendary coach John Wooden. During pre-seminar, make sure the students understand what the quotes might be first saying. Then, an opening question for the group might be: *Which of these quotes would be the best advice for us? Which one would make the best motto for our new school year? Which one would make the best advice for new seminar groups?*

Text Set of John Wooden Quotes

- Don't mistake activity with achievement.

- If you don't have time to do it right, when will you have the time to do it over?

- It is amazing how much can be accomplished if no one cares who gets the credit.

- Failing to prepare is preparing to fail.

- Listen if you want to be heard.

Math Texts

Socratic Seminars tend to be less common in math classes, perhaps because of a seeming lack of interpretive issues. However, math problems with enough complexity can make excellent seminar texts. Many teachers have found that proofs from sources such as Euclid's *Elements* work well. Certain mathematics books, such as *Interactive Mathematics* (Year 1) by Daniel M. Fendel, have complex problems that can work well for middle and high school. Phillips Exeter Academy in New Hampshire, renowned for their Harkness Method, has discussion-based math classes that use complex problem sets specially designed for students to work through together. They have made some of their problem sets available on their website.

Several math teachers I have worked with have had success with a seminar-like activity that I call a Gallery Walk Seminar. To set up this style of seminar, place several complex, multi-step problems around the room with a variety of solutions (either drawn from student examples or thoughtfully crafted by the teacher). The solutions should be short and long, direct and indirect, arithmetical and algebraic, formulaic and geometric, etc.

In small groups, the students then peruse the room museum-style, guided by a discussion question or set of questions, such as: *Which one is most reliable? Which one would be the most prone to mistakes? Which solution is the most elegant? Which is the most efficient? Which one is the best solution? Which is the most beautiful? Which shows the most care? Patience?*

This can remain a small group activity, or after determining their answer(s), the groups can then convene in a circle for a larger dialogue. The students would need some pre-seminar work to first understand what is meant by *elegant* or *beautiful* in mathematics. And of course, the most important aspects of this activity are the reasons and justifications that students have about each of the solutions.

Several teachers at Forest Park High School in Forest Park, Georgia did something similar by showing several graphs to students and asking them which one best matched a specific scenario. In their article "Socratic Seminars for Mathematics," Koellner-Clark, Stallings, and Hoover found "that the method of Socratic Seminars was very effective in encouraging students to assume responsibility for reasoning and communicating convincingly about mathematics" and that the more verbal learners "showed understanding that they had not shown on pencil-and-paper assessments."

For younger students, try *mathematizing* picture books, as Hintz and Smith suggest, in order to begin an inquiry process that could lead to a seminar dialogue. In their three-step process, start by selecting a text that features math, highlights mathematical ideas, or contains visuals for exploring mathematical concepts. Second, explore the text by "engaging students in lively discussion before, during, and after reading" (or reading aloud). In this stage, students pay attention to the mathematics involved, write and share recording strategies, and discuss how and why they represented their mathematical thinking. Their suggested third stage, Extending the Text, can lead to excellent seminar dialogue: "One way to extend the text is to delve more deeply into discussion of key ideas, emphasizing mathematical applications or connections between concepts and personal experience."

Math Texts for Mathematizing a Picture Book

The Hungry Caterpillar by Eric Carle

Double Those Wheels by Nancy Raines Day

Mummy Math: An Adventure in Geometry by Cindy Neuschwander

Ten Flashing Fireflies by Philemon Sturges

The Doorbell Rang by Pat Hutchins

Math Fiction for Seminar

"The Feeling of Power" by Isaac Asimov

The Man Who Counted by Malba Tahan

The Phantom Tollbooth by Norton Juster

The Number Devil by Hans Magnus Enzensberger

Flatland by Edwin Abbott

Beyond Infinity by Charles Fischer

Riddles and Puzzles

Riddles, puzzles, and other texts that tend to have a "right" answer, or a small field of answers, have not worked well for me. Once the riddle is "solved," students relax their thinking or stop inquiry altogether. The task seems finished to them and they have difficulty seeing the value in continuing dialogue.

An example of what didn't work well for me is the well-known puzzle: *Why are manhole covers round?* Once students determined the standard answer, that a circular shape prevents the cover from falling down through the hole, they slowed down their inquiry. (With a square hole, the cover could fall through since the hypotenuse is longer than the sides. A circular cover, with all distances from the center the same, cannot fall through no matter how it's turned). Despite my promptings, they did not generate other ideas, such as: it's round so that it can be rolled; perhaps that's the cheapest method of production; or that a circular shape maximizes area.

With multiple answers possible, this may seem like a potentially good text. But here's the problem. This is a well-known puzzle with a well-known answer. Chances are high that someone may have heard "the answer." What happens then is that someone will respond with what I call the *emphatic hammer*. They may say, "Oh, I've heard this one before. It's because a round cover can't fall through." Since the answer comes with such emphasis and certainty, and because it seems perfectly correct, the other students may feel it's a wrap. As a teacher who wants to promote thinking, I can urge them to discover other possibilities (which may feel like an agenda), but I have found that this does not feel genuine and starts to feel more like filler until the seminar ends.

Videos and Film Clips

Videos and film clips can be excellent sources for texts. Episodes of Rod Serling's *Twilight Zone* and *Night Gallery* have worked extremely well for me. Unlike some television shows, these episodes are powerful, intriguing, and thought provoking. Some of them, like "Occurrence at Owl Creek Bridge" by Ambrose Bierce are adaptations of short stories, and therefore, make excellent supplements to units of study. Clips from the beautiful non-narrative movies *Baraka* and *Samsara* have worked extremely well for me as well.

I had great success with a 7-minute clip from *Indiana Jones and the Raiders of the Lost Ark*, the scene where Harrison Ford's character switches the bag of sand for the golden idol. We enjoyed a rich conversation about the possible symbolic meanings of the idol, Indiana's name and the irony that he's stealing from indigenous people, the fact that two clearly white people are in charge of the entire operation (Indiana and his arch-enemy waiting outside), and much more.

Music videos are challenging, since many of them are inappropriate and some are too visually stimulating. I once tried using the video for *Birdhouse in Your Soul* by the band They Might Be Giants. We had read the song lyrics in the previous seminar and seemed prepared for the video. Even though it was half the length of the *Raiders of the Lost Ark* clip, it was fast-paced, with too many images and scenes flashing past to make comprehension possible.

We watched the video twice, and then focused on a couple of sections to watch again. We attempted some entry points, but there were simply too many and we floundered with where to begin and what exactly to talk about.

However, because of the combination of music, lyrics and visuals, some music videos make fantastic complex texts. Check out "Take on Me" by a-Ha, "The Scientist" by Coldplay, "Do You" by Spoon, "Caught in the Crowd" by Kate Miller-Heidke, and "Karma Police" by Radiohead.

A performance can easily spark hours of conversation, or more with experienced participants. Theatrical performances, such as Jérome Murat's *The Statue with Two Heads*, make great seminar texts. Many animated short films will work well as Socratic Seminar texts, especially because the visual aspects appeal to students. Most of them do not have dialogue, so they lend themselves to interpretive complexities. Some favorite shorts: *Snack Attack, Paperman, The Lost Thing, Feast,* and *The Fantastic Flying Books of Mr. Morris Lessmore.*

> **Seminars based around wildly open questions like "What is mathematics?" might generate interesting ideas and perhaps help a teacher learn about the students, but a full text would likely produce better dialogue.**

A Question as the Text

The text for a seminar can be a single question, such as: "What is boredom?" However, similar to using riddles or quotations, such seminars are more difficult to facilitate. Because there isn't a physical text to cite or talk about, students often must speculate instead of thinking critically. This isn't necessarily a bad thing, though, since provocative questions can often promote new and creative ideas. For example, I once used the question "What is boredom?" for a seminar with middle schoolers. One student noted that he was never bored in the morning, which led the group to the idea that boredom was more about being tired than being interested, which was a thought that many of them had never considered.

Seminars based around wildly open questions like "What is mathematics?" might generate interesting ideas and perhaps help a teacher learn about the students, but a full text would likely produce better dialogue. A slight variation on the question can use a text and still explore the idea: "According to the author, what is mathematics?" The task can be made even more difficult using multiple texts: "According to these texts, what is mathematics?"

In addition, many variations on a basic question are much more engaging for students, so teachers should practice generating questions. Rick Garlikov, in his article entitled "Teaching Effectively: Helping Students Absorb and Assimilate Material," writes:

> I used to hate when teachers began a history or psychology course or some such by coming in the first day and asking "What is history?" or "What is psychology?" That usually puts all but the most avid "teacher-pleasers" into a stupor, usually saying something to themselves like "It is the stuff in this book" or "Who cares?" or "I don't know; why don't you just tell us, since you have the degree in it?" Instead, if a history teacher were to come in to class and say instead something like, "Is it part of history whether Shakespeare owned chickens or not, or whether he ate eggs on the day he began to write *Romeo and Juliet*?" or "Suppose all the history books ever written and all the diaries and journals we have were totally lost, would there still be history? And if so, what would it be?" or "Are the things you have forgotten about your own life still part of your biography or history?" or "What if some of the things in history books are false? Are they still part of history?" or "Commentators and politicians often say things like 'History will judge whether this is the right policy or not.' Well, when does history begin, or get to make that judgment? How long do we have to wait for 'history' to kick in? Or who in the future gets to say?" Questions like those might generate a much more lively and a much more productive discussion than "What is history?"

Science Lab as a Text

In science, Socratic Seminar can still be used in the typical way: The students can annotate a scientific article, generate questions, form a circle, and have a genuine conversation together. Alexis Wiggins writes: "If you are struggling to imagine how to use discussion in your science classroom, the easiest point of entry is to discuss controversial or ethical issues in the news, such as bioethics, climate change, abortion, drugs in sports, genetically modified crops, or vaccination." These issues can often stir up good dialogue, though they can become too heated for some groups. In my experience, many students have deeply-rooted, family-based opinions on topics like abortion, and getting them to openly dialogue about the subject is nearly impossible.

Seminar may also be used in a lab-based science class in a most interesting way. Split the students into lab teams of 4-8 students. From there, split each team into two groups. The first group will do the lab and the second group will observe—essentially similar to forming inner and outer concentric circles. Then they switch roles, which will mean doing each lab twice. I know lab time is usually very precious, but you will probably only need to do this once or twice a year to get powerful results.

When the first group does the lab, the second group can be involved making observations, carefully collecting information, tracking participation, generating questions, and looking for unexpected variables. Think of the observers as quality control. The students can meet as a team after the first lab in order to refine the experiment for more precision or accuracy. They can make inferences based on their observations, make changes to the original hypotheses, encourage members of the team, and even provide feedback to you as the teacher in order to make the lab better.

With the extra structure placed around an experiment, the students will be more reflective about the entire experience and will incorporate more critical thinking as scientists. The students may be able to:

- Find and eliminate unexpected variables.
- Explore the effects of human error in science.
- Discuss scientific methodology.
- Generate questions for further investigation.
- Suggest or create additional or supplemental labs.
- Refine lab techniques.

As an example, imagine a lab where four students, Anders, Samantha, Jamie, and Esa have to mix two chemicals in a test tube and monitor the results in one-minute increments for ten minutes. Anders and Samantha do the lab first, while Jamie and Esa write the following observations and questions.

Seminar-Like Science Lab

Team Observations

- Anders spoke 12 times; Samantha 6.

- Samantha did not get to pour any of the chemicals. She should get a turn next time.

- They couldn't decide how to read the meniscus. We should review our notes.

- They recorded data after 64 seconds one time instead of 60 (third minute).

Questions

- What happens to the data that was four seconds late? Can we use it? Does it ruin the experiment? How do scientists know when an experiment is actually ruined?

- Does the angle that the chemicals are poured at matter?

- How would temperature affect this experiment?

- Our groups all did the experiment at room temperature. What would happen at higher or lower temperatures?

- Does it matter which chemical is poured first?

Lab Reflections

- The meniscus was hard to read on the test tubes.

- Anders and Samantha struggled and argued about it.

- Maybe we should measure with something else first.

- Our corner was dim. We should get a floor lamp or something.

- People in the class used different brands of stopwatches. How could that affect the experiments? Are the stopwatches significantly different? What's the margin of error?

Notice that several of the observations can lead to further exploration. Scientists constantly use critical thinking to decide when a factor is actually a viable variable or whether it is insignificant enough to ignore (at least for the time being). Without certain criteria to rule out, anything could be a potential variable. Even a simple lab experiment would then have to test for whether fluorescent lights affect test tubes, whether the type of brick used at a school affects group dynamics, or whether the brand of air conditioning unit is affecting the experiment.

The teacher and/or the curriculum usually control the number of variables in a particular lab. The students normally only manipulate a few given variables in order to understand the principles of the scientific method. But what is or is not a potential variable could be an amazing and worthwhile critical thinking process for young scientists.

Something Different

Want something completely different? Have your students become too comfortable and overly familiar with discussions and seminars? You could try an activity from a book like Roger-Pol Droit's *Astonish Yourself! 101 Experiments in the Philosophy of Everyday Life*. These activities should shake everything up a bit. Here's a brief excerpted description of one entitled "Empty a Word of Its Meaning:"

> Take what comes to hand, the most ordinary object—a pen, a watch, a glass—or even a piece of your own clothing ... Now take this inoffensive, familiar, safe little object in your hand. Repeat its name, in a low voice, as you look at it ... It shouldn't take long. In a few seconds the familiar word detaches itself, and hardens. You find yourself repeating a series of strange sounds. A series of absurd and meaningless noises that denote nothing, indicate nothing, and remain insensate, formless, or harsh ... Try to observe the moment when meaning dissolves, and how a new, raw reality emerges outside the words ... Is it not marvelous? Terrifying? Funny?

Imagine all of the questions that can arise from such a marvelous activity. What is a name? Why does it "detach"? What does name mean? Is it significant that name and mean are the same letters (anagrams)? Repetition can strengthen (as in practice) or weaken (as in this exercise). Why is that? What are mantras? Who decides what to call things? How do words end up in a dictionary? How do slang and regional idioms happen?

> **Even if the class can "finish" a longer text, it would probably not be at the depth Socratic Seminars target, since it's not unusual for groups to go at a speed of thirty minutes per paragraph.**

Text Length: Start Shorter

In the first few seminars, generally keep the text shorter: a single paragraph or picture book for elementary, a poem or a few paragraphs for middle school, maybe a short story or essay for high school. Of course, in a shorter period, keep the text shorter; a longer period can allow for longer texts. A very long text can be too intimidating and overwhelming for seminar groups. Even if the class can "finish" a longer text, it would probably not be at the depth Socratic Seminars target, since it's not unusual for groups to go at a speed of thirty minutes per paragraph.

A shorter text will allow time for important debriefing and reflection during the post-seminar (chapter 9). With sufficient time to reflect, students can discover why they were successful individually, why the group was or was not effective, and what the process was that revealed the deeper aspects of the text. In other words, they can improve. Reflection can be done for homework, but reflecting as a group directly after the process is most effective.

Remember, since the goal of choosing a text is to develop habits of mind and skills, a variety of short, dense texts will often promote more thinking than one long text on a single subject. A short text can also lead more easily to a sense of accomplishment. Rather than getting lost inside a large text, students can feel good about completing smaller, bite-sized pieces. A simple way to build confidence in any group is to string together a series of small successes.

Longer Texts and Novels

Reading an entire novel at close reading or Socratic Seminar speed would take a significant amount of time, so a typical way to deal with longer texts is to focus on specific passages or excerpts. Instead of dialoguing about the entire text in one seminar, students can instead focus on a few pages that can be applied to the whole. Choose important passages and pivotal moments, such as the green light in *The Great Gatsby*. When in doubt, ask questions: *Which two pages do we need to dialogue about? Which chapters were most confusing? Which pages will help us unlock this story?*

When using entire novels or other long texts for Socratic Seminars, annotating becomes increasingly important. Generally, the longer the text, the more important systematic annotating becomes. Without really good annotations, students will spend large amounts of precious seminar time attempting to find the exact passages or locations in the text. They will likely resort to vague notions and general ideas instead of using specific text references.

While reading long texts, students can first identify some reoccurring themes and repetitive words, and then annotate consistently so that they have a thematic thread. I like to pause after about 10% of the text for the students to identify recurring themes, ongoing examples of connections to essential questions, or multiple instances of "Great Ideas." Once these have been identified, students can stay vigilant for those specific annotations.

One of the best tools I know for this job is Mortimer Adler's list of "Great Ideas" from *The Great Ideas: A Syntopicon of Great Books of the Western World* and *The Great Ideas: A Lexicon of Western Thought*. Paideia Seminars often use these "Great Ideas" and a lot more information and resources are available from the *National Paideia Center*. See the appendices for Adler's original list and additional possibilities.

For example, in the novel *The Alchemist* by Paulo Coelho, students may initially find the recurring themes of chance, happiness, and labor. In George Orwell's *Animal Farm,* the students may recognize change, opposition, and tyranny. In Richard Bach's *Jonathan Livingston Seagull*, the students may discover multiple passages with the ideas of angel, desire, and infinity.

Once identified, the students must then read closely to find additional passages and examples of those same ideas. Let's suppose that the first instance of the theme "angel" occurs on page 4 and the next occurrence is on page 11. When students recognize the theme again on page 11, have them write in the margin or on a sticky note "see page 4." Have them turn back to page 4 and write in the margin "see page 11." By continuing this throughout an entire novel, the students will have a thematic thread that they can navigate and use for dialogue and writing papers.

I always explain to my middle and high school students that thesis papers actually begin during the annotating process. If they annotate properly, they will already have a map of all the thematic citations they need. Additional annotations can be used in the same way, of course. For example, if the students keep finding amazing similes in Ray Bradbury's *Fahrenheit 451*, they can mark an "S" in the margin of the book with "see page 65" as a signpost to a previously encountered simile or "see page 73" as a note to the next simile. From there, the students might be able to develop a thesis around Bradbury's use of the simile.

By reading novels in this way, teachers can differentiate groups of students by interests. Even though the entire class is reading the same novel, the students can annotate for different Big Ideas. Working together in small groups, they can record and share their annotations and explore different ideas that interest them. For example, one group could annotate for the theme of "chance," while another explores "happiness" and yet another "opposition."

Reading Level

There are numerous resources to check the reading level of the written text to use for Socratic Seminar. Some of them focus on vocabulary per page, others on concepts per page. Some measure the number of syllables per sentence, and other systems factor in student interest level. If you have access to this information, it can be useful to help choose texts.

With or without this reading level information, use the following rule of thumb. Since Socratic Seminars are group endeavors, the material should be difficult for a single student to understand the entire piece. In general, a group of middle school students can often be given a text that is normally reserved for high school students to read on their own, high school students can be given college-level material, and an ELL 1 class could be given material that ELL 2 students could handle on their own.

Teacher Interest

Choosing something that you love may seem like a great way to pick a text, but I strongly caution against this for many reasons. A text you love or previously studied is probably something that you know a great deal about. This immediately puts you in a strong authority position—something you are trying to diminish as a seminar facilitator. You want students to develop genuine inquiry into the text, not create a systematic process of guessing what you think.

Using a piece you love will also likely create personal expectations. If the students dislike the piece, you run the risk of taking their comments and the seminar personally. You may find yourself overly biased in the conversation, steering students toward the miraculous interpretation that excited you as a learner, or steering them away from non-traditional interpretations.

In general, I suggest not choosing a text simply because you love it. Choose it because it is complex and difficult for the students, because it raises numerous questions, because it supplements the curriculum, because it has no right answer, but not because you like it.

There is a simple two-question test of whether or not you should use a text that especially applies if you love it: *Can you generate three or more questions on your own about the text that you are genuinely curious about and don't have ready-made answers for? Are you willing to let the students create their own interpretations?* If you can honestly answer yes to these, then go ahead and try it out. Otherwise, choose something else.

It may be a coincidence, but Stephen Crane's "An Ominous Baby" worked very differently for me the first few times I used it with middle schoolers. On the first two occasions, I chose the story because it was full of rich words and descriptions, because it explored the concept of greed, and because it was dense with hints of concepts like social class. In both of the initial seminars, which went two full 90-minute periods, the conversation was rich, packed with excitement, enthusiasm, and discovery. However, the following year I chose it because I liked it, because it was my "old reliable." On this third occasion, the group struggled through a single 70-minute period, and then staggered through part of another. The students were unimpressed and seemed uninterested, with none of the excitement from the previous classes.

Favorite Texts

Here are some of my favorite texts of all time for Socratic Seminar. I apologize if this list is not diverse enough for some readers; these are simply what have consistently produced the best conversations for me over the years. You can find a more complete list on my website.

Elementary

The Zax	Dr. Seuss
"The Land of Counterpane"	Robert Louis Stevenson
"The Blind Men and the Elephant"	John Godfrey Saxe

Intermediate

"Thank You, M'am"	Langston Hughes
"An Ominous Baby"	Stephen Crane
"All Summer in a Day"	Ray Bradbury
"Charles"	Shirley Jackson

Middle and High School

"Sign for My Father, Who Stressed the Bunt"	David Bottoms
"Anyone Lived in a Pretty How Town"	E. E. Cummings
"A Very Old Man with Enormous Wings"	Gabriel Garcia Marquez
"Zaabalawi"	Naguib Mahfouz
"The Ones Who Walk Away from Omelas"	Ursula K. Le Guin
"That Village That Morning"	Akram Haniyyah

Novels

The Journey of Ibn Fattouma	Naguib Mahfouz
The Alchemist	Paulo Coelho
The Phantom Tollbooth	Norton Juster
Animal Farm	George Orwell
The House on Mango Street	Sandra Cisneros

Songs

"The Sounds of Silence"	Simon and Garfunkel
"Lateralus"	Tool
"Daughter"	Pearl Jam
"Cult of Personality"	Living Colour
"The Trees"	Rush
"The Times They Are A-Changin'"	Bob Dylan

Miscellaneous

The Statue with Two Heads	Jérome Murat
The Persistence of Memory	Salvador Dali
Relativity	M. C. Escher
"Living Witness"	*Star Trek: Voyager*
"Eye of the Beholder"	*The Twilight Zone*
"Midnight Never Ends"	*Night Gallery*
The Tao Te Ching	Lao Tzu
Book of the Elements	Euclid
"Autobiography in Five Short Chapters"	Portia Nelson

Socratic Seminar Curriculum Materials

To my knowledge there are three organizations that make curriculum materials specifically for seminars (though each has a different name for dialogue). *The Touchstones Discussion Project* has materials for K-12 and even college. The materials I have used tended to focus on short texts and excerpts from literature, but they have specific collections that focus on math and science. The *National Paideia Center* has materials for all ages and subject areas primarily using Adler's "Great Ideas." They have quite a few free lesson plans available on their website.

The Great Books Foundation also has materials for all ages. The Shared Inquiry process specializes in exploring excellent pieces of literature using interpretive questions, but they also have materials that branch into nonfiction and other areas, with a recent collection focusing on music, film, and television. They have a substantial amount of support materials, such as audio recordings, graphic organizers, assessment resources, and integration suggestions.

Summing Up

1. A "text" for seminar can be anything that will promote a complex thinking process.

2. Good texts generally have multiple possible interpretations, are implicit, unconventional, figurative, allegorical, and/or symbolic.

3. Choose printed texts over digital ones.

4. Generally start with shorter texts so students can stay focused.

5. Novels can be annotated with tools like the "Great Ideas" from Mortimer Adler.

Your Next Steps

- Ask your students what they might want to explore.

- In the beginning of the year, consider using some specific material from your school, such as the school motto (or better yet, an excerpt from history where the motto appears), the school's mission statement, excerpts from the student handbook, etc.

- When in doubt, choose something already in the curriculum, such as a map or chart embedded in a textbook, a painting in an anthology, a diagram in a science textbook.

- When in doubt, try *The Pledge of Allegiance* (or a similar pledge, vow, or national anthem).

- Always be on the lookout for good texts. I tend to come across them in the strangest places when I least expect them.

- Read and research more about text complexity.

- Keep in mind that the text is just one component of the whole Socratic Seminar. A "bad," non-complex text can still generate excellent dialogue with collaborative participants, an experienced facilitator, and provocative questions.

6

Questions

The Quest in Quest-ion

I remember when I first realized that the word question has the word quest in it. I was charged with excitement at the thought that each question could be the start of a quest. It might not be The Quest for the Holy Grail exactly, but each question is the potential start of an entire discovery process.

Some of these quests are short and dull (*Is that a pencil?*); others are long and speculative (*If aliens came to Earth, what advice would they give us?*); some are brief but exciting (*Whoa! How did that just happen?*); and a few rare ones are full of wonder (*Do trees have feelings?*). Perhaps the very best questions are the ones that don't even appear to be answerable but are so full of mystery and intrigue that they never fail to astound (*If the universe is expanding, what's it expanding into?*).

Years later it also dawned on me that the word is quest-ion, leading to the idea that questions are quests for ions. Strangely, it makes a creative kind of sense. Ions are charged particles, and in a general sense can be thought of as excited or excitable particles. Think about a principal being "in charge" of the building. The real quest, then, is to find a question that charges each of us. For teachers, the quest is to find questions that put a charge in our students. In a Socratic classroom, we hope to put the students "in charge" of their own learning.

Quality Follows Quantity

Early in school, students learn and practice the key question words: who, what, when, where, how, and why. Teaching about questions after this, however, often slows or stops. Sometimes students will be exposed to types of questions in textbooks, ones that are labeled "Critical Thinking" or "Synthesis." Some textbooks have pullout boxes and brief mini-lessons that teach about questions, but these are often scattered and disconnected. Opportunities for students to write or ask their own questions are much less frequent, and in fact, in many learning situations, students are even discouraged from asking their own questions.

> Look at the deeper meanings. And ask lots of questions, and respect others' ideas. Don't just think of your ideas, because other people have good ideas too! ~ GP (grade 6)

As early chapters of this book indicate, students do not have enough practice formulating or asking questions—and they certainly don't have enough practice with writing and asking deep, meaningful questions. For example, according to Larry Lewin, most of the questions that students ask "either seek clarification on procedural matters (*Which numbers are we supposed to do?*); attempt to cut a deal (*Can we write two paragraphs instead of three?*); or try to detour the group from the lesson (*What time does this period end?*)."

This means that students must have consistent opportunities to practice asking far more questions. Engel writes, "For children to develop and satisfy their urge to know, they need role models, opportunities to practice, and guidance." I am not suggesting that simply asking more questions will automatically lead to quality questions. More is not always better. But developing a habit of wonder and engaging in more inquiry will provide the foundation for students to get better at asking deeper, more meaningful questions.

The Opening Question

The opening question launches the formal dialogue part of a Socratic Seminar. Because the goal is to have genuine conversation, the opening question should definitely not have a right answer. Instead, it should challenge students to look closely at the text and to think about the ideas and issues in meaningful ways. A good opening question is immediately provocative and engaging for most students, and leads to conversation anchored in the text. A bad opening question polarizes students and potentially results in arguing and debating. A good opening question opens up lines of thinking toward multiple, justifiable answers. A bad opening question forces students down a narrow path of thinking, toward assumptions or pre-established agendas.

There are many characteristics to consider for an opening question. Wanda Ball and Pam Brewer, authors of *Socratic Seminars in the Block*, write that opening questions should be free of judgment and bias. "A Seminar leader must remain neutral in questioning, matching the neutrality of body language and facial expressions. All judgments, deductions, and connections must be made by students if they are to feel truly responsible for the seminar." Matt Copeland writes that he has had great success posing opening questions that focus on the meaning that the author is trying to convey.

Matt Copeland also cautions that opening questions should err on the side of specificity and not generalization because of how they may be perceived with the facilitator's follow-up questions. "Having a specific first question and a more general follow-up question leaves students with the feeling that they are being turned loose to explore the text. Beginning with a general initiating question and following up with a more specific question suggests to the students that you are guiding and leading them through the text by hand."

Howard Zeiderman offers two useful examples of bad opening questions. "Questions like 'Is war good or bad?' and 'Is war more or less important than domestic life?' are almost always ineffective as opening questions. They relate both to the text and personal experience in the wrong way—as evidence for argumentative positions rather than as sources for serious cooperative reflection." He continues, "Questions like 'Did the Greeks think differently about war than we do?' and 'How does our view of marriage differ from that of the characters in the reading?' are also unsuitable. They would be more suitable as essay topics because dealing with them requires a considerable amount of research. Were they asked as opening questions, the teacher would once again become the authority."

"Good" Opening Questions

- Are broad enough to engage all or most students.
- Deal with large philosophical ideas or issues.
- Invite complex conversation with multiple viewpoints.
- Are short and to the point.
- Are colloquial (student-centered).
- Guide students toward the complexities in the text.
- Have multiple right answers.

"Bad" Opening Questions

- Are narrow and only engage specific students.
- Focus only on details or narrow parts of the text.
- Invite simple or shallow answers.
- Present a bias or an agenda.
- Are phrased in teacher language (teacher-centered).
- Steer students away from what might interest them.
- Have embedded assumptions.

Trailheads

Most facilitators prepare several opening questions, and often several types of opening questions, in case the first one falters. If this happens, ask procedural questions in order to rescue the situation. This gets students talking about the seminar itself and not necessarily about the text, but at least they will be conversing. Ask a question like, "How can we make meaning out of line 6?" Or perhaps, "What do we need to do in order to get unstuck?" Questions of this nature help pass the responsibility of the seminar over to the students. When students get better at asking questions, they can get involved in asking opening questions themselves.

Trailheads are different potential starting places for investigating a text, either during the pre-seminar or with the opening question. Think of them as approaches or possible points for guiding inquiry. Just like hiking trails on various mountains, different texts have distinctive features that beg for certain questions or approaches. Some written texts, for example, call for grammatical investigation because of unusual syntax or word choice. Some lead immediately to metaphorical or allegorical inquiry. Others call attention to setting, theme, symbols or other features. The best texts, however, are often rich with numerous starting places, or trailheads.

For example, a trailhead for a poem could be a question about the ambiguity of the title, a specific vocabulary word, a line or a stanza, or perhaps a thematic question about the entire poem at once. For a painting, trailheads could include questions about color, relative position, shape, texture, or potentially all of the above.

Like a mountain with many trails to the summit, the most important part of getting into a text is to start at a trailhead and see where it leads. Mortimer Adler writes: "The 'secret' of *Hamlet* really is a secret, and there is no one line of questioning that will arrive at it. Rather, the seminar leader must circle round and round the play, seeking for an opening here, for an opportunity there, for a point that it would be helpful to make at this stage of the conversation."

Howard Gardner mentions five types of what he calls "multiple entry points" for approaching educational topics. He writes: "Awareness of these entry points can help the teacher introduce new materials in ways in which they can be easily grasped by a range of students; then, as students explore other entry points, they have the chance to develop those multiple perspectives that are the best antidote to stereotypical thinking." Gardner's five entry points are: narrational, logical-quantitative, foundational, esthetic, and experiential. These approaches could be used to generate five different types of opening questions, could be used for pre-seminar activities, and maybe even as a way to help group students by interest.

After facilitating several of the same texts numerous times over the years, I have noticed that it rarely matters which trailhead is taken if there are enough follow-up questions and the students are working well together. What does matter, however, is which trailhead might be more appealing to the students. Certain themes, ideas, or topics will consistently emerge from many texts, no matter where the starting point was for the students. The differences, in my experience, have mainly been how fast we arrived at the standard or traditional interpretation, how long we have to discuss it, how many tangents we went on, or how many new theories we tried on our own. Like trailheads up the same mountain, any initial approach can guide students to the summit.

Generating numerous opening questions can help teachers find one that will really work well for their students. A teacher who wants to have a seminar on the topic of a "perfect circle" should explore variations on the idea.

Please take the time to generate several questions around the idea of perfection or perfect circle. Which ones do you think will captivate the students? Which ones do you think will make good opening questions?

Seriously, take the time.

Here are some of the questions on my list: *What is the difference between a perfect circle and a representation of a perfect circle? Can anything be perfect? What about perfectly human? Can we imagine something perfect If we can imagine it, can we draw it? Can something be practically perfect? Can it be pragmatically perfect? If a panel of experts looked at the circle and decided it was perfect, does it make it so? Can perfection be measured against anything? Would a perfect circle have to be drawn on something perfect using something perfect?*

If you did not make a list of your own, then mine may suffice to make the point that one or several of the questions in the list are probably more appealing than: *"What is a perfect circle?"* Which ones do you like the best? Which ones have you the most curious? If you are going to base an entire seminar on a question, then make sure it is captivating enough to fully engage students.

Closing Questions

Many facilitators use closing questions near the end of the seminar to bring the conversation back to the students on a more personal and emotional level. Wanda Ball and Pam Brewer, authors of *Socratic Seminars in the Block*, write: "An absolute pattern emerging from recent studies of learning and the brain is that if emotion can be tapped, if connections with previous learning can be made, and relevance can be established, retention and learning increase. The sole purpose of the closing question is to create these personal links between content issues and the lives of students... Remember, that this is the only question that may and, perhaps for the emphasis on personalization, should use the word 'you' or 'we.'" Closing questions create relevance and often connect to the real world, especially if the seminar was abstract or historical. A good closing question can also help students think about homework, developing ideas for writing papers, participating in a blog and other follow-up assignments.

There are a few cautions in using closing questions. The first is that poorly crafted closing questions can ruin an entire seminar, either by strongly suggesting a "right" answer or overly bringing the students to too much closure. In addition, closing questions can sometimes feel too personal to some participants. Ball and Brewer write: "While the question's purpose is to connect to the learner's life, it is not intended to pry or in any way force a student to reveal a vulnerability or a sensitivity."

Sample Closing Questions

- How is this useful to us nowadays?
- Would you change The Pledge of Allegiance? Why or why not?
- If you continued this story, what would you write? Why?
- If you were the main character, what would you do now?
- What does this text teach us about today's world?
- What would be different about this text if it were written today?

Types of Questions

In addition to opening and closing questions, there are many other types. There are questions that promote critical thinking, those that promote creative thinking, follow-up questions that drive inquiry deeper, leading questions that have answers embedded in them, and many more. Some probe for shallow answers (What is today's date?), and some probe for deep thinking (*Why are there seasons?*). Some questions ask for an opinion (*What was the best book you read last month?*), while others require guesswork (*What if the main character hadn't done that?*).

There are dozens and dozens of types of questions, but here are some I frequently use.

Closed and Open (open-ended)

Closed questions have a specific right answer, while open questions have multiple "right" answers. Closed questions generally close down inquiry and conversation, while open questions promote more.

Shallow and Deep (sometimes called thin and thick)

Shallow questions probe for surface or conventional answers. They have typical or predictable answers, and elicit regurgitation, even when they seem open-ended. Deep questions search for more than quick answers and demand inquiry, research, and substantiation. Many deep questions are open-ended, philosophical, or existential.

Leading

Leading questions have the answer embedded in them. Because of this, they are antithetical to any thinking process. A quick fix to the habit of asking them is to simply state what you're thinking and then follow up with another question.

Thinking (sometimes known as rhetorical questions)

Thinking questions are like rhetorical questions in that there is not an expected response. They are to be pondered and mulled over by the students, rather than being interrupted by raised hands or overly quick answers. Attach a tag at the beginning when asking them: "This is a thinking question: How do you know you have done your best on an assignment?"

> **Fixed and Emergent**
>
> Fixed questions are those that are prepared ahead of time, such as the questions listed at the end of a typical textbook. They are fixed in the sense that they are unchanging and are not necessarily directly relevant to immediate conversation. Emergent questions grow naturally out of the circumstances.
>
> **Clarifying and Explanatory**
>
> Clarifying questions seek to elucidate something that has already occurred, whereas explanatory questions ask for additional information.

In my experience as an elementary, middle, and high school teacher, *types of questions* are rarely taught—the main exception being when students learn the question words of who, what, when, where, how, and why. But it is vital to teach students different types of questions, not only so that they appreciate and understand different approaches to questions and their expected answers, but also so that they can avoid asking questions that do not help the dialogue. For example, students should not use precious Socratic Seminar time to ask a closed question such as, "What does the word *emergent* mean?" This is something they could have looked up in a dictionary ahead of time during pre-seminar.

Closed and Open Questions

A closed question has a definite answer, something that isn't arguable: *When is your birthday? What is 2 + 2?* The idea here is that a closed question seeks a very quick, very easy answer.

Closed questions are useful because they call for specific information and they can help clarify details such as which character was talking at a certain point, what the definition of a certain word is, or how a word is spelled. Some groups will not be able to proceed with deeper understandings until these details, clarifications, and definitions are dealt with first. Here are some examples of closed questions:

- Is the author still alive?
- What was the title of this again?
- In what year was this recorded?
- Did Edgar Allen Poe write "The Raven"?

Closed questions can be interesting to investigate because they are sometimes not as closed as they first seem—and fascinating dialogue can emerge. Take the question: *What time is it?* Interestingly, if you ask the class what time it is, you will inevitably get watches and cell phones showing slightly varying times. You could dialogue about what the *official* time actually is, who determines that time, why it is official, and how it is calculated.

Take the question, Did Edgar Allen Poe write *The Raven*? It is possible that historians are not entirely sure, and perhaps there is evidence that he co-wrote it. Eventually, such conversations can lead into the reliability of primary resources, or even dialogues about: "When is a fact really a fact?" or "Are some facts more reliable than others?"

An open-ended question is one that does not have a direct or definite answer, and can be thought of as having multiple "right" answers. It's a question that is open to interpretation, invites dialogue, and calls for evidence and reasoning. *Why* and *how* questions are typically open. When I assign Socratic Seminar homework, I sometimes require students to arrive to class having annotated the piece with at least one open question.

Open questions are useful because they are typically the heart of a seminar dialogue and lead to deeper conversation. However, keep in mind that without first dealing with some of the closed questions, students may not reach a complete enough level of comprehension to discuss the text or idea in the first place. So, you may want to have the students ask some or all of their closed questions in pre-seminar before moving to open questions. Examples of open questions:

- How does that memory moment affect the story?
- How does pride or power connect to this story?
- Why don't the people in this lithograph have faces?
- How would you justify the use of repetition in the poem?
- How might each of the characters define the word "honor"?

Shallow and Deep (Thin and Thick) Questions

Shallow or thin questions probe for conventional or surface answers. They are quickly answered by a tiny amount of thinking, research, or inquiry. At first these may seem like closed questions—some people may lump them together—but I find that there are subtle differences. Unlike closed questions that have a specific answer, shallow questions often have a small, but predictable, range of possible answers.

How was school today? is a great example of a shallow question because it could be answered in many ways, but often just elicits a single word, such as, "Good." The question itself does not probe for or demand more than just a shallow answer, nor is it habitually answered with much more than a single word. A question forcing deeper thinking would be: *What are three interesting things that you learned today in school?*

Compare, for example, *Why did the Civil War take place?* or *How did the Civil War take place?* to *When did the Civil War take place?* The first two are deeper and ask for a greater vista of inquiry; the last ask for a more specific answer. At first *When was the Civil War?* might seem like a closed question, but there are a variety of possible answers. What makes it shallow is that many textbooks and websites deal very decisively with the dates involved. By asking a class this question, very often you will get the pre-packaged, standard answer of 1861-1865 without any further questioning or interest. However, many dates are unclear throughout history and different historians find deeper or shallower roots in almost every event.

A question like *When exactly was the Civil War?* may lead to deeper and more substantial inquiry. The standard answer of 1861-1865 no longer seems adequate. So, perhaps April 12, 1861, becomes a more defined start date. The end date is, interestingly, still remarkably unclear. Is it April 9, 1865, when Lee surrendered at Appomattox? Or when Johnston surrendered his troops on the twenty-sixth of April? Or November 4, 1865, when the last confederate naval force surrendered? By inserting the word *exactly*, the question itself is searching, petitioning for more.

Shallow questions typically elicit clichés, regurgitation or mere recall. As far as students are concerned, if they can cough up a pre-packaged answer then the line of questioning is done. No more thinking or discussion is needed because *the* answer was already given. Shallow questions often dead end quickly and by themselves don't lead to fruitful discussion. If you ask twenty-one people a question and they basically all give the same answer, then it was likely a shallow question.

Deep or thick questions ask for more than quick, ready-made answers. They demand inquiry, research, analysis, and/or substantiation. They provoke better dialogue and demand more thought because they tap into what many refer to as "higher order thinking skills." Many deep questions are philosophical or existential in nature, but sometimes they just demand more than habitual or standard answers. *How are you doing today?* is answered shallowly by most people without much thought. *How are you doing today as compared to yesterday?* is deeper and should elicit more from a responder.

Rather than *How was slavery involved in the war?* (textbooks have definite answers for this), deeper questions might ask: *Why do humans fight?* or *When can war be justified?* or *How many types of conflict are there?* These questions ask for more student ideas, invite dialogue and cannot be answered by simple regurgitation or quick reference to a textbook. Deep questions prompt students to profoundly engage with the text, the issues, or ideas.

Bloom's Taxonomy of verbs can be helpful in generating deeper questions. Inserting words such as *analyze, classify, differentiate,* or *justify* into questions helps direct dialogue toward deeper analysis. Carry a laminated copy of the verbs around the classroom to better engage students.

Shallow Versus Deep Questions

Shallow	*Deep(er)*
What is the dictionary definition?	What is a definition that we can synthesize from these three dictionaries?
When was the Civil War?	When did the Civil War officially start?
How are you doing?	How is today different for you than yesterday?
How was school today?	What is a story that captures how things went for you today in school?

Leading Questions

Leading questions have an answer implied or embedded in them, and steer listeners toward an expected answer. Because of this, leading questions are antithetical to a Socratic classroom. They show that you already have the answers and that students should share those same ideas or opinions, or come to those conclusions. A leading question often has a negative sentence construction: *Don't you think greed had something to do with it?*

If you're trying to get your students to think for themselves, then avoid asking leading questions. Asking questions in general is stimulating, but leading questions are deadening and inert since the answer is built in. The message in a leading question is that everyone should think like you do. The danger is that students will fall into the trap of trying to think of what you're thinking, rather than actually puzzling over the question. Some students might find it fun to play "guess what teacher is thinking," but most won't. It's simply not worth it. If they guess wrong, they risk ridicule and humiliation. If they guess right, nothing much happens since the teacher already knew the answer anyway.

Since Socratic Seminar is about developing thinking skills, students must learn to think for themselves. As Michael Strong points out: "As long as the student knows that, whether by didactic instruction or by subtle conversational manipulation, she will ultimately be led to the 'right' answer, she will never rely on her own judgment in the deepest sense." Asking a lot of leading questions can result in a group of students who feel you know the answers and are just holding out on them. With the exception of the students who are engrossed in the dialogue, many students will wait passively for you to deliver the answers.

I have encountered teachers who argued at length with me about this. They suggest that asking leading questions is still stimulating for students, that the method is Socratic and that it gets students thinking. But thinking about what? What I usually observe in these classrooms is that the students are just passively following the transmission of knowledge. They rarely ask their own questions and, when they do, they are mostly clarifying questions. There are few or no student questions that lead outside of the scope of the material being presented. Basically, these teachers lecture in disguise and the students do not take any ownership of the learning.

The worst version of asking leading questions is what I call fishing, or call-and-endorse. This is when a teacher already clearly knows an answer, but asks a question anyway. Of course, hands go up, the teacher calls on people and then approves or disapproves of the answers. You'll recognize the routine: "What were the causes of the civil war mentioned in the book? Tim ... no. Manny ... good, that's one. Keisha ... good, there's another. Molly ... no that wasn't one. Brenna ... good. Susie ... very good, Susie!"

This is fishing and it's a bad habit as far as inquiry and a Socratic classroom are concerned. It's a teacher looking for an answer he or she already has and is mechanically trying to find it in the students. Several students feel stupid for wrong answers and a few get some empty praise. Most students will figure out that you're fishing and they will stop biting on the hook. Observe a classroom where this happens a lot and you will usually see the same few hands go up—and fewer and fewer over time.

Asking leading questions can be a difficult habit to break, especially if you were taught in such an environment. Since leading questions are basically statements disguised as questions, my main suggestion to teachers is to change the leading question into a statement and then follow it with a genuine question. Like trying to break any habit in the classroom, have your students be a police force for you. Tell them that you are trying to stop asking leading questions. If they hear you ask one, they can tell you to rephrase it. I did this early in my career to break myself of asking leading questions and being sarcastic. Believe me, the students will not let you slip. They love catching mistakes.

Thinking Questions

Thinking questions—akin to rhetorical questions—are questions NOT to be answered aloud or in writing. They are to be thought about, pondered, mulled over. Attach a tag to the beginning of the question so that students know ahead of time: "This is a thinking question: *What is the most important question you asked this week?*"

The reason why you would want to do this is because there are times when you don't want hands to shoot up and interfere with the thinking process, and you don't want packaged or preconceived ideas to be immediately regurgitated. You REALLY want students to pause and contemplate.

Add a lot of extra wait time to thinking questions. Three to five seconds is a typical suggested wait time, so add even more. And then more. And then more still. Wait students out until they are unsure of their answers and begin thinking anew. Wait more. Let them squirm around in their minds, wondering why you are waiting so long. Let the daydreamers zone back in and wonder what's going on. Let them doubt their initial answer(s). Wait even more. In a state of being unsure, the students might discover new ideas and make new connections. Try it out someday. It really is magical. Wait two minutes someday. They will wonder what this dreadful, horrible, painful silence is and they will keep searching for more answers. Ask your question again to keep them focused and watch the wonder and magic unfurl.

> **Remember, we want to *uncover* ideas—not cover them— in order to *dis*cover new thoughts and issues.**

Fixed Questions

Fixed questions are pre-written questions that you and your students know about ahead of time. The questions included in a purchased curriculum, the ones at the end of a textbook chapter, those in the teacher's edition or study guide, are all examples. Like shallow questions, they have expected, traditional, or typical answers that are often found within a small section of text or a limited range of thinking.

There are several problems with fixed questions. The first is that, quite simply, they are someone else's questions. They are not questions generated by you and your curiosity or your students and their wonderings. Therefore, they are not often fully relevant, timely, or interesting.

The second is that you and your students probably know the expected answers that are coming, since many fixed questions are recall or search-and-find. In many textbooks, the expected answers are around the vocabulary words in bold. The routine with these questions goes like this: flip back a few pages, *scan* the text (no reading or thinking needed), find the piece of information, and deliver it back to the teacher.

The third problem is the way these questions are usually presented. The most uninteresting questions are usually the first ones listed at the end of every chapter—these become part of a coverage game. Teachers often whip through them to cover the material. Why start a thinking process with boring factual questions? This will surely turn off many students who recognize that the coverage game is occurring.

Many textbooks use leveled questions listed in an order from least amount of thinking to most, from basic knowledge to evaluation. Why not start with the most interesting, most appealing questions first. They will often lead to discussions that include the factual information anyway. Remember, we want to uncover ideas—not cover them—in order to discover new thoughts and issues.

The fourth problem is that fixed questions are potentially mind-numbing for you as a teacher. If you've been teaching with the same text for a while, then these end-of-the-chapter questions are the same ones you asked last year and the year before. Most of the answers that you hear from your students you will have heard before. You know that excitement you get when a student answers with something completely unexpected? Then ask yourself, why isn't this happening all the time?

Try this and see if it works better than plodding through the questions in the order that is prescribed in the textbook. Collect all the questions from several chapters, a unit, or a marking period together. Eliminate the ones that are redundant and have you and your students add some questions to this list. Then have the students start combining and grouping the questions together by putting them into categories.

Start a process of weighting them. Ask your students to vote on the questions that seem to be the most poignant, the most useful, the most engaging or important. I like to do this process in stages of voting. I give my students three votes in the first stage in order to narrow the list and then they each get one vote on the final, reduced list.

Collect together the questions with the most votes and start a series of discussions or seminars with those in an order that makes the most sense to you in your situation. Keep the questions list and check off the "sub" questions that get dealt with throughout the seminars that follow. Post this list somewhere in the room to allow you to refer to it in emergent ways:

"What question(s) from our list would we need answered at this time in order to understand this concept?"

Emergent Questions

Emergent questions spring up organically during conversation. They arise in the moment, because of that moment. These are the unanticipated questions that you and your students are not prepared for. These questions are alive in that sense, growing out of unique circumstances. They are fresh, vibrant, in the now. Emergent questions keep you engaged and on your toes. They keep discussions relevant, alive, personalized, and contextualized.

It takes practice to become skilled at asking emergent questions. Many teachers are nervous about turning over control of discussions and seminars to the students because they don't feel clever enough or fast enough at asking emergent or follow-up questions. Setting up a Socratic Seminar, diving in, and then reflecting on the dialogue is the best way to learn, but I have a suggestion for practice.

You and your students can practice what is called serialized questioning—something I learned from Socratic Seminar International's Oscar Graybill. Have students pair up. One partner asks a question; any question, really. They then listen carefully to each other's responses and choose a word or phrase to form a new question. They actively listen to the new response and follow up with another question. This will create a serialized dialogue that might sound something like this:

> How's your day been?
> **Good.**
> What's **good** about it?
> My first period class went really well—better than I **expected**.
> What did you **expect**?
> I thought the *class wouldn't like* the **poem**.
> What **poem** was it?
> It was "The Hollow Men" by T.S. Eliot.
> Why did you think the *class wouldn't like* it?

Clarifying and Explanatory Questions

When my students give presentations, I like to differentiate two types of questions that are asked from the audience members: clarifying and explanatory. I usually ask for clarifying questions first, followed by any explanatory questions. I do this because it offers another opportunity for me to teach students about different types of questions. The audience members have to think—I repeat, *have to think*—when they ask their questions because they have to decide what type of question they are formulating.

Clarifying questions are those that seek to elucidate something in the presentation: *What was the second reason you gave?* and *Did you say illusion or allusion?* I like to have the clarifying questions come first so that we can proceed to the explanatory questions with a platform of understanding.

Explanatory questions are those that seek more information. These tend to make up most of the questions from the audience. Examples include: *Can you explain why that happened?* and *How did you come up with that idea?*

Follow-up Questions

In Socratic Seminar, the single most important question is the opening question. As mentioned before, an effective opening question immediately engages most or all students and gets the seminar rolling. From there, though, emergent follow-up questions become extremely important, whether asked by a student or the facilitator. Follow-up questions help create group cohesion, drive inquiry deeper, and truly challenge participants to think, find and weigh evidence and justify their thoughts.

Without sufficient follow-up questions, conversations will tend to be shallow and brief. Ideas will not be thoroughly explored or substantiated with evidence. Innovative ideas will likely not be generated or given the time they may need to blossom or be appreciated. Without timely follow-up questions, students are likely to stay confused or unsure of their ideas. Most importantly, the complexities of a text will rarely reveal themselves without follow-up questions.

In order to facilitate better seminars, keep a list of follow-up questions nearby and refer to them throughout the seminar. Keep asking them until the original question is satisfied or until a breakthrough occurs. A good complex text will often reveal itself in layers, like peeling an onion. Like all Socratic Seminar practices, use the principle of *gradual release of responsibility* and get the students to ask the follow-up questions as soon as possible so that you can move on to a new skill.

Reliable Follow-Up Questions

- Could you summarize that in your own words?
- Can you explain that further?
- What in the text makes you say that?
- How did you come to that conclusion?
- What are we assuming about that?
- Are there any alternatives?
- Where are you the most confused?
- What was the most difficult part of this text?
- What other questions are raised by that idea?
- Could you cite an example from the text?
- Who agrees with that idea? Disagrees?
- How does that relate to our essential question?

Introducing Types of Questions

There are many models that may be used to generate different types of questions, such as Bloom's Taxonomy, Webb's Depth of Knowledge Levels, or Gardner's Multiple Intelligences. What I have found important is not to come to a final conclusion about how many types of questions there are in any model, but simply to teach the students that there are, indeed, different types. The goal is to get students thinking about what types are useful for them in various situations. Certain types of questions have a greater value toward thinking and dialogue; some are more useful for pursuing specific knowledge; some types will lead to deeper investigation; and others will generate innovation ideas.

There are various ways of approaching *types of questions*. They can be taught through direct instruction, but I prefer an activity that is inductive rather than deductive. I have the students generate a list of questions in class or for homework—or one of the activities in this book. They can be about the next reading assignment, something that happened in class, or random questions. It doesn't matter what the questions are for exactly, although you may need to encourage a little variety so that they don't all sound the same.

The activity goes like this. Have the students generate 5-8 questions each, so, in total, somewhere between 80 to 150 questions. First, have them look at their individual questions and guide them by asking questions about their questions: *Do your questions have the same power? What are these questions seeking? How are they different? What are the similarities?* Try not to explain much at this exploratory stage. Most of the students have never thought much about questions, so there is much to be discovered.

Then have groups of students put their questions into categories *of their own design*, and give each category a name. Continue asking them about different types of questions and challenge them to search for the central concept that binds the category together. Questions at this stage include: *What are the different types of answers that are resulting from these questions? Does intention matter? Are the answers to these questions equally knowable?*

There are many ways students choose to approach this set of tasks. Some groups look at the obvious language mechanics and might create a "Questions that start with why" category. Some might be simple like, "Tom's Questions." Other groups go more for the abstract and even find subtle differentiations between, say "currently unknowable" and "never knowable." If their names and categories are too broad, challenge them to departmentalize, usually by asking something like, "Are there different types of Tom's questions?" If their categories are too concrete, challenge them to be more abstract because this is a great thinking opportunity, and it should be challenging. The goal is to have them comb through their questions and examine what is really happening when that particular question is asked.

Lastly, have the groups report to the entire class and put all of the small group categories on the board. From the initial questions there might be 20 or so categories on the board. Then have the groups explain their process and decisions, and ask the class to merge similar categories. For example, "currently unanswerable" and "futuristic" might really be the same category and can be combined together. So, those 20 or so initial categories might condense down to 10-15, and then sometimes can be wrestled down to a final total of 5-10.

After this, the class has their own personalized types of questions. More importantly, they have *customized* question types that students feel ownership of, especially if they've created unique names like: Universal Questions, Sleeping Questions, Melt-Your-Brain Questions, and Silent-But-Deadly-Questions. Post the types in the classroom for use throughout the year. Repeat this process with every group in order to have a unique set of types of questions.

As an alternative, have the students create *types of answers*. Use the same process, but focus on the answers instead of the questions. Have the students focus on what the questioning is really asking for—in other words, what results the questions are really seeking. What's important is that the students engage in a very thoughtful process of discovering and ruminating over types of questions and what those questions can achieve.

I certainly encourage you to find a model for types of questions that works for you, whether you create your own, as was just described, or you simply borrow categories from something like Bloom's Taxonomy. The real value will be in differentiating them in the first place, allowing you and the students to broaden your range of inquiry.

Questions for Mathematics

Although Socratic Seminars are less common in math classes, asking powerful questions will still promote strong critical and creative thinking. With the right text selection, students can engage in quality dialogue about mathematical principles and ideas. See Chapter 5 for more on text selection for mathematics.

The characteristics of these deep or thick questions are similar to those that would be in any other thinking endeavor, though many mathematics questions often focus on the process of answering, rather than on the answers themselves. Lainie Schuster and Nancy Anderson in their book *Good Questions for Math Teaching* write that good mathematical questions have seven qualities. What follows after is a list of twenty-one reliable questions for promoting mathematical dialogue.

- Help students make sense of the mathematics.

- Are open-ended.

- Empower students to unravel their misconceptions.

- Help students see and understand multiple potential solutions.

- Not only require the application of facts and procedures, but encourage students to make connections and generalizations.

- Are accessible to all students in their language and offer an entry point for all students.

- Their answers lead students to wonder more about a topic and to perhaps construct new questions themselves as they investigate this newly found interest.

Good Questions for Math - Schuster and Anderson

- Why do you think that?
- How did you know to try that strategy?
- How do you know you have an answer?
- Will this work with every number? Every similar situation?
- When will that strategy not work?
- Can you give a counterexample?
- Who has a different strategy?
- How is your answer alike or different from another student's?
- Can you repeat your classmate's ideas in your own words?
- Do you agree or disagree with your classmate's idea? Why?

Mathematics Questions from PBS TeacherLine

- Can you make a model to show that?
- Is that true for all cases? Explain.
- How would you prove that?
- What would happen if ...? What if not?
- What assumptions are you making?

- Do you see a pattern? Can you explain the pattern?
- Can you predict the next one? What about the last one?
- What decision do you think he/she should make?
- Is there a more efficient strategy?
- Why did you decide to organize your results like that?
- Have you thought of all the possibilities? How can you be sure?

Crafting Better Questions

All of this inquiry into questions leads to an important question: *How do I craft better questions?* More specifically: *How do I craft better opening questions for seminars?*

Some teachers stress about Bloom's Taxonomy or Webb's Depth of Knowledge Levels and try to manufacture better questions through word choice. They deliberate over specific verbs, invert sentences, and play around with semantics. In my experience, this is not necessary at all, although if it already works for you, keep doing it. The best opening questions are simply those that tap into real curiosity and wonder.

The simple answer is *practice*. Have you and your students practice writing questions on as many occasions as you can. Curiosity and wonder drive the art of asking questions, so as mentioned earlier, start with the idea of quantity over quality. Find what you are deeply curious about and start forming questions from your natural curiosity. Then generate a few variations. Ask other people which versions are more captivating and intriguing. Ask questions about your questions and keep the "wheel of wonder" turning.

When you are facilitating seminars in different class periods, ask a different opening question each time. Make sure to save and record questions that work particularly well for various texts. See if there is a pattern to those questions that work well for you and your students.

In addition, as Norah Morgan and Juliana Saxton, authors of *Asking Better Questions*, point out, it is often more practical to be thinking about what function a question has rather than just what type of question it is. Although many types of questions exist and numerous verbs could be used for crafting questions, Morgan and Saxton present three simple categories of questions based on their function.

Asking Better Questions – Morgan and Saxton

Questions that elicit information:

1. Establish the rules or procedures.
2. Establish or help control group discipline.
3. Unify the class in purpose.
4. Supply information or suggest implications.

Questions that shape understanding:

5. Reveal experience.
6. Make connections.
7. Press for accuracy or clarity.
8. Promote expression of attitudes, biases, and points of view.
9. Demand inference and/or interpretation.
10. Explore meanings behind textual content.

Questions that press for reflection:

11. Develop suppositions or hypotheses.
12. Focus on personal feelings.
13. Focus on future action or projection.
14. Develop critical assessment or value judgments.

Try the following activity by perhaps using one of the many question-forming tools mentioned in this chapter or somewhere in this book.

- Bloom's Taxonomy
- Gardiner's Multiple Intelligences or Entry Points
- Webb's Depth of Knowledge Levels
- Morgan and Saxton's three categories

> *The instant you speak words, you miss the mark.*
> **~ Zen proverb**

Write 25 questions about this saying. No, seriously. Do it.

Most people find this challenging. But as with any skill, asking questions gets easier with practice. Here are ten from my list (of several dozen):

1. What's the mark?
2. Who wrote this?
3. What type of mark?
4. Why would someone say this?
5. Is it good or bad that they miss?
6. Do they always miss?
7. Is this saying correct, or does it miss the mark?
8. If it is correct, what's the point of discussing it?
9. Does this count for written words?
10. When is a good time to bring such a quote up?

If it hasn't been abundantly clear throughout this book, questions are absolutely the single most important component of a Socratic classroom. In her article "Piqued: The Case for Curiosity," Daisy Yuhas writes, "Studies suggest it's linked to joy on the job, social skills and even a happy disposition. And in an academic context, greater curiosity generally predicts greater success." Without enough curiosity, without enough wonder, there likely won't be great dialogue, EVER.

Summing Up

1. There are many types of questions.

2. Students need time to practice asking their own questions.

3. An Opening Question—one with multiple right answers— starts a Socratic seminar.

4. Closing Questions near the end of a seminar can help connect the concepts and ideas to students' lives.

5. Introduce types of questions to students by having them generate their own questions, creating their own categories, and then asking questions about their questions.

6. Teachers should practice asking better questions.

7. Follow-up questions are essential for deeper thinking.

Your Next Steps

- Be extremely careful about how you answer questions, not just in the seminar, but all the time. On a very basic level, an answer stops inquiry, especially if it is perceived as THE answer. Body language alone can stop an entire line of inquiry.

- Practice answering questions with questions. In many cases this will help students ask better questions in return.

- Consider never answering a question directly (at least in seminar). This comes with a slight warning since it can appear that you are being annoying or are playing a game. Not providing an answer can drive students to continue searching. You could "answer" with: "Hmm, that's an interesting question ..." Even when you do know *the* answer or *an* answer, you could "play dumb."

- Check out Larry Lewin's *Teaching Comprehension with Questioning Strategies That Motivate Middle School Readers* for great question activities.

- Have students bring in a question every week. Post them in the room or on a blog for various activities. Students could develop research projects, I-Search Projects, etc. Have students use the questions at home for family conversations.

- Buy a "question of the day" calendar or something similar and share with students in order to increase curiosity and wonder.

- Start off the school year with a great questioning activity by Philip Cummings entitled *Prioritizing Thinking* found at his website.

- Consider solutions to "I don't know." Keep in mind this phrase masks several possibilities, such as "I'm not willing to take a risk" or "I don't have enough energy right now." Often the first student will start a chain of "I don't know" comments.
    1. Have them answer as other people.
    2. Say to them, "Pretend you have an answer."
    3. Use a painfully long wait time (beyond 7 seconds).
    4. Ask: "Do you want more time or do you need help?"
    5. Create more options with strategies: think-pair-share and turn-and-talk.
    6. Use quick writes for capturing "Thinking in slow motion."

- Read more on questions, inquiry and the amazing Question Formulation Technique (QFT) at The Right Question Institute.

- As a possibility to increase creative thinking, create restrictions for any answers that the students can give. Some of these may appear to be nothing more than games, but use them for variety and for speaking and listening practice.
    - The answer can't contain any words with the letter "t."
    - The answer must be in the form of a question.
    - The answer cannot use the pronoun "I."
    - The answer in writing can't contain an apostrophe.
    - The answer must be a story or fable.

7

The Facilitator

To succeed as a team is to hold all of the members accountable for their expertise.

~ Mitchell Caplan

THE MAIN FIRST step in facilitating a Socratic Seminar is to begin the journey of moving away from didactic instruction toward facilitation and empowering students. As a teacher, this basically means less talking, and more listening and observing. Facilitating a seminar follows the principle of *gradual release of responsibility*, or helping students take on responsibilities so they can own more of the process.

The problem is that releasing responsibility is unnerving for many teachers, especially when they don't know what to do on a practical level. This chapter will help teachers move step-by-step from "sage on the stage" to "guide on the side," as they say.

One of the fastest ways to transition from teacher to the role of facilitator is to participate in a seminar by *only* asking questions. Ask the opening question, and sit back and watch. The students will most likely struggle, but their learning curve will be steep once they know that these are genuine conversations and not a hidden curriculum. If the initial question doesn't work, ask another until the conversation takes off.

The issue with *only* asking questions is that beginning students may need a great deal of assistance and modeling in order to build skills and improve. They need guidance to stay focused, strategies to get more out of the texts, and they need feedback to reflect on their participation. They may benefit from being assigned jobs, may need disciplinary interventions, and much more. Start by *only* asking questions anyway and note what your students might need from you later.

For teachers and facilitators who love to talk, share their opinions, and/or demonstrate their expertise, it is imperative for them to ask questions, the answers to which they DO NOT KNOW. When they do this, they will be far less likely to hijack the power of the seminar, and they can remain genuinely curious and engaged in the conversation. This requires that facilitators closely examine the text themselves, and carefully and mindfully craft questions that have multiple "right" answers or interpretations.

Another great starting place is to tell the students that they are going to have a conversation, but that you want to try something a little different. Tell them that you are just going to listen and make notes and that they have to lead the discussion themselves. You may want to appoint a student dialogue leader and you should definitely remind the students that they must adhere to discussion norms, use good manners, support each other, etc.

Stages of Group Development

Groups naturally go through stages. Just think about those initial awkward moments of first joining a group and getting to know people for the first time versus the fluidity and ease after working with them for a while. Bruce Tuckman identified four stages that he named: *forming, storming, norming,* and *performing (adjourning* was added later). Briefly, in the forming stage the group comes together to create goals and expectations. In the *storming* stage, the members of the group naturally compete for attention and leadership. In the *norming* stage, the members of the group adjust themselves and their behaviors and reach various agreements. In the *performing* stage, the members actively and effectively work together as a team.

These stages of group process are *very* important to understand. Students need adequate time and effective leadership in order to successfully move through them toward better collaboration. When a group only occasionally participates in Socratic Seminar, they may not have enough time to work through the issues of the *storming* stage. On the rare occasions they get together, they may stay stuck endlessly working out the same group dynamic problems.

Many teachers who try Socratic Seminar only a few times get frustrated because the group is stuck quarreling in the *storming* stage. Without understanding that there are other stages to achieve and work toward, these teachers may give up on Socratic Seminar as a viable class activity. Knowing that there are other stages will help facilitators persevere past the *storming* stage.

Below are some of the indicator characteristics that I have observed over the years at each stage (assuming the group does not change, since even adding or losing a single student will affect group chemistry dramatically). Also, these indicators assume that the facilitator has already established classroom rapport with the students.

The suggested time frames in parentheses also assume that the seminars are somewhat close together and no more than two or three weeks apart. Any greater time between seminars may restart the group back at the *forming* stage, or at least the previous stage.

Forming *(likely at least the first few seminars)*

- Participants have a desire to be accepted by the group.
- Members often stay focused on the rules and procedures, rather than the conversation.
- Participants are awkward and say safe things; many are overly polite.
- Members avoid conflict and let disagreements go.
- Participants generally think only of themselves and their grade.
- Facilitators are busy reminding students of expectations and procedures.
- There is a lack of depth; only a few ideas are explored.
- Artificial tools, jobs, and functions help the group, but conversations are clunky.
- Participants often leave seminars with hope and excitement.

Storming *(often starts around the third seminar)*

- Participants feel comfortable enough to challenge others.
- Members selfishly vie for attention, interrupt and speak over each other.
- Members may attack or ignore other people's views, opinions, and quirks.
- Conflicts and lack of tolerance and patience cause group frustration.

- Disagreements emerge, often with harsh or mean tone.
- Some participants take the conflicts and disagreements personally.
- Lots of competing ideas, but few that are explored.
- Facilitators are constantly solving problems and wonder what happened to the nice forming group.
- Many participants leave the seminar agitated, confused, angry, and/or hurt.
- Many seminar groups do not pass this stage.

Norming *(if this stage emerges, I often observe it starting around the seventh seminar)*

- The group works cooperatively to achieve the seminar goals.
- Members think about ideas and depth, rather than just what they want to say.
- Some impressive ideas emerge and the group pursues them.
- Members tolerate other people's views, opinions, and quirks.
- Student roles or functions are fluid; specific students emerge as leaders.
- Participants discover how they can contribute positively.
- Truly creative thinking emerges as students excitedly share ideas.
- Members are calmer and humor emerges, making the experience more fun.
- Facilitators breathe a sigh of relief.
- Participants usually leave "loud and proud" as dialogue continues into the hallway.

Performing *(if the group attains this level, it is often after 12 or more seminars)*

- The group is highly motivated and could run itself without a teacher.
- Members unselfishly think about ideas and depth.
- Conversations are efficient and effective.
- Members appreciate and value other people's views, opinions, and quirks.
- Participants competently perform a function that helps the group.
- Often a truly ingenious, innovative idea emerges.
- Facilitators can be equal or nearly equal participants.
- Participants walk away amazed, proud, excited, and asking for more.
- Facilitators are awed by the group.

Every group is different, of course, but all of them begin in the *forming* stage. Even a team that returns together after a break will restart at the *forming* stage; however, they will simply pass through the stage faster. Keep in mind that any changes or disturbances to a group may send it back to the *forming* stage. I was once working with a very experienced Socratic Seminar group and they were at the *performing* stage. We got a new student mid-year and immediately the group had to reestablish its identity. The students *reformed* their roles in the group and then briefly passed through a *storming* stage when the new student didn't really understand how to fit in. After a quick *norming* stage where everyone found a productive role, we quickly moved back into *performing* once again.

Facilitator Roles

Teachers know that there are many hats to wear when working with children. There's the scholarship hat for content knowledge and pedagogy. There's the discipline hat for disruptions. There's the entertainer hat for fun, and the serious hat to get back to work. There's a hat for paperwork, hall duty, grading, coaching, working with colleagues, and professional development, and so on.

In looking at the stages of group development, it should become clear that there are different facilitator roles to play at each stage. Just as every day is different and every group is different, your role as facilitator will fluctuate. These roles depend on how much seminar experience you and the students have, what text was chosen, how the students are arranged in the room, how well the students can work together and more.

Michael Strong suggests that there are five roles for a Socratic facilitator: *justifier of the activity, Socratic questioner, provider of synthesis and clarification, process coach,* and *genuine participant.* Ball and Brewer suggest six roles: *listener, facilitator, enabler, clarifier, manager* and *judge.* In both cases, the roles are roughly sequential and cumulative, although they overlap, so most facilitators shift back and forth between several roles.

After twenty years of experience, I have identified nine roles that I have grouped into three clusters of three. Again, they are roughly sequential and cumulative. The first three are called the Constant Three, since they are always active during the seminar process: *sentinel, evaluator,* and *bloodhound.* The next three tend to be Norming Roles: *questioner, clarifier,* and *coach.* The final three tend toward Performing Roles: *invisible midwife, true participant,* and *mentor.* The roles are delineated here to show a general progression and to help clarify what actions to take as a group matures, performs, and becomes more cohesive.

In general, you can feel confident to move on to focusing on a new role when the students have adopted your current role and can do the job themselves. For example, when the students have begun asking a lot of their own questions, then move on to the role of *clarifier* in order to help them focus on accuracy. When they are monitoring themselves and clarifying their own language, then move on to the role of *coach* in order to help them work together better as a team.

Experienced facilitators think quickly, make intuitive decisions and know when to push for more. Wise facilitators constantly practice communication skills and seek to get better at reading, writing, speaking, and listening. Dedicated facilitators learn about and study critical and creative thinking skills and group dynamics. And finally, excellent facilitators are both process- and product-oriented.

Constant Three

Sentinel

Evaluator

Bloodhound

Norming Roles

Questioner

Clarifier

Coach

Performing Roles

Invisible Midwife

True Participant

Mentor

Constant Three: Sentinel, Evaluator, and Bloodhound

As a teacher steps away from didactic instruction and opens up more space for the students, it becomes increasingly vital to make sure they have safe environment to express themselves. Thus, a constant job for every facilitator must be that of *sentinel*. This involves upholding basic classroom decorum and enforcing the school rules, but also involves creating conversation norms or agreements—or having students create them. This includes setting up and being clear about the purpose of Socratic Seminars.

The first seminar will create precedent for the others, so make sure to have a clear plan about how to deal with potential rudeness, cruel comments, interruptions, inappropriate behavior, and so on. The main teacher actions for this role are observation and discipline. Observe the group very carefully to see what their needs are in terms of safety and belonging. This often means stopping negative behaviors, such as students blurting out, general distractions, and engaging in side conversations. Students may need a general safety net, like "what happens in seminar, stays in seminar."

Typical *sentinel* actions:

- Uphold school and classroom rules.
- Establish the purpose of Socratic Seminars.
- Establish and maintain conversation norms and agreements.
- Consistently deal with discipline issues.
- Observe group dynamics and make notes.
- Protect all students and their viewpoints and ideas.
- Create an inviting atmosphere of belonging.

Another constant role is that of *evaluator*. Ultimately, teachers have to provide feedback and often must produce grades for the students, so this role is ongoing. Even if the seminars themselves are ungraded, the evaluator's role is to help students improve through the use of assessments and feedback. Often though, seminar-related grades are established through writing assignments and quizzes, so this role can extend beyond the actual seminar class periods. Common evaluator actions are: tallying student contributions, filling out rubrics, mapping the conversation, gauging equity, and providing feedback.

Typical *evaluator* actions:

- Tally, code and/or map participation.
- Provide feedback to students.
- Set and measure individual and/or group goals.
- Calculate grades.

The role of *bloodhound* is to never let a trail go cold, to relentlessly chase ideas in the seminar all the way to rewarding moments. Adler writes: "seminar leaders should not accept half-minded listening on the part of students or put up with garbled, incoherent speech in their replies. Neither should they rest content with statements that appear to be generally acceptable without also seeking for the reasons that underlie them or the consequences that follow from them. When students give answers that are unsatisfactory in any way, the seminar leader has an easier task than when students give answers that are, on the surface, satisfactory. It is easier to ask further questions that uncover what is unsatisfactory about an answer given; much harder to ask further questions to dig below the surface of an apparently satisfactory answer and discover whether the student who gave it was merely mouthing words or really expressing thoughts."

Bloodhound is a constant role since there is not a single method or strategy to achieve this end. The role of *bloodhound* is personal for the facilitator and often involves challenging oneself as a learner to be more curious and mindful. Those who want challenges can study up on philosophical ideas, logic and logical fallacies, and better ways to ask questions. The main action here is to always pursue learning.

Typical *bloodhound* actions:

- Contemplate, explore, and savor ideas.
- Insist on deeper answers and do not be satisfied with shallowness.
- Stay highly curious and alert through active listening.
- Model wonder and foster curiosity.
- Always be on the lookout for quality texts.

Norming Three: Questioner, Clarifier, and Coach

The Norming Three are roles that dialogue leaders are typically familiar with—roles that begin to help groups develop cohesion and depth. Adler writes: "The task of the seminar leader or moderator is threefold: to ask a series of questions that define the discussion and give it direction; to examine or query the answers by trying to draw out the reasons for them or the implications they have; and to engage the participants in two-way talk with one another when the views they have advanced appear to be in conflict." These three roles are almost always simultaneous. However, those who would like a step-by-step *gradual release of responsibility* procedure can and should work on them in order.

In the role of *questioner*, the teacher focuses on and models wonder and curiosity by *only* asking questions and encouraging the students to participate. Once the students are talking and sharing, the facilitator can work toward getting the students to be equally good at asking their questions. The main teacher action for this role is inquiry: Practice asking questions.

Typical *questioner* actions:

- Prepare opening questions to begin seminars.
- Ask a variety of better questions.
- Model questioning strategies and teach types of questions.
- Ask probing follow-up questions.
- Prepare closing questions to end seminars.

Once the students are regularly asking questions, the facilitator can then focus on and model the role of *clarifier*. In this role, the teacher focuses on listening carefully to the students and using follow-up questions to help students answer more accurately, more eloquently and more succinctly. In this role, the facilitator does not allow sloppy thinking or misinterpretations to slip by. In this role it is extremely important to insist on exact meanings of words.

When the students are asking follow-up questions for clarity, when they are demanding greater accuracy, asking their peers for page numbers and citations, then the facilitator can move to the role of *coach*. A main teacher action here is active listening.

Typical *clarifier* actions:

- Insist on citations, clarity, specificity, and accuracy.
- Insist on exact words and definitions.
- Paraphrase and rephrase.
- Model precise language and vocabulary.

Once students are asking their own questions and are demanding better, more accurate answers from each other, the teacher can move to the role of *coach*. In this role the facilitator acts as a conductor to help orchestrate the group toward better cohesion and teamwork. This will be harder than it sounds and potentially very frustrating. Many students have been and will be passive participants who do not say much. Some of them will talk a lot, but maybe only to hear themselves speak. Some will tell long personal anecdotes that may or may not be relevant to the text. Some of the students will take control of the conversation, steering it toward their personal goals. Some of the students will respond to the change and openness of the class with uncharacteristic misbehavior.

There are a lot of additional actions to take in the role of coach, mainly because this is the primary role that will move a group out of *storming* and into the *norming* stage. Because of these numerous actions, many facilitators get stuck in this role for a long time.

Typical *coach* actions:

- Orchestrate the conversation.
- Balance group equity.
- Increase or decrease a student's participation.
- Code how students participate.
- Summarize and synthesize.
- Use timely turn-and-talk or walk-and-talk.
- Encourage mindfulness.
- Teach mini-lessons (outside of seminar.)
- Share data with students.

- Set and monitor individual and group goals.
- Debrief the seminar.
- Gradually release responsibility.

Performing Three: Invisible Midwife, True Participant, Mentor

The Performing Three are also roles that will likely occur somewhat simultaneously. Again, though, those who would like a step-by-step procedure can work on them in order. These levels may require older and/or highly experienced students, since often the power dynamic between a teacher and, say, kindergarten students is a large gap. It is highly unlikely, for example, that six-year-olds would ever view an adult teacher as an equal in a conversation.

After what is likely a lot of coaching, a seminar group may be ready to move into the *performing* stage. This is possible once the participants are all cooperating together and are coaching themselves. When they are asking each other to speak up, encouraging shy members to speak, listening for and noting repetitions, asking for turn-and-talks, summarizing or paraphrasing each other, reminding each other to listen better, reminding speakers to address the entire group, then the facilitator can be confident to move into the next role of *invisible midwife*.

The *invisible midwife* can appear to be a coach role, but there is a very, very important difference: In the role of coach, the students know they are being coached and guided by the facilitator; as *invisible midwife*, they do not. In this role, the seminar facilitator is acting as an unseen coach. With subtle comments and sly questions, the *invisible midwife* helps students bring out and develop their own ideas. When this role is accomplished well, the students will feel like they fully own their ideas without ever having relied on a teacher.

At this stage, students no longer even notice many of the facilitator actions because they are so adept at helping each other and because they are now focused on the goals of the group, rather than just their own personal agendas. Participants may even (sort of) forget that there is a teacher in the room. The most important teacher action in this role is to stay neutral and unbiased, while bringing out students' ideas for the group to examine.

This role becomes extremely important when considering underdog students. These are the students who struggle to say anything in class, or students who process at slower speeds and have trouble keeping up, especially with fast dialogues. These students may go weeks without participating, even when they know that they are being graded on class participation. The invisible midwife champions these students and helps them bring their ideas to fruition. For students who labor to even speak in the seminar, getting them to publicly struggle through an idea (with the accompanying stutters, restarts, rephrasings, etc.) all the way to fruition can be remarkably challenging.

The efforts are well worth it, however. For the individual student, the moment of courageously daring to speak to the group can be a remarkably formative moment. If the experience does not go well (for example, someone makes a rude comment), then that underdog student may never speak again in class. But if the experience goes well (for example, the idea was valid and relevant), then the student may gain a small dose of courage and confidence that will make the next effort easier.

Typical *invisible midwife* actions:

- Surreptitiously draw out students' ideas.
- Release almost total responsibility to the group.
- Indirectly help students develop courage and resilience.
- Invisibly champion the underdogs and outliers.

Once the group has developed a great deal of confidence, once they are fully capable of functioning on their own, they may not even need a teacher or facilitator present. After dropping the authority mantle and becoming more invisible, the teacher can then adopt a role of equal participant, or *true participant*. The benefit of becoming a *true participant* is that anything you say will *only* have equal value to the participants. This means, for example, that students won't automatically agree with you simply because you are the teacher or authority figure. Instead, they will weigh your ideas, compare them to evidence, and put them in a fitting context.

Once engaged in the seminar process, participants will likely forget that there is a teacher participating. A teacher's viewpoints and opinions are weighed and analyzed by the participants as any other ideas might be.

In other words, the seminar participants are engaging in objective, unbiased critical thinking. They may even begin to act as *coaches* or *invisible midwives* themselves.

Reaching this level is important because the teacher is, in fact, the most informed, the most experienced and (hopefully) the wisest person in the room. You'll know when you've reached this level when the students respectfully and routinely disagree with you and provide you with valid reasons why you might be incorrect. Facilitator actions at this stage have to do with participating as an equal, modeling and sharing experiences, expertise and opinions.

In the role of *true participant*, feel free to contribute to the dialogue in an organic way, adding whatever occurs to you to further the conversation. There is no need to hold back if the students are performing at a high enough level to view you essentially as an equal. Many a facilitator makes the mistake of never saying much during seminars, but this means the students will not be able to benefit from the teacher's experience and wisdom. In the beginning, when the students are learning to perform as a group, not participating (for example, by sitting outside of the circle) may be essential to their development. But as the students become more self-sufficient, the facilitator should move toward becoming a *true participant* so that the group benefits from his/her knowledge, experience, and expertise.

Some seminar facilitators believe that their ultimate role is to stay out of the way and let the students run the entire show. It's not uncommon to see them *always* sitting outside of the circle, coding or tracking participation, and making notes. At first, this is likely a great idea. After all, through *gradual release of responsibility*, the students are running the show. However, the facilitator sometimes forgets that the oldest, most experienced, most educated person in the room is not participating. Imagine how your class discussion would go if you always told the best student not to participate. Imagine how teams would do if they always told their best player to sit out.

Typical *true participant* actions:

- Once again share personal opinions, experiences, and information.
- Raise the challenge level of the group by using expertise.
- Model professional and academic thinking skills.
- Model technical vocabulary and nuanced language.

I include the *mentor* stage for facilitating, although it typically extends beyond the parameters of seminar class periods. I include it because it is good to keep in mind that certain students will make adequate progress in class during the seminars, but some students will not. They may need an adult role model or mentor to help them in any number of ways, including reading, social skills, or executive functioning. Actions for this role include personal coaching or mentoring outside of the seminar or classroom, perhaps during advisory periods or study hall, lunch groups, during detention or after-school clubs, blogging or other means.

Typical *mentor* actions:

- Coach individual students outside the seminar.
- Prepare specific lessons and activities to further help individuals.
- Demonstrate leadership attitudes and behaviors throughout the school day.
- Build rapport with individuals.
- Practice what he/she preaches.

Don't be overwhelmed by all nine roles because they do not have to be undertaken at once and, in fact, probably cannot be. Much like an athlete who works on a specific part of his or her game until it is more or less mastered, a seminar facilitator can focus on one role at a time. Whatever the delineations, the importance is more in understanding that there are varying roles to play that empower the group.

Improving as a Facilitator

The single best way to improve as a facilitator is to just get started. Once you start, the domain will teach you. Trial and error are great teachers. Learn from your experiences and ask your students for their feedback.

Professional development and guidance from experienced facilitators will accelerate any learning process. Many college and university programs do not have specific courses for such guidance, so most teachers will likely need mentors, coaches, or advisors. Mortimer Adler writes: "Knowing a set of pedagogical rules never produces teachers who can perform effectively in any of the three modes of teaching, any more than knowing the rules for driving automobiles or cooking food produces good drivers or good cooks. Good habits of doing must be acquired. They can be acquired only by practice under the supervision of a good performer."

Observing experienced seminar groups is extremely important. Many facilitators stall in the *storming* stages and have never seen what *performing* groups are fully capable of. Without knowing what is possible, many teachers do not have an end in mind. Adler writes: "Beginning seminar leaders should be present as observers of seminars conducted by teachers who already possess the habits of good performance. Observing on one occasion will seldom be enough. A number of seminars, differing in the character of the books read should be observed, and the observers should have a chance to ask the leader why this or that was done. The other prerequisite for beginners is to participate in seminars as students. In no other way can they fully appreciate what is involved in learning from the questions and answers and thus discover how best to question."

I mentioned earlier that some of the best professional development can come through Socratic Seminar. After looking at the stages of group development and the various facilitator roles, it should be clear that there is a complex and varied path ahead for any teachers who truly wish to become Socratic Seminar facilitators.

The Importance of Power ... and Release

The *gradual release of responsibility* model essentially means relinquishing power as the teacher and authority figure and then empowering students to take ownership of their learning. There are many forms of power in the classroom and a teacher who wants to pursue student-led conversation in a major way will always need to be aware of how that power manifests and shifts. A Socratic Seminar facilitator must shed the power of authority in order to become a true participant in the class, but there are many other types of power that must be taken into account. A teacher may work diligently to shed his or her authority mantle, but then may sit at the head of the classroom and thereby reestablish the didactic power dynamic unwittingly.

Power manifests in many forms, even very small ways, such as clothing. I've known teachers who will change their clothes for Socratic Seminar, just to appear less teacher-like and, therefore, less authoritarian. Sometimes this involves simply removing a tie, wearing a hat or adding a scarf, but even such simple changes can be effective.

A specific student can sometimes have most of the power in the room. This person may be the school bully, the coolest kid in school, or the teacher's pet. It may be a group of students who have the power, for example, if you happen to have half of the football team or a small gang in the same class. This can be true of gender as well, if there is a lopsided number of boys or girls in a seminar group. If one group is dominant, then they probably have the power.

> **One of the best ways to deal with basic teacher authority is to require the students to talk to the group instead of to you as the teacher.**

Teacher Authority

The most obvious form of power is that of the teacher and the school hierarchy. There are clear forms of teacher supremacy: the power over passing and failing, of handing out detention or taking away recess, and the power of potentially embarrassing a student in front of his or her peers. Then there are the more subtle forms: teachers are supposed to be right, or "know everything," and teachers use a teacher's guide that has the answers.

There are also levels of power hierarchy in the school: department heads, assistant principals, and superintendents. These are all forms of power that directly or indirectly affect the classroom. Think about when a principal walks into a chaotic classroom. In most situations, the class settles down noticeably with the new presence, even before that adult says anything. Need another example? What happens when you drive past a police car?

One of the best ways to deal with basic teacher authority is to require the students to talk to the group instead of to you as the teacher. When students inevitably talk exclusively to you, avoid eye contact and redirect the student: "Talk to the group, please." This will help all of the participants know that seminars are group endeavors. Observe a seminar carefully and when an idea emerges, especially an unusual one, the students will very often turn to look at the teacher to see if the idea is acceptable or worthwhile. In these moments, stay poker-faced and do not express an opinion verbally or nonverbally. This will force the students to decide for themselves if the idea is worthy of continued conversation and exploration.

Spatial Power

Spatial power is the power of physical position. We all have a sense of it when we meet someone exceptionally tall, when we climb a ladder or look over a cliff. It's the power of potential energy, for example, when an object is lifted above gravity's greed.

In the classroom, this manifests in a few different ways. Sitting in the front of the classroom is one example. The front of the classroom, usually in front of the whiteboard or blackboard, is a main position of power. For Socratic Seminars, teachers should always avoid sitting in any position that can be seen as the "front." Have students take turns sitting there. That student could then be responsible for asking the opening question, so that they adopt some additional authority for the seminar. In a rectangle table arrangement, make sure to sit near one of the corners.

Another form of spatial power is relative position. The three basic arrangements in a classroom are: sitting on the floor, sitting in chairs, or standing. Relatively speaking, each has a feeling of power compared to the one below it. So a standing teacher has a relative power position over sitting students. A teacher sitting in a chair has added authority over students on the floor. Even a teacher sitting on top of the back of a chair has position over regularly seated students. Always try to sit at the same level as the students (or lower). Also, be cautious of having a special chair that you always use. A *perceived* position of authority can be just as powerful a deterrent to genuine conversation as a didactic lecture power dynamic.

Emphatic Power

One sure way to stop genuine conversation is what I call the *emphatic hammer*. This is when something is stated so matter-of-factly that all who hear it assume it must be true (whether they should or not is another story). Teachers should be careful about how they speak so that they do not inadvertently overpower their students. Your whimsical claims as a teacher can outweigh fully substantiated ideas from your students—simply because you are the teacher. I have found that if I remain poker-faced and speak in a bland, almost bored way, then my ideas will often carry approximately equal weight and will be considered as any others.

Names and Titles

Names and titles carry power with them. One consideration that may work for some teachers is to have the students call you by your first name … but only in Socratic Seminar situations. Students may become overly familiar and venture outside of the boundaries, but that can be dealt with as a separate behavioral issue. I taught for eleven years at a school where students called teachers by their first names and I had very few issues with students.

Years ago I worked with a teacher who had a Ph.D. and was somewhat famous in his field (if he wasn't, the students all *thought* he was, which probably amounts to the same thing). He insisted that the students call him Doctor_____ and he constantly made references to famous and powerful people whom he knew. This is obviously his choice, but such a decision makes becoming a facilitator and a *true participant* nearly impossible.

Monitoring and Shifting Power

Imagine you were an alien anthropologist suddenly dropped into a Socratic Seminar classroom. Let's assume that being an alien, you couldn't immediately determine the age of the human participants. How would you determine who was in power? What things would you look for? Take some time right now to create a list.

No—seriously. Make a list.

The items on your list can be tracked and used to shift power toward equity and balance for all participants. For example, if the most powerful person in the room is the one who talks the most, limit the numbers of times he or she can talk. If the powerful person in the room always sits in the same place, then move where he/she sits. If the most powerful person ridicules others, then obviously work to change the behavior. If one group is dominant, split the class into two separate seminars. For example, separate all the boys and girls in different seminars, or separate the students by age or by seminar experience. Clearly, these are temporary measures, since the group apparently can't work well together, so bring the group back together as soon as possible.

S.O.S. — Save Our Seminar!

Imagine this scenario: A soccer coach is watching her team struggle. The players are not working well together. A few players are keeping the ball too long and aren't passing. Some aren't playing their positions and are running all over. Some are passing when they should shoot and others are shooting when they should pass. A few players don't even seem interested in playing. Frustrated, the coach runs out on the field, steals the ball and scores a goal by herself.

Just as this would be a bad idea on many levels, a facilitator should always be very hesitant about rescuing a seminar. This especially includes having the last word. As a general rule, never have the last word in a seminar, especially if you disagree with something or feel compelled to provide *the correct* answer. Instead, make a note to yourself and deal with the issue outside of the seminar, perhaps by assigning homework, re-teaching, or following up with another activity. Don't tell the students they didn't "get it," but instead work on reflecting about what happened and why the students didn't seem to achieve what you had in mind.

Wait Time and Two Types of Silence

Most teachers know that wait time is important after asking a question, but with Socratic Seminar, teachers must go beyond simple wait time (typically go at least 7 seconds). If you want the students to speak and think more, you must speak less. This includes keeping quiet in the uncomfortable silent periods that often occur with every new group. Although the silence might be hard to suffer through, the students are often processing the seminar, formulating questions and preparing to make comments. Give them time. Remember, there are two main types of silence: active and passive.

Active Silence

- "Gears turning" in the minds of the students.
- Tilting heads and nodding.
- Slowly building smiles.
- Gazing with focus.
- Gleaming or widening eyes.
- Leaning in.
- Eyebrows raised.
- Sighing.

Passive Silence

- Slouching.
- Eye rolling or gaze locked downward.
- Arms and/or legs crossed.
- Staring blankly.
- Leaning away.
- Nodding absently or inappropriately.

If the silence becomes painfully long, don't rescue the situation by providing your own answer; facilitate it. Have the students do a turn-and-talk, re-ask the opening question or ask a new one.

Specific Facilitator Actions and Phrases

As a facilitator, there are numerous decisions to make throughout the many roles. I once heard that only air traffic controllers make more decisions per day than teachers. Whether this is true or not, facilitating a conversation involves making and not making a significant number of decisions. Whatever facilitator actions you decide to take, the goals are always the same: *gradual release of responsibility*, better conversation, better teamwork, greater understanding, and stronger skills.

A typical action is encouraging someone to speak, but it may also mean asking someone else to listen more (I prefer to ask students to listen more instead of speak less). Your actions can be as small as a nod or a smile (be careful about endorsing ideas with nonverbal cues), or as large as a complete intervention by stopping the entire seminar in order to reestablish norms or agreements.

Standard Facilitator Actions

- Ask the opening question and follow-up questions. Rephrase as necessary.
- Track and code student participation.
- Ask different types of questions to engage various participants.
- Insist that answers are clear or rephrased until clear.
- Examine answers and ideas critically. Ask more questions.
- Insist on citations, evidence, reasons, and proof.
- Pursue ideas as far as possible.
- Do not insist on consensus and do not demand conclusions.
- Push for or invite additional viewpoints.
- Insist that ideas be strengthened and supported.
- No action.

One of my favorite actions is No Action. What I have come to discover over years of facilitating is something I call the 90% Rule. If I simply don't say anything for long enough, someone in the group will, 90% of the time, say what I would have said. (I actually tracked this data for several years.) This doesn't mean, however, that I am not otherwise actively listening, gauging student interest, and monitoring behaviors. What it does mean is that in an effective *gradual release of responsibility* model, students can and will rise to the challenge and say what you thought or would have said 90% of the time. They actually are doing the thinking work.

Be patient.

It's hard to know sometimes what to say or do as a facilitator during the course of a complex conversation, but the following specific dialogue fragments can help facilitators create better conversations. They are not infallible and still must be used at appropriate times, but they work for a lot of situations. Between these and follow-up questions, facilitators should be able to keep the conversations moving in positive ways.

Keep in mind that certain questions or phrases will encourage creative thinking (*"What's another answer?"*) and others will encourage critical thinking (*"What in the text supports what you're saying?"*). Creative thinking will expand possibilities (divergence), while critical thinking will eliminate possibilities (convergence). Both are needed for productive conversations and quality seminars.

Also keep in mind that the following are only suggestions and that you should develop your own reliable actions through reflecting on your style of facilitating and your Socratic Seminars. The first four are examples from Chick Moorman and Nancy Weber's *Teacher Talk: What It Really Means*, which is an excellent resource for thinking about the hidden messages behind talking to students.

> *What's another answer?*
> (Moorman and Weber)

This is a perfect phrase for Socratic Seminar since the goal is to generate and explore ideas and issues, not arrive at a single right answer. Moorman and Weber write: "Different right answers enhance creativity by encouraging fluency and flexibility of thought ... Students' self-esteem is enhanced when they realize that they are valuable members of the group; their opinions are respected and sought; their ideas valued. Different right answers help students become cooperative problem solvers. They develop the talent of looking for more than one solution, and they learn to look to each other for supportive ideas and alternate points of view."

> *Thank you for taking a risk.*
> (Moorman and Weber)

Speaking in front of peers and having to sound intelligent can be extremely hard for many students. It is important that teachers recognize that participating in a seminar involves a great deal of risk. Moorman and Weber write: "Throughout the school years and throughout their lives, people must be willing to step out of the safety and security of the familiar in order to make the changes necessary for growth and learning. You can help students increase their willingness to take those steps by choosing language that encourages and validates students' efforts."

> *Do you want some help or*
> *do you want more time?*
> (Moorman and Weber)

If you use a talking stick, call on people, or otherwise take turns in seminar, there will come a time when a student is put on the spot and doesn't know what to say. Even with significant wait time, some students need *even more time* to compose their thoughts. Moorman and Weber provide an example where a student consistently needed twenty- to twenty-five seconds in order to process answers. This phrase can help take the pressure off and, importantly, offers the child a choice and a way out of a potentially embarrassing situation.

Do you want some help or do you want more time? gives the student an important and empowering choice. Whenever a student asks for help, have them call on someone for support. If that next student has a sufficient answer, go back and call on the student who asked for help and have them repeat or rephrase.

Use this strategy especially when students answer, "I don't know." This will send an important message to the group that this is a hard-working, thinking class and that they can't get off the hook with easy replies like, "I don't know."

> *Act as if.*
> *Play like you can.*
> *Pretend you can.*
> (Moorman and Weber)

At some point in the seminar process, a student may say the dreaded words, "I can't" or "I don't know." It may be about reading aloud, interpreting the text, speaking in class, or any number of other possibilities. Moorman and Weber suggest the following:

Many teachers reply, "Sure you can, come on, *try*." Teachers believe that if students try, they will prove to themselves that they can. It sounds logical but it does not work. Typically, students respond with "I'm trying." Neither the teacher nor the student realizes that trying does not work. *Doing* works. "Try" is too often used as an excuse for giving up. Anybody busy *trying* is not busy *doing*.

We recommend "act as if" as a strategy to get your students doing rather than trying. The next time one of your students looks up to you and whines, "I can't do it," resist telling them to try. Say instead, "I want you to 'act as if' you already know how to do this." Then step back and watch what happens.

> *What in the text supports what you're saying?*

This phrase keeps the conversation objective and grounded in the text. This is a useful phrase no matter what the outcome ends up being. If there is sufficient evidence, then the participant can cite the text. If the student is not sure, then other participants can always search for the references. By using page numbers, line numbers, times (for songs and videos), and grids (for visuals), everyone can follow along. If the text does not support the claim, then the idea should be clarified, modified, or dropped. Dropped ideas are still potentially useful, since even seemingly irrelevant points can lead to new discoveries.

> *Who would like to add to that?*

I like to use this phrase whenever a student answers a question with incomplete information or with a highly unusual or creative answer. This response does not invalidate the previous response, but does encourage others to build on the answer. With interpretive texts, there are almost always multiple right answers and additional evidence, so more ideas are often better and more supportive.

> *Speak to everyone, not just to me.*

This is a classic facilitator phrase to deflect students from constantly checking how right they are by making eye contact with and speaking to the teacher. This also helps the group listen better because everyone will feel more included in the conversation. When you say this, make a circular gesture that indicates the whole group so students have a visual cue. This way you can eventually just make the gesture and silently remind students to speak to everyone.

> *Please direct your respect and best listening to...*

This is my favorite way to direct or redirect students to listen to a particular speaker. Students obviously need to first know what respect truly means and how to actively listen.

> *What's an example of that?*

Examples are powerful tools for understanding ideas, especially abstract ones. Keep in mind that anecdotes might very well move the conversation away from the text and possibly away from anything useful. But sometimes examples and personal experiences help students on practical levels.

> *I'd like to hear from someone who hasn't spoken yet.*

This phrase invites new participation without spotlighting someone. In my experience, students who are put on the spot rarely contribute meaningfully to dialogue. Instead, the vacuum of "negative space" created by this phrase is often inviting enough for shy students to participate. This phrase is especially powerful when used right after a turn-and-talk (the two combined work 95% of the time to get someone new speaking). In addition, because students are not put on the spot, their contributions are almost always more relevant and meaningful.

Conventional vs. Viable Interpretations

As mentioned earlier, teachers should not have a specific agenda for the interpretation of the seminar text. A well-chosen text will certainly help the students explore a territory of concepts and potential interpretations. But even without a specific agenda, there are often standard or conventional interpretations to many texts. It can be difficult not to intervene when a group of students is circling around conventional interpretations and even harder when they completely deviate.

Seminar groups will often start down false interpretive trails or dead ends, but they should be allowed to explore as far as reasonable for two main reasons. The first is that if the trail really is a dead end, then the students can learn an important lesson about thinking and learning: that not all ideas produce adequate results. They can also get an intellectual sense of whether an idea truly has potential or not.

The second is that some of those trails may have seemed like dead ends, especially to you as the facilitator, but turning some last corners may result in some amazing discoveries. Facilitators must find a good balance that works for them and their students. Intervening too early can curtail these opportunities, but a long tangent will often cause students to lose interest.

Although it can be difficult to suffer through many "wasted" minutes, seminar facilitators must be willing to endure these explorations in order for the students to discover new ideas and insights. This is especially true with complex texts, where the students may struggle to piece together their own understandings that may be completely unconventional.

Instead of being focused on conventional interpretations, which can be handled effectively through lectures, facilitators have the wonderful opportunity to encourage new and creative ideas. In fact, this is one of the benefits for facilitators, since seminar students will often renew and invigorate stale texts with innovative interpretations.

Standard interpretations are important, don't get me wrong. They form the basis of understanding cultural literacy, the common ground upon which people have conversations. In addition, standardized tests often look for typical or conventional interpretations, as do many teachers and employers.

Socratic Seminars are powerful forums and should allow for and encourage both traditional interpretations and new insights. By allowing both, the facilitator creates a situation where the students must decide for themselves when an interpretation has enough evidence to be valid and convincing. They may find, for example, that the traditional interpretation has twelve solid pieces of evidence, whereas one of the new seminar interpretations has five. Although they may conclude that five is enough to make the new theory viable, they may also begin to understand why the standard interpretation is conventional.

In addition, they may begin to ask questions that explore these issues: *Why do so many readers consistently find the twelve pieces of evidence for the conventional view? Why do some readers miss or undervalue the five that we found important? How can different interpretations for one text coexist? Did the author intend to have multiple interpretations, or are we just accidentally finding stuff? Are interpretations consistent across cultural or socioeconomic lines? Why or why not?*

> **If you endorse what the students have to say with praise such as, "Nice job" or body language like a nod or a smile, you will maintain and reinforce your power and authority role.**

Endorsements, Praise, and Encouragement

As a facilitator it is important to consider the effects of endorsements, praise, and encouragement. It's easy to fall into habits of praising students in class or endorsing their ideas with comments or body language (consciously or unconsciously).

In the beginning of the Socratic Seminar journey, students will seek endorsements from you as the authority figure, especially when they are unsure about themselves or what they have to say. They will speak and then make eye contact with you, the authority figure, in order to find out if they are right or on track. As they are directed to do so, and as their confidence grows, they will address the group more and you less. Very confident students may even address the seminar in a bold, somewhat confrontational manner, challenging others to disprove their ideas.

If you endorse what the students have to say with praise such as, "Nice job" or body language like a nod or a smile, you will maintain and reinforce your power and authority role. Even a raised eyebrow can be enough to give the recognition or endorsement the student is seeking—and not just for that student. The rest of the class will view you as an approval machine. If an idea or question has merit, then you may nod, smile and/or say something like, "Great idea!" If it doesn't have merit, then you may shake your head, frown, and/or say something like, "Hmmm ... where'd you get that idea?"

Positive comments like "good question" or "that's an excellent insight" still set you up as a judge of ideas and values. Instead of thinking for themselves and deciding what is "good," the students will rely on you to do the work. They won't have to be critical about the evidence presented because you are the gatekeeper of "good" and "bad." In short, they won't have to think because you'll let them know what is "good."

If you are interested in having students decide what ideas have merit, what questions are worth pursuing, and when there are enough facts and reasons to support a viewpoint, then you must remain neutral. By staying poker-faced, not endorsing ideas and handing out praise, you force the students to turn their attention to the ideas and issues themselves. Thus begins the shift of authority from you to the group, from the "certainty" of you to the "uncertainty" of the group.

The students will have to test the waters to seek proof and clarification from their peers. They'll have to determine for themselves what's valuable and important instead of just turning to you for the endorsed answer. They'll have to ask their own questions to continue the inquiry. In short, they will have to make meaning for themselves.

What about students who need praise and encouragement? What about those students who bravely took risks? How do you give them the recognition and encouragement they might need? I suggest doing it outside the containment and sanctity of the seminar. Do not say much, if anything, to students during a seminar. When students need praise or encouragement, speak to them after class, before or after lunch, right after school, etc. Send them an email. This way they get the praise or encouragement they need without direct connection to the seminar process.

What follows are three examples of conversations I might have with students outside of seminar. The strikethrough words might easily come to mind or mouth, but aren't choices I want to make.

To a student who needs encouragement:

Me: Hey, Sam, you had a lot of great things to say. I was really impressed! I liked how you were strong and didn't back down from your position.

* Fragile students may lock onto the word *today* and hear a criticism that they haven't ever participated well in the past.

Sam: Uh, thanks.

Me: We definitely passed a hurdle when you asked that question. I want to thank you for taking a risk because we broke through at that point and the conversation really took off. That was a very insightful question. When did you think of it?

* Specific and honest feedback is important, otherwise the student might think you don't really mean it and are just trying to falsely encourage them. If I didn't really think the question was "good" and useful, pick another day where you can provide honest feedback.

Sam: Yesterday.

Me: Nice. I'm glad you brought it up to the group or we wouldn't have been able to interpret that passage.

* I think it best to word things as strongly as possible.

Sam: Thanks.

To a student who didn't speak in seminar:

Me: Ari, hold on a sec. (In private) I noticed you didn't speak today. I am wondering, though, what were some of your thoughts while you were listening?

* The word *you* can feel accusatory and off-putting.

Ari: (Shrugs shoulders)

Me: What was one thing you were thinking about today?

Ari: The stuff at the end—I liked the surprise ending.

Me: What did you like about it?

Ari: I liked how none of us saw it coming.

Me: That was something you could have shared.

Ari: (Shrugs shoulders)

Me: ~~You know~~ I'd like to remind you that it's an expectation in seminar to contribute at least once.

* Many people suggest using "I" statements instead.

Ari: Yeah.

Me: So, I'm going to ask you to start the next seminar by asking the opening question. I know it will be nerve-wracking for you, but you can ask it to the group and then the pressure will be off. You know Mary will have something to say!"

Ari: (laughs)

Me: So prepare a question, one that is open enough to get things rolling. I can help you if you want. Is that okay with you?

Ari: (nods)

Me: Okay, so you'll be ready with an opening question for next seminar?

Ari: Y   eah.

Me: And maybe you'll add a comment as well ... I'd like you to challenge yourself and speak a bit more every week.

Ari: I'll try.

Me: I'd like you to DO it, not just try.

* If the conversation were full of tension I would probably quote *StarWars* using a Yoda voice or something to add a bit of humor: "Do or do not, there is no try." Humor is good medicine.

Ari: Okay ... can I go now?

Me: Yeah, see you, Ari.

To a student who dominated:

Me: Hey, Chris, can I talk to you?

Chris: Yeah, what's up?

Me: You had a lot of great things to say today.

* I like to start with something positive in case I have to be direct and possibly criticize the decisions in class—always the decisions, not he person.

Chris: Yeah, thanks—that was fun.

Me: What was your favorite part?

Chris: I don't know. The last paragraph, maybe.

Me: Why?

Chris: I had a lot to say and it was cool.

Me: Were you challenged enough?

Chris: What do you mean?

Me: Were you challenged enough by the other students?

* Key question. I'm hoping to guide him to his own realization.

Chris: Oh ... uh ... not really. They didn't really say much.

Me: Why is that?

Chris: Uh ... I don't know ... I think maybe I spoke too much.

Me: Is that bad?

Chris: No ... maybe. I should probably let other people talk a bit more.

Me: Why?

Chris: 'Cause then I can get more ideas from people and learn more.

Me: Can you help me get the other students more involved?
        I could really use your help to get them talking. Any ideas?

* Asking for help is a positive way of getting a student to positively
engage, instead of framing the whole thing as a problem.

Chris: Sure, I can—just ask them.

Me: Sounds good. Thanks, Chris.

Making Adjustments

After every seminar there are a lot of questions to consider. How did it go? How did the seminar leave you feeling? How was the conversation? How deep was the analysis? Did everyone participate? How will you assess and give feedback to the students? How did you perform as the facilitator? And the list goes on.

These reflective questions help highlight positives and negatives. If the seminar went well, a teacher may simply want to tweak a couple of aspects, such as encouraging a few more people to speak, cutting off lengthy anecdotes a little faster, and asking a better opening question. Or perhaps a teacher may want to add something new, such as having the students bring in their own opening questions, using a new rubric, or adding more time at the end of class to journal or reflect as a group.

But if the seminar flopped for some reason, it can be difficult to rebound, not only for the facilitator, but for the students as well. Don't give up! Facilitating Socratic Seminars is a learning process and you have to start somewhere. Reflect on the process and make some key adjustments so the next one is better. If you have a few bad seminars in a row, take a break, do some more planning and prepare another series. If you start to lose faith, remember that Socratic Seminars are for the benefit of the students. They need a chance to develop their thinking and interpersonal skills, something that will serve them well the rest of their lives. You may benefit from rereading the introduction of this book to reconnect to the purpose of a Socratic classroom, and, of course, there is the rest of the book to offer support.

If you need to make any changes, don't worry! Make a plan for the new procedures and introduce them to the class. When possible, have the class practice the new procedures before actually starting the seminar. For example, if the students were interrupting each other a lot, you could have the students write their questions or comments down while the other person speaks. If the students had trouble listening, have them rephrase what the previous speaker said before making their own contributions. Before the next seminar begins, introduce any new norms and have the students reflect on the previous seminar.

Having the students reflect as a group can also be valuable in the learning process. Not only will the students appreciate being part of the process, they will flood you with excellent suggestions.

> **No written word, no spoken plea**
> **Teach our youth what they should be.**
> **Nor all the books on all the shelves,**
> **It's what the teachers are themselves.**
> **~ Anonymous**

Embodiment

What follows is perhaps the most important concept in this book.

If your students arrive to school in the morning without breakfast, you would want to feed them. If they arrived without jackets or shoes, you might try to gather some for them. If they came without pencils, you probably would provide them in class. As teachers, it's natural that we care. We probably wouldn't be teaching otherwise. (Interestingly, the word *teacher* anagrams to *the care*—and, perhaps, implies that education starts from the platform of caring.)

What happens, though, when your students arrive without confidence, passion, wonder, curiosity, or dozens of other qualities? Where are they going to get those? Who is going to provide for them? *Parents?* Probably not if your students don't already have these qualities, or glimmerings of them. *Peers?* Perhaps, if there are circumstances to promote collaboration. *Naturally or accidentally developed over time?* Perhaps, but where are they going to get the initial seed or push? Where are they going to get the daily dose they need in order to struggle past whatever is inhibiting them?

The answer is *YOU*, of course—and all the other dedicated teachers, coaches, tutors, and important people in a student's life. It works through the important concept of *overspill*. You, the teacher, must have enough curiosity, wonder and passion for you and your students. You must have enough courage, resilience, kindness (and anything else) that you are in an overspill situation, flooding the banks of your mind to provide a flood or fountain for everyone in need. You must have enough to give away to the needy and yet remain strong enough to stay balanced and secure.

Warning: If you give everything away, if your stocks of passion and courage are depleted through cynicism, inaction, depression, defeatism, or any other factors, then you will dry up and BURN OUT.

Overspill is not a new concept. It might be a different metaphor, but experienced teachers will, I think, know what is being identified here. We all know that we need to recharge our batteries—hey, that's what summer vacations are for. I'm not accusing people of not being passionate about teaching. I assume you are. What I want to encourage here is for you to think about what your students need and how you create an overspill process in *yourself* for them. I want to encourage you to find other areas of your life where you can further develop yourself.

If your students, for example, are not curious enough, then you need to be the one to make the difference. Walk around your house or yard and ask questions of everything around you. Become a *questioner* of everything. Write down a list of 200 questions. Look at your list and categorize the questions. What types are there? Ask enough questions for you *and* your needy students. Embody wonder and inquiry and help the students develop these qualities.

If your students are not clear enough with their ideas, then you must help them by becoming a *clarifier*. Work on making *your* ideas as clear as possible with the right words at the right times expressing specific ideas. Ask people around you to be as clear as possible. Become a *clarifier*. A great place to start with this is in giving and receiving directions …

If you want your students to be more cordial and considerate in your conversations, then you had better start with yourself. I have observed many teachers at conferences and trainings who interrupt each other, turn their backs on speakers, raise their voices, check their email and behave in ways that I know they would NOT want in their classrooms. How can they expect better behavior from their students, how can they demand respect from their students when they themselves don't embody it? Do they think respect only occurs in the closed environment of the classroom?

Practice what you preach.
You must have extra to offer your students.
You must regenerate if you wish to last.

Summing Up

1. For Socratic Seminars, teachers start the transition to the role of facilitator typically by either only asking questions or by sitting outside of the seminar.

2. Bruce Tuckman suggests that groups naturally go through four stages: forming, storming, norming, and performing.

3. There are multiple roles and actions for the facilitator:
   - Constant Three: Sentinel, Evaluator, and Bloodhound.
   - Norming Roles: Questioner, Clarifier, and Coach.
   - Performing Roles: Invisible Midwife, True Participant, and Mentor.

4. There are many forms of power in the classroom to consider for *gradual release of responsibility.*

5. Teachers must practice what they preach and generate extra for their students.

Your Next Steps

- Reflect on how coaching a sports team and coaching a Socratic Seminar group compare and contrast.

- Use a sociogram or a website like *Sometics.com* to help strategically assign seats and place students within the seminar.

- Reflect on the various roles that you play as a teacher, as a facilitator, as a coach, as a family member. How many of these roles could be turned over to others through the gradual release of responsibility model?

- As a teacher, what procedures do you have in place to turn roles and responsibilities over to the students?

- Read about and research de Bono's *Six Thinking Hats* model of facilitating.

- Interview the coach of a sports team. Ask about various coaching actions: when and why to call a time-out; how to get players to work together; how to maximize potential; how to increase or decrease participation, etc.

- Who were your favorite teachers when you were a student? What traits did they have? Were they easy or challenging? How did they make you think and work?

- Reflect on how mentoring or tutoring is different than teaching.

- What do you do to stay balanced and healthy?

- What is your professional development plan for the next year? Three years?

- What Professional Learning Community (PLC) or Critical Friends Group (CFG) could you join?

- What are three new professional books you could read? What are three new blogs you could follow? What professional organizations could you join?

- What certificates or endorsements could you get to better yourself?

- Consider exploring the many aspects of group dynamics through resources such as Maslow's Hierarchy of Needs or an excellent set of lesson plans such as *Belonging to a Group* found at the website Science Net Links.

8

The Students

If we value independence, if we are disturbed by the growing
conformity of knowledge, of values, of attitudes, which our
present system induces, then we may wish to set up conditions
of learning which make for uniqueness, for self-direction,
and for self-initiated learning. ~ Carl Rogers

SOCRATIC SEMINAR STUDENTS must conduct themselves as indicated by the norms, expectations, and procedures established for the classroom in general and seminars in particular. Participants must stay engaged by actively listening, posing questions, drawing conclusions, summarizing and synthesizing information, and much more. All of these may seem intimidating in terms of where to begin, so I usually start by telling my students that they simply need to participate in the conversation at least once.

Students must always feel safe and have enough confidence to participate. The feeling of safety is often established by prior experiences. The most sensitive students will not speak at all until they first see what happens when (if) others are ridiculed, whether or not sarcastic comments are allowed, and if there are such things as "dumb" questions or comments. Teachers must establish a culture of genuine, safe inquiry in the classroom before attempting Socratic Seminars so that everyone will be willing to contribute.

Because seminars are different from typical class periods, for example, because the teacher steps back from an authority position, expect many of the students to behave in new and unexpected ways. The "good" students, who have developed strong school habits with a teacher in the authority position, may suddenly become hesitant to participate. The "bad" students, who are often bored, may suddenly become surprisingly interested because they can share their own understandings. The confident students, used to finding "right" answers, may suddenly become unsure of themselves. And the list goes on. Observe carefully and make notes.

Homework

If homework is assigned before a seminar, then it is highly recommended that you require its completion in order to participate in the seminar. This is an absolutely crucial point. It may seem like a good idea to have students participate even if they have not done the homework. After all, more people participating would create better dialogue, right?

> I think the three most important things that I ever learned in Socratic Seminar would be:
> 1. The knowledge that everyone has a valid point in some way.
> 2. When you are talking, get to your basic facts first; then run off on tangents.
> 3. The knowledge that you cannot have an active conversation without answering everyone's questions. If you truly have a clear mind and understand everyone's ideas, you will easily/naturally be able to contribute to the discussion.
> ~ MS (grade 6)

The problem is that students who don't do their homework are apt to deviate from the text (having not read it). Their ideas will be at best partly substantiated, and their ability to cite the text will be minimal. Instead of using and staying focused on the text, students who don't do the homework often drift, and unanchored by the text, they wander into anecdotes.

When students don't do the homework, I usually have them sit at a different table, listen to our conversation and make notes. I grade them on the notes they make, but do not give them full credit for the seminar. Generally, the students greatly dislike sitting apart from the seminar. The result, in short, is that students eventually give seminar homework very high priority because they want to have interesting and powerful conversations with their peers.

I can't stress this point enough. Students don't often have many opportunities to have engaging conversations. A few years ago, I had a sixth-grade student visit one of my Socratic Seminars. My principal spoke to his mother, who described him as "philosophical." He was reading Robert Pirsig's challenging book *Zen and the Art of Motorcycle Maintenance*, and he was looking for more of a challenge from school. He was exhilarated by the conversation in our Socratic Seminar and participated a lot, especially considering he only knew one person in the class and he had never been in a seminar before. After the seminar, he sat in his chair, elated and stunned. Finally, he looked at me and said, "I didn't know kids my age could talk like this."

> **It's definitely worth stressing that students should NOT raise their hands during Socratic Seminar.**

Participation Norms or Agreements

Teachers should begin by establishing specific conversation norms or agreements for what *to do* and also what *not to do*. Things to do: take turns, "listen with your eyes," cite the text, ask questions, stay focused, and build upon what others have stated. Things not to do: raise hands, repeat what's already been stated, interrupt others, engage in side conversations, and share irrelevant stories.

It's definitely worth stressing that students should NOT raise their hands during Socratic Seminar. There are many reasons for this, but for starters keep in mind that in general, a raising hands system creates an environment of optional participation. The students who do not raise their hands can essentially disengage from the conversation because they do not feel involved. In addition, raising hands can be intimidating and discouraging to other students who are not quick thinkers.

Raising hands also distracts students from active listening, mainly because they are too busy "holding" their idea while waiting to speak. Instead, students should focus on the conversation and how they can more genuinely contribute, and if they need to hold a thought, they can write it down.

Not raising hands keeps everyone more engaged and involved, as evidenced in 2010 by researchers led by Professor Dylan William who found that students who stopped raising their hands and instead wrote their answers down on whiteboards had increased confidence and test scores.

Norms or Agreements for Dialogue

- Actively listen to each other.
- Build on other ideas (even if you disagree).
- Stay positive and assume the best.
- Paraphrase and ask clarifying questions.
- Cite the text whenever possible.
- Be as specific and accurate as possible.
- Politely insist on evidence.
- Respectfully disagree with ideas, not people.
- Speak to the group, not the teacher.
- Contribute original ideas.
- Resist just sharing the first thing that comes to mind.
- Stay on topic and search for strengths.
- Support each other (this is not debate).

Groups that struggle can use a number of strategies until they are ready to try not raising hands. Individual whiteboards, clickers and voting systems, talking sticks and other turn-taking strategies, such as simply going around clockwise, can help with procedures. However, in keeping with the seminar thought process, the best approach is probably to pass the responsibility over to the students. As an example: "Today we are going to try not raising hands. How do you think we should handle this? How can we ensure that we take turns and that everyone is able to contribute?"

What follows are examples for participation norms or agreements, the first for elementary students and the second for middle, high school, and beyond. Keep in mind that each teacher should develop specific norms based on the needs of the students and the particular goals for the seminar or course.

Older or more experienced students may want to start by developing their own norms, in which case I recommend instead calling them "agreements." Since Socratic Seminars work on the principle of *gradual release of responsibility*, this could be an immediate move for students to take ownership. In fact, the very first seminar of the year could be focused on how to engage in group dialogue in the first place. These questions may help: *How should groups behave in order to achieve their goals? What norms should we create for ourselves this year when we want to engage in dialogue? What are the ingredients of a good discussion? What stops a conversation? What is the difference between gossip and discussion? What is the best conversation you've ever had? How did it happen?*

Participation Norms for Elementary Socratic Seminar

1. Do not raise hands, but take turns speaking.
2. Actively listen to others.
3. Speak at least once.
4. Speak to each other, not to the teacher.
5. Ask questions.

Participation Norms for Middle and High School Socratic Seminar

1. Be fully prepared for seminar.
2. Do not raise hands, but still take turns speaking.
3. Work together respectfully and collaboratively.
4. Actively listen—stay relevant, search for strengths, and build ideas.
5. Speak at least once.
6. Speak to each other, not to the teacher.
7. Ask questions, seek clarifications—do not stay confused.
8. Agree or disagree with completed ideas (not people).
9. Refer to the text whenever possible.
10. Be willing to change your mind.
11. Improve what others have to say (even if you disagree).
12. You are all responsible for the quality of the seminar.
** Do your seminar job (if you have one).

Ways to Participate

There are many ways to participate in a Socratic Seminar besides forming and sharing an opinion, citing a tex,t or asking a question. Because of the complexities of the texts and the intricacies of group dynamics, there are dozens of potential actions that students could take at any given time. A list of the most common ones is presented in the Ways to Participate in Socratic Seminar.

> This year I have learned to trust my gut more. I have learned that if I have a question I should ask it, no matter how silly it may sound, because it usually benefits me. I have learned that not everything I say in seminar has to be perfect, and that even a confusing jumble of words can generate great ideas.
>
> For example, almost all of my statements in seminar end in, 'Did that make sense?' or 'Well, that sounded better in my head.' Yet, somehow quite a few of those statements have helped 'decode' the text.
>
> ~ BC (grade 8)

Make copies of this list and hand out to students. Have them identify which ways to participate are easy for them and which ones will be more difficult. They can then set goals for themselves, such as: "I will try to take two risks today by asking a question and citing the text at least once." Or: "I am usually scared during Socratic Seminars, so I will smile, have fun and ask my burning question."

The Ways to Participate list could also be used as a checklist, especially if there is an outer concentric circle of observers. Participants could then check off the actions on the list as they are used as a means to monitor the quality of the seminar. For example, a participant may note that the group hasn't drawn any conclusions yet (not necessarily good or bad), an observer may note that only two people continuously volunteer to read, or the facilitator may notice that the group keeps adding examples and broadening an idea without going deeper.

The ways to participate can be broken down into specific jobs (see later section) so that students can focus on specific ideas and skills. As they get comfortable with various jobs, students can add additional jobs until, ideally, all of the participants are routinely participating in multiple ways. Keep in mind that even the Ways to Participate in Socratic Seminar handout could create interesting dialogue: *What is the difference between deepening and broadening an idea? When might repeating be good? How do you appreciate another viewpoint?*

Two ways to participate of note are that of the anagrammer, who would explore language through anagrams, and the task of mathemagician, who would explore counting and numbers. These two are elaborated upon in the seminar jobs section.

Ways to Participate in Socratic Seminar

TAKE A RISK

ASK A QUESTION

ASK A FOLLOW-UP QUESTION

PRACTICE ACTIVE LISTENING

PROVIDE EVIDENCE

SMILE AND HAVE FUN

STAY FOCUSED

Cite text or help someone else cite text.

Share an annotation.

Give someone specific praise.

Make a relevant comment.

Volunteer to read.

Add an example.

Ask for a turn-and-talk.

Ask for evidence from the text.

Ask for clarification.

Weave together a few ideas.

Summarize what has happened.

Make a connection to personal life.

Make a connection to another text.

Support another person's idea.

Encourage someone to speak.

Appreciate another viewpoint.

Draw a conclusion.

Help a peer stay focused.

Keep the group on track.

Point out that we are repeating.

Look up a word in a dictionary.

Paraphrase or rephrase someone else.

Use relevant or specific vocabulary.

Offer to make notes for someone else.

Help deepen an idea.

Help broaden an idea.

Anagram a word or phrase.

Count or calculate something.

Speaking and Listening Sentence Frames

In addition to the ways to participate, students often need even more concrete means to successfully contribute to Socratic Seminar. Speaking and listening sentence frames, or sentence stems, can help students practice the thinking and collaboration skills needed for academic dialogues. However, as with many thinking tools, make sure to wean the students off using them once they have developed sufficient habits of thinking and collaborating.

Make a copy of the sentence frames for the students to keep in front of them, so that they can refer to them for ideas. However, as with many scaffolding tools, conversations that rely heavily on sentence frames will often be clunky, somewhat disconnected and may even sound artificial or lifeless. This is because the students can become overly focused on just using a sentence frame instead of truly listening to others, responding organically, and helping the dialogue move on. Overuse of the frames amounts to talking for the sake of talking, instead of creating genuine dialogue that moves toward a purpose.

Although it might be tempting to give each student one or two sentence frames, this will likely result in students forcing their sentences into the conversation without relevance. Make sure to focus on the necessary listening skills that will help students choose a relevant and useful sentence frame that will enable them to contribute meaningfully and relevantly.

Speaking and Listening Sentence Frames

Statements and Questions

- I wonder why …
- How could we look at this differently?
- What in the text makes you say that?
- How does that support the idea about …
- In my imagination I see …
- Based on _____, I infer that …
- I am still confused by …
- My prediction is based on …

For Clarification or Paraphrasing

- _____, could you please rephrase that?
- Could you please say more about that?
- I have a clarifying question about that …
- Could someone please paraphrase that?
- In other words, are you saying …

For Building Ideas

- I agree with _____, and I'd like to add …
- I really like that idea because …
- That idea is important because …
- If we modify that a little, we can see …
- A text to text connection of that is …
- This reminds me of …
- This relates back to our essential question because …

For Different Viewpoint

- I agree with the part about _____, but I think …
- On the other hand, what about …

- The evidence seems to suggest something different, such as …
- I politely disagree with that idea because …

Partners

- During the turn-and-talk,_____ pointed out to me that …
- After our think-pair-share, _____ I believe I have a new idea …
- After conferring, we were all thinking that …
- My walk-and-talk partner was saying that …
- We can't seem to agree on …

Problem-Solving

- I think we should do this step-by-step starting with …
- I feel like we are missing something here because …
- Maybe we can rethink this by …
- Which thinking map could we use to help us?
- Can someone draw a picture of this for us?
- What Notice and Note Signposts are on this page?
- Where do you see a theme?

Summarizing

- I'd like to go back to what was saying and …
- So, the "Great Idea" is …
- What can we conclude from this?
- So what's the effect of this?
- What does this mean for us in today's world

Group Dynamics

- How can we take turns better?
- Who hasn't spoken yet?
- Can we do a turn-and-talk right now?
- I think we are repeating ourselves and …

Table Manners

There is nothing quite as derailing as getting into a fascinating conversation only to have someone raise their hand and instead of contributing, they say, "Can I go to the bathroom?" Laughter ensues and the flow—the essence of the seminar—can come to an unfortunate halt. In terms of interruptions, bathroom breaks, and people otherwise having to leave the seminar for some reason, I suggest you develop hand signals. For example, I teach the students to use the American Sign Language hand signal for "bathroom" when they need to go. They make eye contact with me, make the signal, and I just nod or shake my head based on the timing.

> I have learned that engaging yourself in the conversation is very important. I have learned that deep thinking is very important ... because now whenever I read a book, I think harder about it and I get more out of it.
> ~ EP (grade 7)

Set up a system where students can go to the bathroom without interruption, have a gesture for sharpening a pencil, and another for leaving the seminar and sitting outside of the circle for a while. You will find it is useful when you encounter an amazing discussion and do not want it to stop.

Interest Management

In the simplest possible terms, a student's primary job in a seminar is to manage his or her own interest and engagement. As teachers, we can do a lot to get students engaged, but we cannot be inside the heads of our students. It is up to each participant to find connections into the text or dialogue, and only he or she knows what will work.

Teach the term "interest management"—a term I first heard from Margarete Imhof—or something similar that will work for your students. Students should understand that they are responsible for the quality of the seminar, and that the quality is affected by their ability to participate. As facilitators, we can then get students more metacognitively aware by asking them questions like: "How are you managing your interest in this dialogue?" or "What are you doing to stay connected to the process?"

The most important component of managing interest is curiosity. If students are curious about something, they are likely to engage. This is why it is extremely important for students to generate their own questions, particularly during the pre-seminar stage. Students can also get powerfully interested in seminar when they are able to emotionally connect. For example, texts on the topic of animal testing have almost always worked for me to get students engaged.

Throughout seminar, encourage students to continuously monitor and manage their interest levels. By majority, this metacognitive monitoring has to do with active listening and removing barriers to listening, to which chapter 11 is dedicated. Here are some typical metacognitive questions that students could ask themselves to help manage their interest levels:

- How does this connect to something that interests me?
- Why is this important?
- How is this relevant to us today?
- What does this mean for me as a learner?
- How does this connect to my other classes?
- How will this discussion make me a better person?

There are many other strategies that can help students stay focused and engaged in the seminar process, some of them have been noted already, such as having a seminar job, using specific sentence frames, and finding relevant ways to participate. The important thing to remember is the principle of *gradual release of responsibility*. Students must be encouraged to manage their interest more and more as they experience seminars.

Other positive metacognitive techniques include: setting individual listening and speaking goals; making detailed notes and/or using thinking maps; connecting prior knowledge and identifying gaps; using anticipation guides; and thinking about filling out an exit ticket.

It's important to note to students that often they must simply do the hard work of learning and doing things that aren't inherently interesting. Studious people do the work anyway. But arguably the smartest students find personal connections to whatever it is they are learning and studying. In other words, they work to make the material always relevant. Many students feel that this is the teacher's responsibility, but operating with the *gradual release of responsibility*, students should of course be expected to manage themselves and their interest levels.

Anecdotes and Personal Stories

At first, sharing anecdotes and personal stories can seem like a good idea. After all, that student is participating and he or she is making a connection. If the anecdote is clear enough, then the entire group can benefit. Perhaps the story will trigger another participant's story and then that person will speak, triggering another story ...

In the best situations, these chains lead to a series of stories that further illuminate some aspects of the text. But, in my experience, only sophisticated students can string together several stories that remain relevant to the text. Far more often, what happens is that the students hear a word or idea in the previous story and then connect to that instead of connecting back to the main idea of the text or the previous speaker. This is especially true of young children or inexperienced seminar participants. Maria Nichols writes:

> How familiar does this sound, primary teachers? You are reading aloud a fabulous text, such as *Chester's Way* by Kevin Henkes. You've just read the part about Chester's breakfast, which is always the same: toast with jam and peanut butter. Suddenly, a voice leaps out from the circle. "I like jam with my peanut butter. Strawberry's the best. Once, my mom ..."
>
> And, you know that if you let this sharing continue, soon every child in the circle will be weighing in with their favorite jam flavor and jam story. Yes, this is thinking and talking, but is it purposeful talk that will help us to build bigger understandings about Chester, the classic control freak? The stronger conversation would be about why Chester is this way, and how this affects those around him.
>
> If we have cultivated a caring and respectful environment in our classroom, we can say to our young jam enthusiast, "Wow, I like jam too. But I'm wondering if thinking about jam right now is going to help us to understand Chester? Some-times things pop into our head as readers, and we realize that it's taking our thinking away from the text, rather than pushing us deeper into the text. When that happens, we park our idea on the side of our brain, and refocus on the story."

Overall, I have found that anecdotes and stories are often not useful. For starters, many students are not effective storytellers and do not know how to engage an audience, so unless you want to teach that skill as well, then the stories drift and wander and often don't even make a significant point. A lot of students who tell stories like to hear themselves speak, so rather than driving to a specific point they may, like Scheherazade, carry on for quite some time. It can be difficult to cut them off, particularly if the story is well connected to the text and seems to be leading to a significant point.

A few ideas may help make the storytellers able to participate more effectively and purposefully. For example, you could create a procedure for telling stories where students have to actually preempt their stories with the phrase, "I have a story that relates to this." You can then start a timer. The students must have the story completed by the end of the timer or they must stop immediately. This will frustrate students a lot at first, but will eventually train them to use words more efficiently.

Definitely consider limiting the number of anecdotes for a particular idea. I would suggest three is sufficient to make a point effectively. Again, having everyone contribute can at first seem like a good thing, but only if the examples build upon the previous ones, instead of simply being a collection of similar examples. I suspect, too, many similar anecdotes are a symptom of not listening effectively to each other.

Seminar Jobs

As mentioned in the previous chapter, becoming a better facilitator and having more productive Socratic Seminars involves adopting new and additional roles as the teacher. When a teacher feels ready for a new role, then he or she can gradually release responsibilities to the students. One specific way to do this is through seminar jobs.

The goal of seminar is to have a genuine conversation about complex ideas or issues. If that goal can be met without jobs, then you might not want to use them. Some groups may already have the skills necessary to have quality conversations. Others may need serious and dedicated work on specific skills in order to know how or when to participate.

You may want to start without jobs and then add them slowly to the process to refine the process, build unity and perhaps expand the students' knowledge of logic. If you can jump directly to quality conversations, then jobs may only slow down the start-up process. You may want to observe the roles that students play in seminars and create jobs that will help them develop skills.

In any event, I have the following suggestions about using seminar jobs. Keep in mind that if you are using an outer circle of observers, they could be doing any or all of these jobs in addition to helping a partner or small group in the inner circle.

First, get a sense of the group and then consider the roles that various students play. Assign individual students jobs that will help them become better, more balanced thinkers and contributors. The jobs may just become the medicine certain students need.

Second, rotate the jobs so that the students practice and develop a wide range of skills. Ideally, all of the students will get an opportunity to do all of the jobs. Similar to adding roles as the facilitator, students can add jobs to their list of responsibilities, as they are ready.

Third, don't always assign all of the participants a job. This way some of the students can stay focused on the dialogue without having the extra layer of responsibility. If you use an inner and an outer circle, many of the jobs could be assigned to the outer circle, leaving the inner circle able to converse freely.

Fourth, assign some of the jobs to more than one student. The jobs vary in complexity, so some need to be further broken down. Sarcasm Watch is fairly simple and may be done by one student. However, a job such as Logician calls for listening for up to 22 logical fallacies and/or 27 barriers to logical thinking. In those cases, there could be several logicians who are each assigned a few.

Most importantly, be vigilant that the jobs do not become overly consuming. They are supposed to help the seminar, not become the seminar. Here are some brief descriptions of some seminar-based jobs. Keep in mind that all participants should be questioners and listeners.

Sample Seminar Jobs

1. Sarcasm Watch
2. Citation Insister
3. Bias Detector
4. Peer Pressure Sensor
5. Summarizer (of the conversation, not the text)
6. Logician
7. Paraphraser
8. Encourager
9. Clarifier
10. Statistician
11. Graphic Organizer
12. Process Coach
13. Sociologist
14. Anagrammer
15. Mathemagician

Sarcasm Watch

Sarcasm Watch involves listening for sarcasm or potentially sarcastic comments. Sarcasm generally hurts people and will stop some students from participating, since they know it will only be a matter of time before they are the target. Explain to the class ahead of time that you want seminars to be a safe environment for thoughts and ideas and that sarcasm has no place. The Sarcasm Watch listens for sarcasm and when he or she thinks it occurred, simply states objectively, "That was sarcasm," or as a question, "Was that sarcasm?" From there, the sarcastic comment can be re-phrased, and apologies can be issued.

Citation Insister

Citation Insister listens for any text-based claims that occur in the seminar and then politely insists for the source if one wasn't provided by simply following student's comment with: "What in the text makes you say that?"

or "What's your source for that idea?" If a weak citation is used, the insister can also ask for additional sources. Such a job will help prevent weak reasoning, will help differentiate strong from weak sources ("I read it somewhere" from "I read that in last week's issue of *Time* magazine, page 37"), and may even help curb students from lying about sources to save face.

Bias Detector

Bias Detector involves listening for bias, prejudice, and preconceived notions. Explain to the class ahead of time that one goal is explore new ideas during Socratic Seminar. Have the student listen for bias and when he or she thinks it occurred, can simply state objectively, "We seem to be biased right now." Or as a question, "Are we being biased against this?" From there, the group can explore more objectively.

Peer Pressure Sensor

This job involves listening and looking for potential peer pressure. The student's job is to try to determine if the answers and comments in the seminar are being driven by peer pressure instead of by logic, reasoning, and evidence. The student can say, "I think we're experiencing peer pressure right now" or ask participants to provide evidence to move away from the peer pressure.

Summarizer

The summarizer's job is to periodically summarize the conversation (not the text). When there is a quiet moment, or perhaps in specific time increments, the summarizer recaps what has been said during the seminar. This is a great job for someone who needs to practice the skill of active listening.

Logician

The logician listens for logical fallacies, such as overgeneralization. The student may need a participation card to help him or her remember the different types of logic errors and what they're called. In this way, participants can benefit not only from seeing logical errors or inconsistencies, which is a skill in itself, but they can also work toward making stronger and better arguments.

Paraphraser

The paraphraser's job is to make sure that ideas are restated in a different way before moving on to a new idea or argument. Restating a complex idea can help the speaker refine or clarify his or her thoughts, and will provide extra layers of meaning for students who may not be fully comprehending the point. Sentence starters may help the paraphraser with how to do his or her job: "So, what I'm hearing you say is ..." or "So, your four main points were ..."

Encourager

The encourager is supposed to offer genuine praise and encouragement to the seminar participants. Praise in this case refers to positive feedback—which should be heartfelt and sincere—since few people enjoy false praise and it is often interpreted as sarcasm. Encouragement here refers to trying to get quiet people to participate or to continue. Cold-calling on students in Socratic Seminar rarely works, but the encourager can look for nonverbal cues to know who to try to draw into the conversation.

Clarifier

The clarifier seeks to prompt people toward greater precision, accuracy, and clarity. This may take a corrective form, such as fixing vagueness or dispelling ambiguity, or may take the form of asking for more or better examples. The clarifier likely needs a list of follow-up questions to help him or her respond.

Statistician

The statistician tracks data during the seminar and may draw the conversation map, tally student participation, count the number of questions asked, determine gender equality, and time how long certain trains of thought last. As the teacher, decide what information would be useful and start having some of the statisticians collecting the information. My students have often enjoyed counting "likes," "ums," and other filler words, which I always allow because I have found it increases the students' awareness of their speech patterns and often results in better, clearer dialogue.

Graphic Organizer

The graphic organizer's job is to create visuals that can somehow assist with the seminar. These can be drawings that illustrate certain points (which may be necessary for seminars in math and science, for example), conversation maps (which can be a separate job), or even traditional graphic organizers that may assist students in the class. These resources could then be used to help with comprehension, making notes, reflection, and studying for tests.

Process Coach

The process coach is a junior facilitator. This person listens for things like repetition, side conversations, overly long anecdotes, tangents and other features of the conversation that do not help the dialogue proceed. The process coach can make facilitator-like comments to steer the dialogue:

- "I think we are repeating ourselves. Does anyone have a new question?"
- "We should speak to the group, not just the teacher."
- "We're not supposed to have side conversations."
- "How does this story relate to our question?"
- "Could someone summarize this? It seems like we are a little lost."
- "Maybe we could use a turn-and-talk right now."
- "Is there another way to phrase that?"

Sociologist

The job of sociologist is to investigate and record various data about the group's performance. Similar to the statistician, the sociologist would collect information primarily geared toward the equity of the group. For example, investigating how often the genders spoke. The data can take many forms based on the needs of the group. For example, a sociologist might record the number of times the boys spoke and the number of times the girls spoke, or the number of times the boys were interrupted versus the girls. What needs more equity in your group? Track the data and seek ways to improve.

Anagrammer and Mathemagician

These two jobs involve searching for creative connections in new ways—the anagrammer by moving letters around in words or phrases, and the mathemagician through searching for numbers and patterns. These potential connections provoke the discovery of new territories for dialogue by linking seemingly disparate elements together.

My favorite anagram example is from the short story "Oliver Hyde's Dishcloth Concert" by Richard Kennedy. The story is about a man named Oliver Hyde who has been mourning the death of his bride. A friend asks him to play the fiddle at a wedding and Oliver reluctantly agrees, but only if the participants wear dishcloths over their heads. My students have sometimes struggled to determine the theme of the story ... but not when an anagrammer is on the job. Students as young as fifth grade soon recognize that the main character's name is Oliver Hyde—by anagram ... Live or Hyde ... and that, of course, is one of the themes of the story. Oliver has a choice—we all have a choice—when tragedy strikes: We can either choose to live or hide.

The mathemagician is looking for connections through mathematics, patterns, and numbers. This can involve counting things, like the paragraphs in a short story, the syllables in a poem, or seeing patterns in a painting. My favorite example where a mathemagician has come in handy is in the lyrics to the song "Lateralus" by Tool. The song is sung in a way where the syllables create the Fibonacci sequence—a connection that completely opens up the song's meaning.

Summing Up

1. Students must stay engaged by actively listening, posing questions, sharing ideas, managing interest, and much more.

2. Students must be physically and mentally prepared for seminar.

3. Unprepared students should not participate.

4. Teachers should establish norms for participation.

5. There are numerous ways for students to participate in a Socratic Seminar.

6. Students can be assigned specific seminar jobs.

Your Next Steps

- Use a sociogram from Sometics.com to help assign seats.

- Record a seminar and have students watch themselves or another group. They could then debrief, create goals, and assign themselves jobs.

- Watch *12 Angry Men* by Reginald Rose and have students discuss the roles they saw in each of the 12 jurors. Then have them assign jobs to those characters based on what would be "good medicine" for each of them. Which seminar jobs did that group need the most?

- Create analogies to sports teams. Much like a sports team, seminars function best when all the participants know their own skills and contribute unselfishly to the team. What are the different roles on various teams?

- Read about and research de Bono's *Six Thinking Hats* model.

- Have the students observe a meeting and have them focus on the process. What worked well? What didn't work well? What roles and jobs did various people have?

9

Post-Seminar

*By three methods we may learn wisdom: first, by reflection,
which is noblest; second, by imitation, which is easiest; and
third by experience, which is the bitterest.* ~ Confucius

THERE IS ALWAYS a need for a post-seminar debrief or extension simply because many seminars are never long enough to thoroughly explore complex ideas. Just think about philosophical ideas that have been discussed over the centuries with no sign of concluding any time soon. In addition, Socratic Seminars are very focused on a large number of skills, and those take years of practice to hone. Ball and Brewer write: "A post-seminar assignment enriches and extends the learning, and thus maximizes all the foregoing efforts of students and teachers ... Teachers should use the post-seminar activity to increase learning and to satisfy curricular objectives."

There are two main post-seminar activities: **reflection** and **extension** (assessment and grading are dealt with in the next chapter). For post-seminar reflection, participants should think about how to improve the seminars, both personally and as a group; and the extension component is for expanding the thinking work students did beyond the seminar. The reflective practice may be informal and ungraded, such as simply sharing feedback and observations around the circle about what worked and didn't work, or formal and graded using rubrics, observation sheets, participation goals, and reflective writing. Extensions can take many forms, from short homework assignments to huge projects.

Either or both reflection and extension can be applied to the two basic outcomes of the seminar: the **product** and the **process**. The product is the text and the group's deepening understanding of it. Participants could reflect on the text ("That story wasn't complex or deep enough.") or could extend it in some manner by: deciding to continue the seminar another day, rewriting the ending, adding another chapter, doing research, blogging, writing papers, and soon.

The process is how well the group worked together, how effectively the seminar was facilitated, and how harmoniously the inner and outer circles worked if there was a concentric circles or fishbowl set up. Keep in mind that, in general, it is the inner circle's job to discuss the product, and it is the outer circle's job to help coach the process. Participants can reflect on many aspects of the process by focusing on specific skills ("We didn't summarize enough."), personal goals ("I am proud that I reached my goal of speaking three times."), or group goals ("We still need to work more on not interrupting each other."). Extending the process often involves coaching or direct teaching of interpersonal social skills and mini-lessons on how to reflect or provide feedback.

> My advice
> for future students is to
> ask every question that comes
> to mind, but still expand on
> other people's questions.
> ~ MS (grade 8)

Sample Reflection Activities

- Use an exit ticket to reflect on personal participation (see examples later in chapter).

- Blog about ways the group could improve.

- Use a journal to reflect on current and future goals.

- Annotate the text (again) to highlight the easiest and hardest parts, along with a few reasons why.

- Engage in a think-pair-share about the pros and cons of the seminar.

- Pair up with someone from the outer circle to hear feedback about your participation in the inner circle.

Sample Extension Activities

- Write an essay that explores or explains ideas that were not addressed during the course of the seminar.

- Add other viewpoints and opinions shared in the seminar to an existing paper or assignment.

- Analyze another text and write a compare/contrast paper.

- Research group dynamics and make suggestions about improvements for future Socratic Seminar participation.

- Rewrite, redraw, or reorganize a part of the text.

- Creatively express ideas in the text using a different medium: painting, sculpting, song writing, acting, etc.

- Write a letter to one of the characters in the text.

- Create a parody of the work, making sure to emulate the style.

Debriefing

An essential element of a Socratic Seminar is the post-seminar debrief, which is the major vehicle for improvement. Groups should always seek to be better, especially with Bruce Tuckman's stages of group development in mind. Alexis Wiggins writes: "Remember that it's a team sport: if the conversation didn't go well, it's everyone's responsibility to figure out why and to try to remedy the problem."

Many facilitators stop with 10-15 minutes remaining in class in order to reflect on how the seminar went, usually measured against a rubric or some other set of goals. This usually involves going around the circle and having students take turns sharing what worked and what didn't work, or "popcorn style," where students share out as they have something to contribute. Students could also be selected randomly (for example, using dice or popsicle sticks), especially when there is limited time remaining in class.

A typical debrief can be done orally or in writing with questions such as: "What did we do well today?" and "What do we need to improve on next time?" This often involves going around the circle and asking each participant for a pro or con. Students can be asked to journal about individual or group goals with reflective questions, such as:

- How was your participation?
- How well did we stay focused?
- Did we improve on not interrupting each other?
- Did you achieve your goal?
- Were you able to share everything you wanted to say?
- What should we focus on for next seminar?
- Should we continue this text next class, or are we done with it?

The debrief can take many forms using best practices as long as the comments and ideas help improve the process. For example, students could be given sticky notes and then walk around the room writing down their thoughts and placing the notes in categories, such as "I Observed," "I Think," and "I Wonder." Students could use technology like Twitter to quickly share their thoughts, or *Padlet.com* to post digital sticky notes.

Students could move around the room to various pre-made stations. For example, one corner of the room could be for "I fully met my goal," another for "I mostly met my goal," a third for "I sort of met my goal," and the last for "I did not meet my goal." Once students are positioned in the corners, they could then turn-and-talk in order to talk about how they succeeded or what they could learn from others in order to improve.

Debrief reflections can be personal (*I could have spoken more*) or group related (*We interrupted each other a lot today*). Without being specific, however, many reflections are rarely useful and very often focus on the negative. Perhaps it is a cultural phenomenon where finding fault is easier than finding praise. Perhaps students remember being interrupted more than they remember their own positive contributions. Whatever the reason, without more guidance, comments made during the debrief are often general and tend to be negative.

Make sure the students are as specific as possible when they are reflecting and don't let them make empty comments. If someone says, "This was a good seminar" then ask what was good about it. One strategy to help with being more specific is to have a more thorough requirement for reflecting, such as having the students provide two positive comments, one criticism or needs improvement, and a goal for next seminar—or use color-coded sticky notes for different types of reflection.

Another thing to be careful about is repetition (often so students don't have to actually think). A certain thought can enter the debriefing process and be repeated so many times that the students will assume it must be true—for better or worse. As negative feedback, this can snowball to the point where students have a sense that the seminar was a complete failure; as positive feedback, the students can leave with a false sense of accomplishment or mastery.

My best example of this occurred after what I considered a very productive and collaborative seminar. I felt very positive and buoyant: The students had dialogued effectively about the text; successfully interpreted several symbols in deep and meaningful ways; and cooperated well together. During the post-seminar debrief, the first student complained that the conversation had been choppy, full of interruptions, and that the group had not listened well. The next student in the circle agreed with the first, particularly about the interruptions. Then a chain of agreement occurred around the circle, each student agreeing with the first that there had been too many interruptions. At the very end of class, my buoyant feeling disappeared as I watched the students mope out of the classroom, convinced that things had gone poorly. I was shocked to say the least.

I went through my tracking notes later and realized that there had only been ONE interruption in the 45-minute period, and that it had been that first student to talk in the debrief who had been cut off. This student had probably taken the interruption personally and generalized the experience of being interrupted to the entire class. Then the repetition of negativity had created the illusion that everyone had interrupted each other the whole time.

The main point of the post-seminar debrief session is to improve the quality of future seminars. Certain practices, such as dwelling on past mistakes, heavily criticizing certain individuals, or spending significant time on what *didn't* happen rarely help. A good balance between positive feedback, constructive criticism and neutral observations is best.

Exit Tickets

Exit tickets are also a very popular way to check for understanding and to have students reflect on the seminar experience. I use exit tickets of all kinds depending on what feedback I want from the students.

Favorite Exit Tickets

- Identify one classmate who made a point that helped you to better understand one of the questions. Be sure to include how their answer gave you better understanding.

- Identify one classmate who made a point that you strongly agreed or disagreed with. Explain why you agree or disagree with his/her idea.

- What is one new idea you heard that you would share with your family?

- List one thing you learned today and one thing that you are still wondering about.

- List one thing you did well today and one thing you would do differently next time.

- Identify a page or section of the text that you are still confused about and write two questions that you would like answered.

- Write down two pieces of advice for future classes you have regarding this text.

By getting immediate feedback from the students, teachers can decide how to proceed with planning. Are the students "done" with the topic? Are they ready for the test? Are they prepared for writing their papers?

Should the seminar continue next class? Students can also reflect on their contributions to the process and their personal goals. They can make suggestions and create solutions for making future seminars better, suggest possible texts, and generate additional questions.

Data Debrief

Presenting and sharing data with the students can help them stay focused on objective criteria. Experienced seminar facilitators often track data, often as some type of conversation map, or by using an app like Equity Maps®. The collected information can be nearly anything, such as: the total number of times people spoke, the number of interruptions, the number of questions that were asked, and the average time per speaker.

The data itself could lead to interesting conversations and future seminars. Having an entire seminar on the group's data could lead to fascinating reflective insights. Is the data telling us what we want to know? What do we want to know? What are our dialogue goals? Does better balance create better conversation? What is a "good" conversation? Is the data helping us understand the text better? How much silence is good?

Reflection and Deepening

A popular post-seminar activity is to have the students revisit a pre-seminar piece of writing to see if they changed their minds or wish to add to it. After listening effectively to peers, most students are able to add citations, deepen their ideas, counter other claims and otherwise make their writing much stronger. Typically, students would write their initial opinion about the opening question beforehand, and then write their new opinion or additions after the seminar.

> There is always another answer.
> ~ MS (grade 8)
>
> Keep an open mind. Explore an idea before you dismiss it.
> ~ TD (grade 7)

This before-and-after practice helps students use *Listening For* to appreciate other viewpoints, keeps their thinking open and flexible, and encourages them to listen better. As a general rule, the more participants who change their minds the better the seminar went. This is because changing your mind means that you listened effectively, weighed the new viewpoint against your old one and then determined that there was enough evidence to adopt a new idea.

If the students have set goals for themselves, then they should reflect on how well they achieved their goals, and if they were assigned jobs, then they should consider how well their job contributions added to the seminar. Exit tickets are a fantastic way to quickly reflect on either or both of these.

Reflective Questions for Students

- Did I speak loudly and clearly to the group (not the teacher)?
- Did I contribute new ideas?
- How well did I take turns?
- Did I ask questions when I was confused?
- How well did I do my seminar job?
- How well did I cite reasons and evidence for my ideas?
- How well did I actively listen to others?
- Did I try paraphrasing and summarizing others?
- Did I support others and build up ideas (even if I disagreed)?
- Did I make connections to other texts?

Visual Seminar Debrief and Goal-Setting

My current favorite technique for debriefing how well the group performed is by using a conversation map and then having the students add their thinking to what they observe. This process has several levels of reflection, so a great deal of student thinking can be revealed. Here's the process on paper, though the Equity Maps app is incredibly useful.

1. First, facilitate a Socratic Seminar. As you do, draw a conversation map by drawing a line between each speaker and responder.

2.   Add facilitator notes around the perimeter. These might include: a tally of the number of interruptions, the number of questions asked, side conversations, writing ideas or issues raised next to a student's name, etc.

3.   Finish the seminar and then attach the conversation map to the middle of a large poster. Place the poster in the middle of the floor or on a table where students can circle around it. If space is an issue, students could use sticky notes and take turns attaching them.

4.   Silently, have students make observations about the map. Then have them create bubbles of their thinking by drawing a line from an observation point on the map onto the poster where they write what they think about it. For example, a student may draw a line from a note on the side of the map "Turn-and-talk at 12:44" and write in the bubble: "I think the turn-and-talk really helped us get closer to that theme." Encourage them to generate questions as well.

5.   They may also create links to other people's ideas or questions, even if it is as simple as, "I totally agree." This should create clusters of bubbles.

6.   Use a turn-taking system to allow students to write comments or questions all the way around the poster. I suggest having them shift clockwise every minute or so and using a "tap in/out" system. If someone can't fit around the poster, they can tap someone on the inside to exchange places.

7.   Once the process slows down, have the students step back and verbally make observations on the clusters. They may say things like, "Wow, I guess that turn-and-talk really was useful." Facilitate the conversation at this point with questions such as: "Do you think we should use turn-and-talk more often? Okay, who is willing to take that on as a job?"

8.   You may want to highlight or circle the main clusters extra times so that they stand out. If you want to establish goals as well, these main clusters will likely be useful. For example, if the students noticed that they interrupted a lot, you may need to teach them nonverbal

turn-taking and turn-yielding cues, or you may need to employ a talking stick or other strategy.

9. Finally, use an exit ticket for students to set goals. I typically ask them to set a personal goal and suggest a group goal as well.

10. Review the map, the thought bubbles, the exit tickets and any other notes or observations before the next seminar.

Moving Past Like and Dislike

In the beginning, the students are usually not very good at reflecting. As Michael Hale and Elizabeth City, authors of *Leading Student-Centered Discussions*, write, "Reflective activity is arguably one of the least emphasized intellectual skills in the United States. Although it is certainly developed in many classrooms around the country, it is usually practiced through writing (essays, journal writing, reading responses, etc.). Reflective activity is rarely honored in a group setting or as an aspect of discussions."

Like everything else, students need instruction and practice, and may not have gotten a lot in the past. Without specific guidance, the students will often stay at the like/dislike, good/bad, or cool/uncool stage of reflection, which is often virtually pointless except as a beginning to develop a habit of thought. A typical first round of unguided reflection often sounds like this:

"I liked this seminar 'cause it was cool. I thought we did a good job."
"Today was good. I thought it was cool that we were able to understand the first stanza."
"I liked today's seminar because it was fun."

At first, this level of reflection is at least developing a habit of reflection. The students will know it is important if you stop every seminar early for reflective activity. However, general comments like these do not help students understand how to do better next time, and the main idea behind reflection is to understand how to get successively better. In the above examples, a few follow-up questions can get to more specific details.

"I liked this seminar 'cause it was cool. I thought we did a good job." Follow with: *What did you like about this seminar? What exactly did we do to make this 'good'? What made it 'cool'?*

"Today was good. I thought it was cool that we were able to understand the first stanza." Follow with: *What was 'good' about today? What did we do to arrive at an understanding of the first stanza? How do you know it was good?*

"I liked today's seminar because it was fun." Follow with: *What did you like about today's seminar? What exactly made it 'fun'?*

Even with such follow-up questions, students may struggle to reflect in a useful manner. Many students are remarkably adept at criticism, but they are sorely lacking in the ability to make positive observations and comments, particularly about themselves or people who are not their friends. For some reason they can hardly resist adding the dangerous conjunction "but" into whatever they say. "We did well today, but ..." or "I like what you said, but ..."

I have preferred to steer participants away from such constructions by having them state each one as a separate proposition. I often do a round of reflective feedback just for focusing on "needs improvement" and another separate round for "what went well." Some teachers refer to these as "cool feedback" and "warm feedback," respectively.

The goal of post-seminar is to improve the quality of reflective thinking at as many levels as possible in order to improve dialogue through better collaboration. Participants can deepen the reflective process by looking at seminar data or "feedback frames," as Dave Nelson from Equity Maps calls them. These data sets or frames can include how often participants spoke, how long they spoke, the number or types of questions asked, the number of citations to the text, or any other frames through which the participants may want to objectively view the seminar. See Chapter 10, *Evaluation*, for more on tracking data.

By reflecting on seminar data, students can dialogue about specific elements of the seminar itself, rather than speaking generically about each other. A good post-seminar is essentially another mini-dialogue where students can continue learning how to better collaborate. Dave Nelson shared this illustrative story:

> ... after viewing the Feedback Frames one student noticed that there had been virtually no silence during the 30 minute seminar, concluding that continuous speaking of the 16-student-group was a sign that they had done really well. When asked who sees silence in the same way, some students agreed, while others opened the reflection further,

suggesting that the dialogue moved too quickly and didn't allow for everyone to build on ideas because they didn't really try to understand them.

The most profound comment came from a quieter student who shared that he simply wanted to take in what people were saying and wanted to "really try to hear them" before adding his own piece to the dialogue.

In the end, the class had pivoted and agreed that more silence would be much better and would allow the group to slow down and truly listen—the goal for the next seminar was set!

Facilitator Reflection

In order to improve their skills, facilitators must always reflect upon the seminar, so that the next one can be incrementally better. In general, facilitators should ask themselves a series of reflective questions to gauge the quality of the seminar from three perspectives: the process, the product, and the leadership. In terms of the process, how well did the participants do? How well did the text work in conjunction with the opening question? How did I do as a facilitator?

Reflective Questions

About the participants and the process

- How well did they speak one at a time? How many interruptions were there?
- How well did they do their seminar jobs?
- Were there clarifying questions for greater accuracy and precision?
- How well did they cite reasons and evidence for their ideas?
- How well did they listen to others actively and respectfully?
- To what degree did the participants take control of their learning?
- How well did they paraphrase and summarize accurately?
- Did they support each other and build up ideas?
- How many students left excited, awed, and wondering?

- Were the students making connections to other texts?
- How balanced and equitable was participation?

For the seminar text and opening question

- How engaging was the text?
- How well did the opening question work?
- Was the entire text used in the discussion? If not, which parts remained unexplored?
- Did the students discover themes, symbols, "Great Ideas," or deeper meanings?
- Did the participants get stuck on certain parts? If so, why?
- How well did the pre-seminar prepare the students to work the text?

For the facilitator

- How well did I listen and ask follow-up questions?
- How well did I protect the safety and integrity of the seminar?
- How well did I manage the group for balanced participation?
- Did I consistently insist on citing the text?
- How well did I draw out reasons and evidence?
- Did I have to call a time-out or otherwise intervene in the process?
- How close was I to an equal participant?
- Do we need to have another seminar or a follow-up assignment?

Of course, these questions must lead to making decisions about further actions for improvement. If the text was engaging but the students only discussed the first two pages of a six-page text, then consider only using that two-page excerpt next time. If the students got stuck on certain parts of the text, then they likely need more pre-seminar work targeting those parts. If the students were interrupting each other, consider providing them with a talking stick, a listening mini-lesson or other intervention.

Hale and City further suggest that there are four fulcrums to consider for seminar improvement: *safety, authentic participation, challenge* and *ownership.* They write, "We call these four dimensions *fulcrums* because they are the leverage points on which seminars should be balanced; you can use them to guide your decisions." According to the authors, problems in seminar are often due to one or more of these four fulcrums being out of balance.

In my experience, these four fulcrums are roughly sequential in importance to the health of a seminar group. In other words, issues of *safety* will likely prevent the development of the other three; issues surrounding *authentic participation* will prevent the last two; and issues of challenge will probably prevent the students from developing *ownership*. So I recommend investigating any problems or barriers in Socratic Seminar in the order stated. When in doubt, start asking the students: *Were there any issues of safety? What about problems with participation?*

> **There are two simple but reliable ways to tell if a seminar went well: the number of students who changed their minds, and how much conversation continued on after class.**

After thoughtful reflection, a good facilitator will realize there are a million things that could be better next time. Sometimes this reflective practice can lead to analysis paralysis. So, how can you quickly know if the Socratic Seminar went well or not? There are two simple but reliable ways to tell if a seminar went well: the number of students who changed their minds, and how much conversation continued on after class.

The first is to simply ask the students how many of them changed their minds during the seminar. In general, the more students who changed their minds, the better the seminar went. This is a great measuring stick because of all of the ingredients that would be necessary for a change of mind: actively listening to other students; understanding the other person's ideas and evidence; being willing and able to let go of biases and personal opinions; and appreciating that the new viewpoint has strong enough merit.

A second quick way to tell if a seminar went well is to see if the students kept the conversation going out into the hallway after class. Socratic Seminars employ open-ended questions and complex texts that combine for exciting conversations with multiple "right" answers. By the time the class period is over, many students are often still unsure about how to think about the text. Even better, you could check with the next period's teachers to see if the students kept the conversation going into their classes. I also like to walk the halls and wander through the lunchroom to see if the students are still talking about the text.

Extensions

A common practice for the post-seminar stage is to have the students further their understandings from the seminar through additional research or new applications. With this activity, the seminar is used as a springboard for further inquiry. The students could look over their questions from the annotation stage and see which ones are still unanswered, or the class could generate additional questions to explore.

Often post-seminar activities ask students to apply their knowledge to new situations. For example, after a seminar on an excerpt from Machiavelli's *The Prince,* high school students could write about what advice Machiavelli would give to new presidential candidates. After reading *The Zax*, by Dr. Seuss, elementary students could write about how the situation resembles events on the playground and students could then write potential solutions to their problems. After reading *The Pledge of Allegiance*, middle school students could create their own pledges specific to the classroom or their goals as students.

Extending Learning

Homework assignments can be good extensions for seminars, but there are a number of cautions. Remember, the skills involved in homework assignments are often different than those in the seminar itself. For example, homework is often an intrapersonal written product, whereas seminars focus on interpersonal speaking and listening skills.

Keep in mind that the purposes for homework before and after a Socratic Seminar are different as well. Essentially, assignments before a seminar are often designed to prepare the students for the most effective participation possible. This often includes: defining new vocabulary, exploring key concepts, organizing information, and generating questions. After a seminar, teachers are often looking for analysis and synthesis. Typically, teachers assign reflective papers that ask students to expand a viewpoint, synthesize several positions, or justify an interpretation of the text.

Before a Socratic Seminar, when students are typically exposed to a text for the first time, they are primarily dealing with Bloom's first two or three levels of Knowledge, Comprehension, and Application. Without further discussion or instruction, many of them would have a lot of difficulty moving into the higher levels. When the students come together as a group, however, they begin to tap into the higher levels of Analysis, Synthesis, and Evaluation. Because Socratic Seminars tend to focus on developing skills, many teachers value the higher levels more, and, therefore, assess and grade those with greater weight. Pre-seminar work, therefore, might carry 40% of the homework grade, and post-seminar work 60%.

Work can be collected over time in seminar portfolios. This allows for another grading consideration. Due to the cumulative nature of knowledge, many students do their best thinking at the end of marking periods. Giving those assignments more weight may result in a more accurate evaluation of the student and his or her progress. This is not always the case, however, so I have developed a system where I have the students collect their work in a folder and then they revise and edit a number of pieces at the end of the marking period. This gives them an opportunity to choose what they think is their best work.

Journaling: Writing Is Thinking in Slow Motion

Journaling can be a powerful tool for critical and creative thinking, but like any tool, must be used effectively. A great practice is to have the students keep a questions journal. In general, students do not have enough practice asking questions, so these journals can help students immensely, not only in formulating the questions themselves, but also in building a greater sense of wonder and curiosity about the world.

Determining the exact purpose of the journal can focus the questions. For example, if the journaling is to give students an opportunity to practice asking (better) questions, then any questions may suffice: *Why are stop signs red? Why is school mandatory? Why does ice float?* If the purpose of the questions journal is to practice asking a greater variety of questions, then the students can collect different types: open and closed questions, shallow and deep, or mortal and immortal. If the purpose of the journaling is more focused on a particular text, then the entries can be directed to specific parts: *List ten questions about the first stanza. Generate five questions about imagery in the poem. List five questions about symbolism.*

Double-entry journals are a great way to provide students with extensive direct and personalized feedback. In this style of journaling, have the students either fold the pages in half to create two columns, or use even or odd pages. The students write on one side, posing questions, defining vocabulary, and interpreting parts of the text. Then another person responds to the writing in the other column. If two students swap double-entry journals, they can have powerful and effective dialogue. Teachers can write in the other columns, not only to respond, but also to provide the student with direct feedback.

Blogging

Blogs and forums are a great way to extend seminars outside of the classroom. Because Socratic Seminars generally use complex texts and open-ended questions, students often leave the seminar without definite answers, so having a blog will allow them to keep engaging with the ideas and issues from class.

Students sometimes prefer blogging over other writing assignments because they are more interactive and often offer students a choice of topics or threads. Students can often earn badges, become monitors, create avatars and much more. Perhaps best of all, students can often get feedback very quickly from their peers and their teachers.

Blogging does present some challenges, so read more in Chapter 10.

Reflection Portfolios

Over the course of a quarter or a semester, students can keep all of their annotated papers, entrance and exit tickets, copies of conversation maps, and notes and reflections collected together into a portfolio. Alexis Wiggins writes: "I've had positive experiences asking students to reflect on their learning twice a year, generally at the end of each term. I ask them to pull out portfolios of their written work, their rubrics, and their feedback over the term and ask them to note, in writing, how they feel they have grown and what they think they have gained as a learner. As part of that same reflection, have students compare the first couple web graphs of the year with the most recent ones, asking students to reflect on their collaborative and individual growth over the course of the term with regard to discussions."

Students can then reflect on their growth and development over time, as individuals and as a group. I often like to have students revisit a previous text in order to explore their expanded skills and ideas. Here is an example I used for middle school students.

Socratic Seminar Reflective Portfolio Piece

Seminar texts from this trimester:

Picture	*Think*	Author unknown
Math Proof	Proposition 1	Euclid
Nonfiction	*Rules for Being Human*	Dan Millman
Quote	"The instant you speak words …"	Proverb
Math Proof	Proposition 2	Euclid
Pledge	*The Pledge of Allegiance*	Francis Bellamy
Song & Lyrics	"Birdhouse in Your Soul"	They Might Be Giants
Music Video	Birdhouse in Your Soul	They Might Be Giants
Philosophy	*Tao Te Ching 43*	Lao Tzu
Poem	"a glazed mind …"	E.E. cummings
Poem	"Vanishing Point"	Billy Collins
Story	"The Ingenious Patriot"	Ambrose Bierce
Song & Lyrics	"Moon Over Bourbon Street"	Sting

Part 1: Annotations

Choose one of the pieces above to re-annotate to the best of your ability.

For most of you, this assignment involves writing rather than speaking, so focus on your thoughts and ideas more than your questions. You will use these annotations to assist with writing, or for conducting a seminar at home for part 2. You will be graded on your annotations based on our anchor papers.

Key question: How do your new annotations compare to your old ones?

Part 2: Interpretation

Written: Interpret the text using your new annotations. I will be looking for a line-by-line analysis, along with an overall understanding. Use your annotations to focus. This is the same practice we have been doing in class—only in a written form. Provide examples as possible.

Video: Those of you choosing to have a seminar at home will organize a time where you and your family and friends can enjoy the text for 30 minutes or so. Your job will be to use your annotations to ask questions, cite the text, and make connections during the conversation. You have a leadership role here, so make sure you facilitate the conversation, while also providing your own ideas. Along with the input from your family, you will be evaluating yourself using the Socratic Seminar rubric. Much of the grade, however, will be focused on the reflection in part 3, since your family does not necessarily have Socratic practice.

Part 3: Reflection

This reflection is very important. It has often been said that you don't really know something until you've reflected upon it. This piece should be 5-7 paragraphs of well-written and thorough reflective writing about what you've learned in Socratic Seminar this trimester.

Reflective questions:

Have you noticed approaching reading or thinking differently? Are you listening to songs more carefully? Are you appreciating words more? Are you able to listen better? Do you appreciate other ideas more now?

Mini-Lessons from this trimester:

- How to annotate and read closely.
- How to ask better questions.
- Separating emotions from discussion.
- How to disagree with someone.
- How to organize your thoughts before speaking.
- How to consider ideas.
- How to dig deeper.
- Ways to participate.
- Building more self-control.

Summing Up

1. There are two main post-seminar activities: reflection and extension.

2. There are two basic outcomes to reflect upon: the product and the process.

3. A typical post-seminar activity is to debrief what went well and what needs improvement.

4. Facilitators should reflect on their own participation, as well as how the text and Opening Question worked.

5. Students often seem to reflect on the negatives and can get stuck in the simple dichotomy of like/dislike.

6. The seminar participants can set individual and group goals.

Your Next Steps

- Matt Copeland has a great idea to have current students write letters to future students about Socratic Seminars and their experiences. This awesome assignment serves two purposes: Current students can reflect on the seminar process, and future students get the benefit of wisdom from their peers.

- Similar to coaches watching game tapes, record a seminar and then have the students watch in order to debrief. You could actually use the video as the text for another seminar.

- Watch and debrief the movie *12 Angry Men* by Reginald Rose. Have the students consider how the entire process could have gone better. What goals would they establish for each of the characters?

- Have former students come watch a seminar and assist with the debrief.

- Based on the outcome of the seminar, consider having the students make suggestions for or choose the next text.

- In the debrief, also consider what DID NOT happen during the seminar. This can sometimes be a more useful thought process than looking at what DID happen.

- Use a suggestion box in the classroom for anonymous suggestions. Sometimes students are simply not willing to share with their name attached.

- Use the app Equity Maps (it's the best app I have found for the job) to help collect data about the seminar and then to assist in debriefing and goal setting.

10

Evaluation

The greatest sign of success for a teacher ... is to be able to say,
"The children are now working as if I did not exist."

~ Maria Montessori

THIS CHAPTER OUTLINES the basics of evaluating Socratic Seminars. For purposes of clarity in this book, the term *evaluation* breaks down into three separate but connected categories: tracking, assessment, and grading. **Tracking** here refers to the quantitative (sometimes qualitative) process of data collection, such as tallying how many times a student speaks in a seminar. **Assessment** refers to the ongoing reflective practice of providing students with the formative feedback they need to improve, such as the comments on an observation form. **Grading** refers to the summative process of creating grades for the students and/or the group.

Three Connected Categories of Evaluation

Tracking: the quantitative (sometimes qualitative) process of data collection, such as tallying how many times a student speaks in a seminar.

Assessment: the ongoing reflective process of providing students with the formative feedback they need to improve, such as the comments on an observation form.

Grading: the summative process of creating grades for the students and/or the group.

Teachers who grade Socratic Seminars will encounter numerous questions. How do you grade a conversation? Clearly, a productive comment is better than a redundant or irrelevant comment, but how much better? How do you grade listening? Is a question better than a statement? If seminars are group endeavors, how do you grade an individual? Is a concise comment better than a long comment? Should you grade the whole group? When is a student improving, and how would you know? Is one comment from a shy participant better than three from a talkative student?

Before getting into the details about tracking, assessing, and grading, it is important to keep it simple when first starting the Socratic Seminar journey. There will be an overwhelming confluence of many factors in the beginning, such as text selection, seminar procedures, facilitating strategies, and student management. With many other variables to juggle, and because seminars are often only occasional activities, evaluation tends to get a backseat.

TRACKING

Tracking, sometimes known as coding, is the very useful process of tallying and monitoring student contributions. The data collected can range from a very basic system of counting student contributions, to tallying the types of contributions, such as positive, negative, and neutral. More complex systems of tracking may include: statements, questions, procedural comments, redundancies, new ideas, volunteering to read, or monitoring any other skill that the students are working on.

Such data can help a teacher assess each student, can help direct feedback, and may assist in the grading process. However, it is not by itself normally detailed enough to form an accurate grade for a student's participation in Socratic Seminar. For example, are three questions from a shy student worth more than three statements from a talkative student? Are six useful comments (positives) and two distractions (negatives) the same as four contributions? How might a student's contributions in the beginning of the year compare to those at the end of the year?

After my very first few seminars, I started with the simplest version of tracking: merely counting every time a student contributed to the seminar. Although this seems easy at first, the reality is that even such a crude system can be remarkably convoluted by personal decisions. For example, if a student uses a conjunction in a contribution to class, does that count as two separate ideas or one sentence? Does a long anecdote with one main point count as one contribution or several because it is a lot of talking? Does a question count the same as a statement? In general, each facilitator should make his or her own decisions on these and then stay consistent.

I quickly realized the limitations of simple tallying. I began to wonder what I wanted to see in my students. I valued inquiry above general comprehension because I wanted all of my students to wonder and question. I figured the students who were good at literary analysis would contribute their excited thoughts anyway, but that reluctant students may only share questions about what they didn't understand. In this way, I got everyone more involved to create better equity and balance.

A slightly more complex version of simple tallying involves deciding if a participant's contribution has a positive, negative, or neutral influence on the conversation. Positive additions that move the conversation along get a "+" mark as a tally; remarks that interfere with or hinder the conversation get a "—" mark; and comments that neither advance the conversation nor take away from it, such as a reiteration of something that was already stated, get an "N." Such a system, which can be as simple as making these marks next to a class roster, is a little more accurate, but demands more from a facilitator who must make very quick decisions about the content or effect of every comment.

I soon realized that I did not have a clear idea of how each student contributed to a specific seminar. I could tell parents how often their children were participating, but I didn't have data that told me more than that. As I became better at juggling my many roles as a facilitator, I began adding categories for types of contributions. I started with statements, procedural comments, questions, and reading from the text, or an S-P-Q-R coding system.

Because tracking occurs during the seminar itself, teachers should choose a system that they can manage, keeping in mind that they have other hats to wear simultaneously. Facilitators may need to manage behavior, ask questions, curtail tangents, coach the process, or any number of other tasks.

Name	Statements					P	Questions					R	O
	Unrelated -1	Redundant 0	Relevant 1	Insightful 2	Remarkable 3	1	Unrelated -1	Redundant 0	Relevant 1	Insightful 2	Remarkable 3	1	
1													
2													
3													
4													
5													
6													
7													
8													
9													
10													
11													
12													
13													
14													
15													
16													
17													
18													
19													
20													

S = Statement   P = Procedural   Q = Question   R = Reading / Citing Text   O = Other: _____

S-P-Q-R

The general system I have used for many years is an S-P-Q-R chart. Supplemented with basic informal notes, I find that the system provides me with most of the information I need. The **S** is for statements, and I add a tally mark based on the quality of the contribution, from unrelated to remarkable.

The **P** is for procedural comments and I tally any contribution that focuses on helping the dialogue. Some students will show great charisma in Socratic Seminars without necessarily analyzing the text, but they are still helping the group. Examples of student procedural comments: *I think we should move on now. Does anyone else want to say anything about line 6 before we move on to line 7? Should we read the whole thing first or go line by line?*

The **Q** is for questions. A student who asks a question gets a tally mark, again based on the perceived quality. If the participants did not pursue a question, I will usually add a procedural comment or question, such as "What about Mira's question before we move on?"

The **R** stands for reading from or citing the text, and I tally any time a student refers to the text, either volunteering to read or citing the text to prove a point. Many students are intimidated by oral reading, especially in front of peers, so I find tracking this potentially useful for measuring confidence.

I reserve the **O** or Other column for anything else I want to track during the dialogue, such as when students use specialized vocabulary, demonstrate good manners, seek first to understand, etc.

For statements and questions, I use the *relevant* category for any contribution that is related to the current dialogue. On the less productive side, the *redundant* column is for when a student repeats an idea. This is important because some students might talk a lot, but they may simply repeat what others have said. This not only wastes precious seminar time, but also might indicate that the student is not actively listening or thinking about the current question. The *unrelated* category is for those contributions that detract from the seminar, either because they are side conversations or because they off topic. When I notice a few *redundant* or *unrelated* contributions from a student, I meet with him or her outside of seminar to check in about potential issues.

I use the *insightful* and *remarkable* categories for questions or comments that surprise or amaze me. In general, I use *insightful* for those contributions that stand out for some reason in that class or grade level. I use the *remarkable* category for those students who stop me in my tracks and cause me to see the text in new ways. With proficient seminar groups, I might have two or three *insightful* tallies per seminar and perhaps two or three *remarkable* tallies per semester. For me, a *remarkable* contribution is a big deal and often involves sending a positive note or email home.

Conversation Mapping + Coding

Conversation mapping along with coding is my current favorite tracking method. To map a conversation, write the names of the students in a circle or square, just as they are arranged in the room. Start your pencil at the first student to speak and trace a line to the responding participant. Keep drawing connecting lines throughout the course of the seminar. If someone asks a question to the group, wait until a student picks up the question and then draw a connecting line. If a question or comment goes unanswered, then you may want to put a tally mark next to the speaker's name to track that attempt even though it wasn't part of the conversation sequence.

As a facilitator, you will need to decide what merits a contribution. For example, if several students mutter "I don't know," they may not get sequential lines or tally marks, since they didn't actually contribute to the conversation. Most teachers use codes next to the students' names and sometimes even code the connective lines as well.

See the Post-Seminar chapter for how to use a map specifically as a debriefing tool.

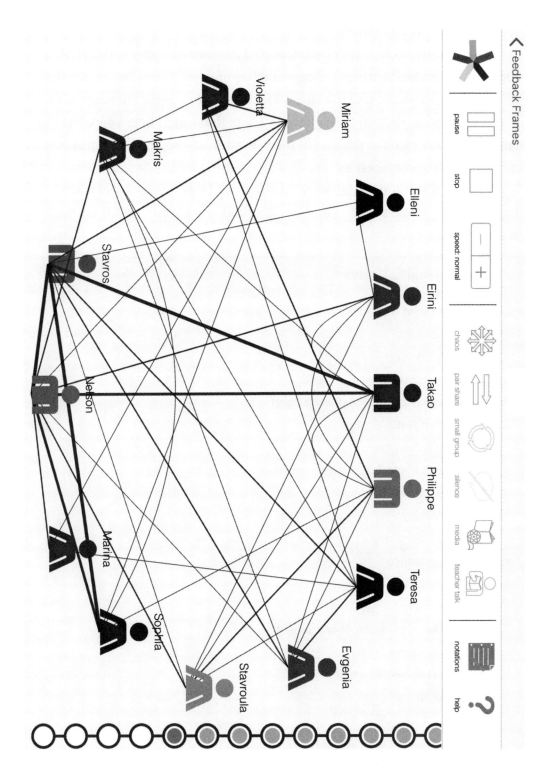

Screen Shot from Equity Maps App

Additional Coding Symbols

Finally, for those who may be interested in more complex systems of symbols and colors, there are a huge number of possibilities based on what information you would like to collect. Track what you need, but keep an end in mind. For example, you can collect any data that might help you write narrative report cards at the end of the semester, or keep coding notes to help with parent conferences.

Although these codes may vary across grade levels and subject areas, the following sample symbols and tracking codes are likely useful for most conversations.

Sample Tracking Codes	
+	Relevant
−	Irrelevant
A	Agreement
AN	Anecdote
B...	Begins talking, but doesn't finish
C	Cited Text
D	Disagreement
E	Eureka! Breakthrough comment
I	Idea to revisit
L	Listening
LF	Logical Fallacy
Q	Question
R	Redundant
S	Statement
S+	Powerful Statement or Thought
SC	Side Conversation
T-T	Text-to-Text Reference
V	Vocabulary Use
Red Line	Line of Disagreement
Blue Line	Line of Agreement
Green Line	New Idea or Question Ventured

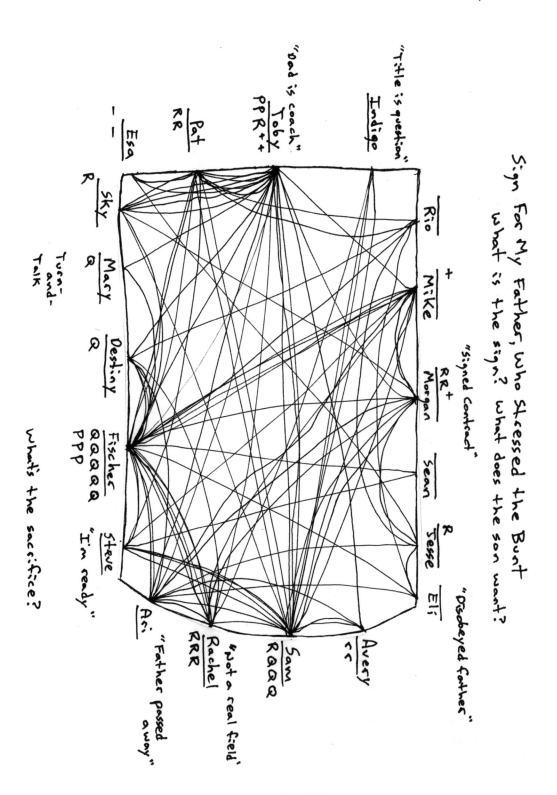

Conversation Map

Tracking Over Time: When 4 > 8

Because tracking is mainly quantitative, tracing a student's contributions over time can help illuminate trends and patterns. Some students work better in the morning, while others think more clearly in the afternoon. Some students will participate a lot when the text is a poem or song, but not when the text is longer. Others will suddenly become animated and insightful when the text is a visual.

Tracking over time will help demonstrate progress (at least in the quantitative sense). For example, a student who consistently averages eight contributions per seminar is not showing growth over time—at least quantitatively. However, another student may go several seminars too shy to contribute at all, only to develop enough courage to speak four times a seminar near the end of the year. In this case, four contributions from a shy student may be greater than eight from a talkative student.

> **If you share your tracking system with the students in order to provide feedback, make sure that it is not connected to a strictly quantitative grade.**

Problem-Solving

The main problem with tracking occurs when students ask questions or add comments for the sake of getting more tally marks, rather than for the purposes of facilitating genuine conversation. A few measures can fix this so that the conversation can be organic. First, tracking should not be the only means of grading. A tracking system is mainly an observational tool used to inform practice and to set goals.

If you share your tracking system with the students in order to provide feedback, make sure that it is not strictly connected to a grade. For example, six comments earn an A, four comments is a B and so on. This will usually encourage talk for the sake of talking. Work the concept of progress over time into the system so that you do not automatically penalize shy students. This way two contributions from a shy student can be an A and eight comments from a talkative student could also be an A. Students could also have individualized goals to aim for in order to earn specific grades.

Have a conversation with your students to remind them that Socratic Seminars are group endeavors. The analysis and conversation are what is actually important, not individuals acting in isolation. Place value on the things that will improve your seminars. If your seminars need more questions, then try grading those higher for a few weeks. If there aren't enough examples from the text, then weigh those more for a while. Create new categories that the students can strive toward. For example, if a student interjects irrelevant comments into the conversation, then begin tracking irrelevant and relevant comments. Over time, this will make all of the seminars better and will give students the focus on the skills they need.

ASSESSMENT

For the purposes of this book, assessment is the process of giving formative feedback in order to improve the seminar process for individuals and groups. Assessment starts with an effective tracking system so that teachers can provide basic feedback to the students, such as: "You spoke three times." In addition, you can use the information to achieve better balance. For example, in a particular seminar perhaps one student dominated the conversation with seventeen contributions, while the average was four, and perhaps three students didn't participate at all. In this case, the teacher and the students can work toward better balance by encouraging some of the students to speak more and the one student to listen more (notice this is not phrased as speak less).

Sharing Data

By sharing your tracking system with your students, you can set very simple and manageable goals together. A student who asks two questions one seminar can try to ask three the next time. A student who cites the text once in a while can attempt to use citations regularly. Although this may seem overly simplified considering that one insightful question can be vastly better than three comments, tracking quantity is still a powerful tool.

The students could even track their data in learning logs or spreadsheets. Dennis Li, in his 2017 Edutopia article "Why Student Data Should Be Students' Data," writes: "Having students enter their own scores into a spreadsheet was intended to help teachers by gathering the data in one place for them to view and analyze. But what we observed was that the process was having a profound effect on the students: They became very interested and engaged with their own data and tracking their learning … When I surveyed students who were tracking their data, they were substantially more likely to respond that they were trying their hardest and felt in control of their learning than students in other classrooms."

Track what you want to measure, share the data and help students improve. Some apps like Class Dojo and Equity Maps are great tools for the job.

Confidence, Then Skill

A first step in seminar is getting students to start participating. Once students get involved, once they are excited by genuine conversation, then helping them to refine their contributions through effective feedback is fairly easy. A student I had years ago is a good example. When she first started Socratic Seminars in sixth grade, she was extremely quiet. She had low reading comprehension skills and was not widely read, so she could not contribute much intellectually at first. However, she did speak from personal experience once or twice a seminar. Over the course of her sixth-grade year, she developed more confidence, ranging into three or four contributions per seminar by the end of the year.

In seventh grade she started the year strongly, taking a leadership role in nearly all of the seminars. Although she still wasn't able to analyze the texts well on her own, she encouraged others to speak, asked for clarification when people weren't clear, and began asking very insightful questions. Like a bloodhound, she developed a sense of when a line or sentence had significant or metaphorical meaning. By now she was contributing seven to twelve or more times per seminar, effectively guiding the conversation like a skilled facilitator.

Her confidence grew in eighth grade and, as she contributed more and more, the quality of her leadership improved. She completely stopped interrupting people and politely stopped others from interrupting. She stopped criticizing people's ideas and instead began encouraging them to develop their thoughts, even if she disagreed. With practice came confidence and with confidence came skill.

Facilitator Notes

Some facilitators like to make notes during the seminar, but I have found note-making (not coding) to be most intrusive during seminars. Generally, it affects my ability to actively listen. However, occasionally it can be a productive way for giving students useful feedback and perhaps for writing report cards as well. When a student says something useful, insightful, or interesting, write the sentence down verbatim. If it's particularly long, just ask the student to repeat it. If the conversation is moving too fast, have the students slow down, either by repeating the main idea of the person who spoke before them, or by simply waiting 3-7 seconds before speaking. This is a great technique for gathering quotations for newsletters, narrative report cards or parent meetings.

I still consider note-making to be a form of tracking because at the end of the seminar I still only have bits and pieces of conversation, some of it connected and some of it out of context. It still allows for a bit of quantitative tracking because some students might have 7-9 quotes, others 3-5, and some may not have contributed a single quotation. Having quotations to draw from, at least once in a while, makes assessment and grading easier to some extent because you have a little more of the student's thought process captured. Like the other forms of tracking, however, recording notes cannot stand alone to create an accurate picture of a student's performance in Socratic Seminars.

Teachers who want to have extensive notes can record their seminars and then extract the quotations and jot down notes at a later time.

Students Making Notes

One year I tried having middle school students make notes during Socratic Seminars. Some things worked out well. Because the students were busy writing, there was time in between each speaker and, perhaps because of that, the students listened better and retained more. However, the conversations were often jagged and clumsy, with slow periods where students had to ask for things to be repeated so that they could write things down. The students had a difficult time keeping up and many struggled with handwriting or typing issues.

I have abandoned the practice of student note-making during seminars because it took too much away from the natural flow and analysis of the conversation. Ultimately, the notes seemed to reflect more of a student's ability to multi-task, to write quickly (and legibly), and to write for a long time, rather than anything to do with critical thinking, reading, or listening.

Now when I want the students to have notes for some reason, I stop the seminar briefly, have the students write for a minute or two, and then resume. Using a graphic organizer or fill-in-the-blank notes can help speed the process along.

Outer Circle Feedback

If you are using the concentric circle model, or want a few students to sit outside of the seminar to collect data, you can always pass over some of the assessment responsibilities. Students can track participation, can fill out rubrics or checklists, help their inner circle partners set and measure goals, and otherwise share feedback about the process with the class. Think of the outer circle participants as process coaches and get them involved in improvement strategies. Matt Copeland writes: "Rather than focusing their attention on what is being said, students in the outer circle should focus on the human behavior of how those ideas are presented. Students should look for such things as who speaks the most, who speaks the least, who asks the best questions, who offers the most insightful answers, who leads the group, who distracts the group from achieving their goals, and so on."

Group Data and Goal Setting

Similar to tracking individual student contributions, there are aspects of conversation that can be measured at the group level. Facilitators can use the Equity Maps app to track different group categories, including: chaos, pair-share, silence, and teacher talk time—all which can be used to establish group goals. For example, a recent group I was working with had 28% chaos in their last seminar—obviously a lot of lost time and a need for better listening skills and habits. The next time we met, we set a goal to reduce the chaotic interruptions by "listening with our eyes" to have a better idea of who wants to speak. With this emphasis we had only 5% chaos and probably the best seminar of the school year.

GRADING

Just as tracking helps inform assessment, both tracking and assessment help with the grading process. However, extracting a grade from Socratic Seminars, especially a series of them, can be complicated. A student could participate effectively in a seminar, yet fail to synthesize the material into a coherent form later. Test and quizzes, for example, tend to test more of a student's written abilities than his or her other skills. Homework tends to be intrapersonal and focuses on reading and writing skills, whereas Socratic Seminar is interpersonal and mainly involves speaking and listening.

Over the years I have tried a lot of different techniques to assess and grade students in Socratic Seminar. Early on, I did not specifically grade the students or the seminars, although using tracking methods, I did provide the students with a lot of feedback in order to improve. Instead of grades, I wrote narratives based on my notes that incorporated the students' contributions and their thoughts and insights from their journals. But that process was extremely time-consuming and forced me into a role where I was making too many notes instead of facilitating the dialogue.

Establishing reliable grades for Socratic Seminar can be achieved through multiple measures. The chart that follows has eight different ways to create a grade, keeping in mind that communication has four forms: reading, writing, speaking, and listening. In order to evaluate students as accurately as possible, we can triangulate reliable grades combining at least three techniques.

Because Socratic Seminars involve getting the students more and more invested in their own learning, I like to have the students involved in the grading process as much as possible. After a practice seminar or two, I like to have the students converse about the weight that they think each category of grading deserves. The percentages listed after each category are based on feedback from my students over the years.

Evaluation	Communication Forms	Examples	Suggested Percentage
Individual Contributions	Speaking, Listening	Mapping, Goal setting, "Two cents worth," Tallying, Transcripts, Recordings	20-40%
Group Grade	Speaking, Listening	Debriefing, Rubric, Goal setting	20-40%
Written Work	Reading, Writing	Journaling, Blogging, Thesis papers, Writing prompts, Annotations	10-30%
Annotations and Anchor Papers	Reading, Writing	Student-generated, Teacher-generated, Exemplars	10-30%
Observation Forms	Speaking, Listening	Outer circle forms, Checklists, Random selection	10-30%
Rubrics	Reading, Writing, Speaking, Listening Participation rubric,	Participation rubric, Personal goal rubric, Comprehensive rubric, Listening rubric, etc.	10-30%
Self-Assessment	Speaking, Listening	Checklist, Paired checklist, Goal achievement	10-30%
Quizzes or Tests	Reading, Writing, Listening	Text-oriented, Process-oriented	0-20%

Evaluation Forms Chart

Personally, I prefer to use at least three grades for the seminars themselves: an individual participation grade, a group grade, and a grade for annotations. For the individual grade, I either have the students do a quick self-assessment, or I set up a participation threshold. In the beginning of the year, for example, I require students to speak at least once. If they do, they get full credit. If they don't, I still give them half credit for listening (assuming they didn't detract from the dialogue).

> **"Fairness is not equality; fairness is meeting the needs of all students." ~ Author unknown**

Later in the year, I often set up individualized participation targets, so one student might need to speak four times for full credit and another might need to speak twice. I create these baseline numbers by observing and meeting with students. Some teachers are uncomfortable differentiating like this, but for me, one comment from a painfully shy student is equal to several from a talkative student. And as long as I thoroughly explain the policy, students never seem bothered by it.

After several seminars, I like to add a group grade, especially for older or more experienced students. I wait a while because ideally I want to grade the students when they are in the *norming* stage after they have tasted success, not while they are struggling through the *storming* stage of group development. I introduce a group grading rubric a few seminars in advance and then use the rubric along with student input.

Because annotations are so vital to prepare for a quality dialogue, I usually grade the students on those as well. After a seminar early in the year, I create five anchor papers or exemplars for the students to grade themselves against. See the examples in the appendices. If students are using sticky notes instead of annotating directly on the text, then the sticky notes could be graded in a similar way.

Individual Contributions

Tracking individual student contributions, especially different types of participation (such as SPQR), will make grading students easier and more comfortable than using a vague and generic "class participation" grade. In the beginning, I recommend grading the student contributions in one of three ways: setting a minimum threshold, setting individual goals, or tracking over time to view improvement. As the students come to know the process better, as they feel safe enough, and as they see the value of contributing, more can be expected of them—and the grading process can reflect that.

First, consider whether you need to grade the individual contributions at all. Many students want to be heard and understood, so they don't often need to be motivated by a grade. Others are literally unable to speak in large groups, so assigning a participation grade is harsh and probably counter-productive, since they may meet with failure almost immediately and give up. The remarkably shy students must be coaxed out slowly and delicately. Remember, sometimes four is greater than eight.

As I cautioned in the Tracking section, grading students strictly on their number of contributions may encourage talking for the sake of talking.

On the other hand, students who don't know how much they are speaking, or how they are contributing, can't set goals for themselves.

One grading method is to set a minimum contribution threshold for students and either give them credit for reaching that goal or not. Keep the number low at first so that everyone has a legitimate chance to speak and be successful. For example, you could set a goal of one contribution per seminar in the beginning of the year, moving to two per seminar later. Those who meet the minimum can get the full ten points (or whatever weight you assign). When I first introduce seminars to a group my initial requirement is always to speak once, since for some students once is challenging enough.

After facilitating and tracking a few seminars, you should have a good idea of how much each student tends to contribute. Once you know the students well enough, you can assign them individualized goals: one student could be assigned nine contributions, another six, and someone else might be one. Although this may not seem fair at first to some students, if the goals truly challenge everyone in the class, then nothing is fairer than that. Keep in mind that there's only a finite amount of time in a period, so don't set the goals too high. The students could also create their own goals, and could even track their own participation. If you track types of participation, such as SPQR, then the goals could be based on types of contributions. A student goal, for example, could be to ask two questions and cite the text at least once.

If you're planning a series of seminars, then the students could focus on improving the amount they contribute over time. At the end of the marking period, if they have demonstrated growth, then they earn their individual contribution points. Keep in mind that how much students contribute will fluctuate a great deal, depending on what the topic is, family issues, attendance, and so on. But like the stock market that fluctuates but tends to grow over time, the goal for the students is to demonstrate progress over time.

Despite many efforts and strategies, there may be students who simply won't speak in class. One solution is to have the students record their thoughts and notes in two columns. In one column, the students should briefly write down what's going on in the seminar. In the other, they write down what they think about the conversation. They can turn their notes in for their participation grade.

Participation is still highly subjective. Although quality tends to follow quantity, more is not always better. A serious student may, for example, become more discerning of when to listen and respond. Instead of talking a lot and not really saying anything, a student may seek to simply say the right thing at the best time, or to practice active listening more.

Group Grade: All for One and One for All

Working together cooperatively is difficult, but is arguably the most important element of Socratic Seminar. After all, what would all of the skills be for if not to ultimately interact with other people? Stephen Covey put it this way when describing what he called the Maturity Continuum:

> We begin each life as an infant, totally *dependent* on others. We are directed, nurtured, and sustained by others. Without this nurturing, we would only live for a few hours or a few days at the most.
>
> Then gradually, over the ensuing months and years, we become more and more *independent*—physically, mentally, emotionally, and financially—until eventually we can essentially take care of ourselves, becoming inner-directed and self-reliant.
>
> As we continue to grow and mature, we become increasingly aware that all of nature is *interdependent*, that there is an ecological system that governs nature, including society. We further discover that the highest reaches of our nature have to do with our relationships with others—that human life is also interdependent.

Because seminars are group endeavors, and because the participants should be held responsible for the quality of the conversation, a group grade for the entire class should be considered. Grading the class as a whole raises immediate issues for many teachers. What about the students who don't say anything? What about the students who do their share of the work, but get penalized for a poor seminar? What if the text was too hard for the students? What if only a few students ruin the seminar?

After being clear about the purposes of Socratic Seminar, my students have often concluded that the group grade should get the highest weight, typically averaging between 25-40%. However, I have heard enough stories of teachers getting into trouble with parents and administrators for assigning group grades to know that this may not be a desirable option. Even so, I strongly urge teachers who grade Socratic Seminars to assign at least a nominal 10% group grade in order to place some value on the collective process and experience.

For parents or students who are upset by the apparent unfairness of grading the group, point out that a major part of seminar is working together, being polite, listening respectfully, asking useful questions, and following lines of thinking. If these goals are made clear to the students, then grading them on those expectations is not only fair, but is also to be expected.

Inequities in participation can be handled by having individual grades as well. Even if 30% of a student's grade is a group grade, the remaining 70% can still be based on the individual. Such percentages send the message to everyone involved that in order to achieve the very highest grades, students must actively listen, assist others, build ideas, and help the group. I strongly believe that encouraging such balanced equity is a tremendously important endeavor.

If the text appeared to be too difficult, or if a seminar is somehow sabotaged, either on purpose or accidentally, do not feel obligated to grade the group. First, if the text was so thoroughly difficult that the students "failed" to discuss it properly, then keep in mind that you likely chose the wrong text or asked a poor opening question. Don't penalize the students for something that was your fault.

Second, no matter how difficult a text is, the students can still think about it, ask questions, politely challenge each other, analyze bits and pieces, and otherwise engage in the text on some level. If they demonstrate good manners and critical thinking skills, it doesn't really matter how far they get or whether they achieve a traditional or acceptable interpretation. They should be graded on what they achieved as a group, not what they didn't or couldn't achieve.

Third, students who attempt to sabotage the process should not be allowed to continue interrupting. If these students are treated as a behavior management issue and, for example, are asked to leave the room, then the seminar should be able to continue just fine.

Despite all of these measures, a teacher may find that there is still too much opposition to a group grade. If this is the case, just drop it for a while. Some teachers do not even grade seminars themselves, so a group grade is not necessary. Alexis Wiggins writes: "I believe that using the group grade as a 'doesn't count, weighted zero' formative feedback mechanism is more in sync with practices that include grading to standards and avoiding unfair group-grading scenarios. If you explain to students, parents, and administrators that the purpose of the group grade is feedback toward specific goals related to collaboration, speaking, and listening, and that the grade doesn't affect individual GPAs because it is weighted 0 percent, you shouldn't have too much difficulty implementing the method where you work."

If you do decide on a group grade, begin with the end in mind, and help students understand what is expected. Use rubrics and goal-setting to determine success. Students should reflect on questions such as: Did I feel listened to? Did the conversation flow naturally? Did I reach a point of understanding? Was it useless chitchat or something worthwhile? Was it uncomfortable or enlivening?

There are also intangibles to consider. After a "good" seminar there is an *espirit de corps*, a buzz, an excitement, an electricity that fills the room. There should be a strong sense of accomplishment, a sense of having worked hard to achieve a worthwhile goal. After a good seminar, I check the pulse of the class by looking to see if the students leave the room still talking about something from the seminar. I check to see if a majority of them are happy and smiling. And, in a great seminar, there is often a student claiming, "My brain hurts!"

Most participants are aware when a discussion or seminar falls flat. There are uncomfortable silences, redundancies, chaos, and interruptions. There are students who may argue for the sake of arguing, or arguing just to win an irrelevant point. There are frustrated students who wanted to speak, but couldn't figure out how to enter the conversation. Students may leave the room mumbling things under their breath, rolling their eyes and blaming others. Instead of feeling a sense of accomplishment and hard work, there is a sense of frustration, anxiety, and tension. These signposts indicate a "bad" seminar.

I started with the intangibles for a very good reason. Tangible measures, such as rubrics, are typically created ahead of time and are, therefore, a measure of one's previous expectations. In my own experience I have rarely been able to create a satisfactory rubric ahead of time, even when I borrowed heavily from an experienced teacher or an expert in that area. Every text, every group of students, every situation is different, and I have always found the need to customize rubrics over time to meet unique circumstances or to focus on specific aspects that the group is working on.

Once you develop a rubric, the intangibles not only help adjust the grade to be more accurate, they can also help modify the grading tool itself. For example, you may find that the students did particularly well on a rubric you developed, mainly because the analysis of the text was excellent, but the conversation may have been stilted and full of interruptions, and the students left the room frustrated and complaining. Add a new category to the rubric for the next seminar.

Written Work and Blogging

Written work, such as journals, reflective papers, and essays, can be great sources for creating grades related to seminars, but there are a few things to keep in mind. Students tend to find translating their experiences in seminar to written work quite difficult. If the writing assignment does not soon follow the seminar, some students may forget too much to be effective, and making copious notes during seminar brings up other issues. Writing and participating in a seminar are different skill sets, so evaluating students only on written work is not a complete measure of the student's efforts and abilities.

Written work can also take the form of blogging or otherwise contributing to some kind of online discussion board. When I first assigned a blog, I thought that the students would naturally extend our amazing conversations outside of class. I dreamed that they would rush home every day and keep participating in deep and meaningful ways. But that's not what happened.

What I noticed was that the students had a much more difficult time having a quality "conversation" online than in person. Many of the blogs and the responses were shallow and uninteresting, especially compared to the deep dialogues we had in class. Students who participated a lot in class were often quiet online. Students who were remarkably insightful in seminar were unusually bland on the blog. What I discovered probably should have been obvious, but blogging at home and talking in class are very different.

We had to spend a lot of time clarifying that the purpose of the blog was to extend our amazing conversations in deep and meaningful ways. I identified the good bloggers and recruited them to act as monitors to help keep the online conversations provocative, robust, and useful. We created polls, added supplemental graphics and visuals, and included links to keep participants engaged in better online thinking behaviors.

A big part of improving our online conversations was focusing on quality instead of quantity. Originally, I required high school students to blog daily, thinking they would enjoy it, but they quickly became indifferent, so we eventually settled on two contributions per week. For some classes, I would think once a week would be plenty. With fewer contributions to make, the online conversations improved dramatically, although they never reached the depth and dynamism of in-class dialogues.

Here's how the students were graded on the blog contributions:

Grade	Quantity	Quality
A+	More than 2 quality contributions per week	Profound questioning that many respond to Valid research using links and sources Leadership Creating useful polls Using QUOTE function to be clear **New knowledge**
A	2 quality contributions consistently 2 quality contributions consistently every week	Some connections to information outside text Consistent links and sources Questions are usually followed **Consistent initiatives**
B	2 useful contributions inconsistently averaged over the entire semester	Questions not followed (perhaps not your fault, but did you phrase them thoughtfully?) Occasional links and sources **Some initiatives**
C/D	1 useful contribution per week average	React only to other postings No new thinking generated **General habitual thinking** **Few or no new initiatives**
F	Less than 1 contribution per week average	No new initiatives Few comments

Annotations

As presented in the pre-seminar chapter, anchor papers or exemplars can be used to grade student annotations. They can, of course, be used to grade writing assignments, notes, and reflections. Students could use a before and after anchor paper to grade themselves twice, once before the seminar and once after the seminar. In addition, students could be involved in the process of grading sample annotated papers to better understand the thinking processes involved in quality annotating. See the examples in the appendices.

Outer Circle Observation Forms

In the concentric circle model, the outer circle provides valuable coaching feedback for the seminar. Even with a single circle, a few students could be assigned to sit out of the seminar to help coach and provide feedback. This advice can take many forms, but should always be focused on improving the process or the product. Keep in mind that the observation forms themselves can (and should) be graded because they can be a valuable resource for group improvement.

Matt Copeland writes: "Many students take the comments of their peers much more to heart than they do the comments of a teacher. And the knowledge that the outer circle will be evaluated in the same manner as the inner circle later in the class period helps to keep the feedback constructive and more positive in nature."

> **The biggest problem I've seen with rubrics is that they are often confusing to students.**

Rubrics

Whereas tracking is more quantitative in nature (keep in mind that quality follows quantity), a well written rubric can focus more on the qualitative aspects and can make a path for improvement much clearer for students.

The biggest problem I've seen with rubrics is that they are often confusing to students. Sometimes the distinctions between each level are not clear enough, so students flounder back and forth between scores, unable to determine accurately where they stand. If the levels are not clear to students, usually because of dense language, then they cannot effectively set goals for themselves.

Another issue I have seen is that teachers try to cram numerous seminar skills into one rubric. The result is a wall of text that is intimidating and often incomprehensible to students. A single box may contain three or four separate skills, and even if the students are clear on the meanings, they may still be confused. Two descriptions may apply from one box and two from another box, leaving them somewhere in between.

If you use rubrics, then I have several suggestions. First, go over the rubric with the students. Examine each part and make sure that the delineations between each level are clear for the students. If your students are like mine, they'll say they understand the rubric, but they really don't. Saying they get it is easier than having to do the comprehension work. They may benefit from putting some of the language into their own words.

Second, focus the rubric on a narrow set of skills instead of trying to capture everything from a seminar into a single rubric. This will make the rubric easier to understand and will allow students to focus on skills. Use an active listening rubric, one just for annotating, and another for citing the text.

Third, if you have time, create the rubrics with the students. Going through the entire process should make them comprehensible and clear to the students. If you don't have that much time, collect or create several rubrics and have the students choose the one that makes the most sense to them as a class or as individuals.

Self-Assessment: Mirror, Mirror on the Wall

In my experience, students are not very good at self-assessment, although they get better with experience. Like every other learning opportunity, they need a chance to practice, combined with timely and effective feedback. When I do have students self-assess, I also like to use the same assessment so that our results can be compared. If the results of my assessment and the student's self-assessment are close, I accept the grade without further feedback. However, when there is a large disparity, I like to follow up with a personal conversation.

Some students are overly critical of themselves, grading what they wish or think they could do rather than what they have accomplished. Sometimes the disparity is baffling. One year I had a student who graded himself consistently 20 points lower than my grade on our rubric. This prompted several useful conversations over the course of the year, and led us to rewrite our rubric several times until we were both in agreement about the expectations of the specific language in each of the boxes.

Some students are not critical enough of themselves or their work, inflating their grades 10-15 points. Sometimes their standards are too low. Sometimes the students are not clear enough on the expectations. Sometimes they simply don't care enough to be accurate. Whatever the reason, the disparity is worthy of a conversation or further instruction for the class.

Quizzes and Tests

I caution against using quizzes or tests for assessing or grading the conversations in Socratic Seminars. Certainly a two-week unit can culminate with a Socratic Seminar and then a unit test, but quizzing or testing students specifically on the seminars themselves will likely backfire on the constructivist *gradual release of responsibility* model that is Socratic Seminar.

Socratic Seminars are meant to be organic conversations where the collectivity of the whole is greater than the sum of its parts. With an entire class endeavoring to discover more about the text, everyone benefits from the greater number of connections, insights, and questions. However, if students believe they will then be tested on the conversation itself, they may develop habits that are antithetical to a good seminar. They may begin to listen more and participate less (not necessarily a bad thing unless everyone is mostly listening). They might steer the conversation toward subjects that are easy or likely to be on the test, rather than those that genuinely interest them. They may start making detailed notes and interrupt the dialogue by asking people to constantly repeat themselves. In other words, they won't be having an organic conversation.

Summing Up

1. For the purposes of this book, Evaluation involves tracking, assessment, and grading.

2. Tracking, or coding, is tallying or collecting data about how students participate.

3. One tracking system is SPQR for (S)tatements, (P)rocedural comments, (Q)uestions, and (R)eading from the text.

4. Conversation maps with lines drawn between students and additional codes are great for visually collecting data.

5. Share seminar data with the students to aid in reflection and goal setting.

6. There are several categories to consider for grading:
   - Individual contributions
   - Group grade
   - Written work and blogs
   - Annotations
   - Observation forms
   - Rubrics
   - Self-assessments
   - Quizzes or tests

Your Next Steps

- As a guiding principle: Always grade what you value.

- Triangulate grades using at least three categories.

- Involve students in the assessment and grading processes.

- Share data with the students.

- If there is time, have the students help create rubrics for assessing and grading themselves. This is a lengthy process, but can be valuable at the beginning of the year.

- Consider having Socratic Seminars with your students about the complications of assessment and grading. Present them with fictional scenarios of various student contributions and see what they value as participants.

- Consider watching a recording of a seminar and have the students grade themselves.

- There are numerous Socratic Seminar rubrics online. Some grade and value positive attributes, while others focus on subtracting points for not doing things. As a constructivist approach, I HIGHLY recommend using positive strategies for Socratic Seminar. In any event, find some rubrics that work well for you.

- Try using three different rubrics across three different seminars and then have the students synthesize the elements of each rubric into one that they like.

- Use an app like Equity Maps to collect various data that could be used for feedback and to create grades.

- Find out how other teachers at your school deal with grading groups.

- Keep in mind that the ultimate goal of the seminar is to better understand the text and to work together more cohesively.

11

Active Listening

One of the most sincere forms of respect is actually listening to what another has to say.

~ Bryant H. McGill

OF ALL THE skills in Socratic Seminar, active listening is arguably the most important and the least practiced or appreciated. For those reasons alone, I feel active listening deserves its own chapter. It is tempting to assume that students know how to listen considering they have been doing so for years (even before kindergarten, of course), but active listening is a skill that must be practiced and honed, just like any other. Assuming that students will naturally develop quality active listening skills is like thinking that throwing a soccer ball to a group of children will make them a soccer team.

Considering how often students must actually listen in school—Ball and Brewer suggest up to 97% of class time—it is surprising that there is rarely direct teaching or practicing of active listening as a skill, especially past primary grades. Perhaps in the lower grades there are too many other language development skills that take priority. Perhaps in the older grades, teachers assume that the students can listen well since they have had hundreds of hours of listening. Perhaps, as Leonard points out, it is because much of our sensory learning is self-taught when we are very young. Whatever the reasons, many students do not know how to actively listen.

I will even suggest that many older students actually listen *less* effectively. This is because after years of the habit of *passive* listening, they struggle to actively process sounds into personalized, meaningful thoughts or ideas. As David and Elizabeth Russell put it, "To listen is to process what is heard," but many students do not take responsibility for their listening habits.

Listening is a vital component to any Socratic classroom. Leonard writes: "There can be great excitement in a classroom where ideas are merely presented—but there can be no discussion unless students are encouraged to absorb and reflect as well as to speak. Then ideas can be expanded, criticized, and sharpened. For such discussion, the capacity to listen is a precious resource. At any given moment, after all, all members of the group but one is engaged in listening." Because Socratic Seminar is tremendously dependent on quality active listening, students must be taught stronger listening skills and they must be given opportunities to practice.

Listen and Silent

I always like to point out to students that the words "listen" and "silent" are anagrams (they have exactly the same letters). It's a simple and elegant way to suggest to students that to truly *listen* requires that the mouth and mind be *silent*. To be effective listeners, we must first silence our own thoughts and filters in order to actively listen to what is being said—and not just the words, but to the entire message.

Levels of Listening

Introduce students to the idea that there are multiple levels to listening, roughly based on the amount of engagement or effort required. They range from the simple unconscious hearing of sounds, to the conscious decision to listen from another person's perspective, known as *empathetic listening*. People can move between these levels, but they probably have listening habits primarily lodged in one of them.

> I've learned that a simple two words could have more depth than a paragraph, and that you should listen to people more closely because the words that come out of their mouth can help you with your understanding.
> ~ JP (grade 6)

Five Levels of Listening

1. **Hearing:** the automatic, passive process of registering noises and sounds.

2. **Assumed Listening:** the common misperception of listening.

3. **Listening For:** the conscious act of anticipating and focusing on specific sounds or ideas.

4. **Active Listening:** the deliberate action of attempting to understand the total message, complete with nuances, nonverbal communication, asking questions, etc.

5. **Empathetic Listening:** active and open-minded listening from another person's perspective.

> *The single biggest problem in communication*
> *is the illusion that it has taken place.*
> *~ George Bernard Shaw*

Hearing and Assumed Listening

The main difference between passive hearing and active listening can be quickly differentiated. As Michael Opitz and Matthew Zbaracki, authors of *Listen Hear!* quote from a friend Doug Resh: "Hearing is a sound; listening is a thought." Hearing is the automatic, passive process of registering noises and sounds. As such, there is no accompanying thinking that is required. We can hear while asleep, but we aren't listening.

I like to include *assumed listening* as a level because many students and teachers believe they are good listeners—though people in their lives might disagree. In my experience, when most people think they are listening, they are instead just directing partial awareness and attention toward a speaker. Just ask most people to repeat what a previous speaker said and you will discover who is at the level of *assumed listening* and who may be exerting more energy toward *active listening*.

Assumed listening could also be called pretend listening, especially with younger students. As teachers, we can ask students questions to help them orient their listening: Are you actively listening or pretend listening? Are you fully listening or assuming you are listening? Are you using whole-body listening?

Listening For (Discriminative Listening)

In our daily lives we are often listening, consciously or unconsciously, for certain sounds in the environment around us. On the way to work, for example, we might be listening for different sounds from a car's engine or a bike's tires. Although sometimes this listening is unconscious at first, the moment we hear a siren, for example, we instantly become hyper-vigilant and listen for the source.

Students are also often in a state of listening for certain things (consciously or unconsciously). For example, the day before an exam, students might specifically listen for what will be on the test. During attendance, they are (briefly) listening for their name to be called. In a debate, participants might listen for weaknesses, mistakes, and inconsistencies in the other person's argument.

Listening For, also known as discriminative listening, is the best level for coaching students. Just as sports coaches break complex tasks down into specific parts to practice, teachers can break the complex task of active listening down into specific focus areas based on needs. Students can then begin to practice better listening skills.

When we are listening to other people, we often have two basic choices: We can listen for what's right and good, or we can listen for what's wrong and bad. In discussions and Socratic Seminars, many participants have the habit of immediately disagreeing with an idea, even though that idea might not have come to fruition. Instead, students should withhold thoughts as long as possible: "I'm not sure I am going to end up agreeing with this, but I will keep listening."

Because Socratic Seminar is a cooperative process of building and supporting ideas, the students must practice their listening skills in order to maximize the group's intelligence, experience, and wisdom. As a general principle for a Socratic classroom, students should listen for:

- the good in someone else.
- strengthening and developing ideas as far as possible.
- agreement and points of interest.
- what is right.
- what is *not* stated, implied, or asked.
- nurturing fledgling ideas.
- hints or clues toward new ideas.
- being inspired.
- the entirety of a thought process or "train of thought."
- the message (not how the message is communicated).

Active Listening

When we move to the level of Active Listening, we attempt to put all the pieces together and listen for everything at once. *Listening For* is great for practicing and honing one's listening skills, but like in sports, we must eventually put all of the practice together into a coherent game. In school, this formal listening "game" can be Socratic Seminar.

When in the Active Listening level, the goal is to understand the total message. Jiddu Krishnamurti put it this way: "So when you are listening to somebody, completely, attentively, then you are listening not only to the words, but also to the feeling of what is being conveyed, to the whole of it, not part of it." This level almost always requires the listener to ask clarifying questions, and to prompt the speaker in various ways in order for full comprehension to occur. In other words, the students must negotiate toward clearer, broader and/or deeper meaning. As a Socratic Seminar facilitator, you can recognize this level when participants are addressing each other and are consistently asking each other relevant questions in order to bring ideas out in the clearest possible ways.

Empathetic Listening (or Empathic Listening)

The most involved level of these five is empathetic listening, or the idea of "listening with the heart." When we listen empathetically, we are trying to "walk a mile in another person's shoes" by truly understanding that person, his/her viewpoints and ideas. This level of listening requires extreme effort for most people because they have to push aside their own beliefs, judgments, disagreements, and opinions to let an entire message through. Sometimes this is made even more difficult when the idea is foreign or threatening.

When students are able to listen on this level, they will be able to participate in the best, most sophisticated way possible: objectively take in new ideas, add evidence, strengthen the idea as much as possible and then evaluate the final outcome against other ideas that were similarly built up. As a Socratic Seminar facilitator, you can recognize this level when participants change their language from things like, "I disagree with you" or "I agree" to "Looked at from that viewpoint, I think I would disagree as well" and "If I were you, I'd probably agree as well."

Redefine Listening as an Active Decision-Making Process

As readers, many of us are familiar with the idea that we must monitor our reading process in order to make sure we comprehend what we are reading. With any given text we might: monitor reading speed, reread, create useful notes, check for comprehension, track main ideas, and generate questions.

Active listening is also full of decision-making moments, though many students aren't always aware of or appreciate them. For starters, there are always factors that affect a person whenever he or she is in a listening situation: Why am I listening (or not)? Is something more interesting going on? Do I understand the words being spoken to me? Do I understand the entire message? What is the speaker not saying? Were there words that I didn't understand?

Inside this initial framework, at any given moment, listeners are constantly making decisions, even if some of them are passive or unconscious. Teach students that quality listening is an active, decision-making process. Below is a list of active listening decisions by Wolvin and Coakley.

- Not to listen
- To listen
- To listen for a purpose
- To set aside biases and attitudes in order to understand the message
- To concentrate on the message, not the speaker

- To overcome emotional barriers to listening
- To know why he/she is listening at a given time
- To know how he/she is listening at a given time
- To understand the process of listening—and the process of communication—to know what he/she is (or should be) doing as a listening communicator throughout this process

It is worth repeating that students should NOT raise their hands in Socratic Seminar. Instead, they should learn how to otherwise appropriately listen and take turns. Teach Socratic Seminar students that there are subtle nonverbal cues from both speakers and listeners to look for instead of just raising hands. Students can familiarize themselves by observing other groups, re-watching their own seminars, and watching movies with the sound off. Wolvin and Coakley describe three sets of *regulatory cues* students can practice looking for and using.

Speaking and Listening Regulatory Cues

Turn-Yielding Cues

- A hand gesture of termination.
- The speaker relaxing.
- Falling pitch (completing a statement).
- Rising pitch (indicating a question).
- Making prolonged eye contact.
- Speaker trailing off.

Turn-Maintaining Cues

- The speaker raising volume and/or increasing speed.
- A slight raise of the hand or finger.
- The speaker avoids eye contact.
- Hands remaining in mid-gesture.
- Speaker fills in pauses in speaking with *uh, um,* etc..

Speaking and Listening Regulatory Cues *(continued)*

Turn-Requesting Cues
- Raising an index finger.
- Inhaling audibly.
- Moving from a slouching to an upright position.
- Leaning in.
- The listener nods rapidly or agrees repeatedly (*yes, yes, yes ...*).
- The listener engages in a stutter-start (*I... I th ... I think ...*).

Whole-Body Listening

Introduce students, especially younger students, to the idea of whole-body listening (to my knowledge, first articulated by Susanne Poulette Truesdale in 1990). Whole-body listening shows evidence of active listening and will strengthen the speaker-listener connection by allowing the speaker to feel more confident. In addition, whole-body listening will give the listeners their best opportunity to actively listen. A great place to start is to watch the fabulous TED Talk *How to Truly Listen* by Evelyn Glennie, a deaf percussionist who speaks about listening with the whole body. By introducing whole-body listening, we can help students maximize their listening efforts.

Whole-Body Listening

- **Head:** Thinking about what is being said.
- **Eyes:** Tracking the speaker.
- **Ears:** Ready and willing to actively listen.
- **Mouth:** Quiet, but ready to ask questions.
- **Heart:** Caring about what is said; empathetic listening.
- **Hands:** Quiet and still; ready to indicate turn to speak.
- **Knees:** Quiet and still.
- **Feet:** Still and flat on the floor.

Keep in mind that some students might need a quiet fidget toy, and that some students may actually be unable to maintain eye contact. In a more recent article, Truesdale cautions that for children who have been diagnosed with autism spectrum disorders, "listening with the eyes" is essentially eye contact, and this expectation should be modified or deleted depending on the child's individual needs and goals.

> **One common barrier to effective listening in discussions and Socratic Seminars is that students do not have a lot of practice listening to and learning from each other.**

Barriers to Listening

The first barrier to listening that students face is to understand themselves as learners and participants. How aware are they of their listening skills and habits? What effective habits do they have? What ineffective habits have they formed? What goals could they set for themselves as listeners? An important part of self-assessment is determining barrier words and barriers to effective communication.

The speaking-listening communication is very complex and many things can interrupt the process. One of the very first barriers is the misconception that listening and hearing are synonymous. In general, hearing is an automatic, passive process. Listening, on the other hand, is an active process of making meaning out of what is being heard. Listening is not a passive process since we must assign meaning to the sounds and words we hear.

One common barrier to effective listening in discussions and Socratic Seminars is that students do not have a lot of practice listening to and learning from each other. The expectation in many classes is that the teacher will disseminate the necessary information—especially the vital information that will be assessed. Leonard writes: "Our students have been taught largely in a lecture format, and so have we. They expect their teachers to tell them what they need to know, and they have been conditioned to learn this material and repeat it when asked. Students typically listen to instructors only along a limited dimension—largely for facts and theories—and to each other hardly at all." After all, student comments, critiques, and insights made in class are almost never on quizzes and tests, suggesting that they are not important.

Another barrier to listening is the environment created by the teacher. Many teachers, for instance, have the habit of repeating what students say. They may add to what was said, simplify it, or connect it to the textbook. Nichols writes of one example where "the teacher is repeating everything the child says, and in a clearer, more concise manner. Why would any member of the learning community listen with intent to a peer, putting in the effort to understand their thinking, if the teacher is going to repeat and clarify? A smart learner would wait for the teacher!" In seminar, we must get the students to listen more to each other, and pass skills like paraphrasing and summarizing over to the students as soon as possible.

Another common barrier to effective listening in seminar occurs when students "hold" what they want to say so firmly in their minds that they are essentially unable to listen. They're so eager to share what they want to say that they leave no room in their minds to listen. This is why students are encouraged to not raise their hands in seminars. This is easily seen in many inexperienced groups when students repeat, sometimes nearly verbatim, what another student just said. Having the students jot down reminders on paper so they don't forget, or having each student paraphrase the previous speaker can remedy this barrier.

Another common issue occurs when students do not wait for previous speakers to finish—sometimes known as *listening with your mouth open*. Kevin Murphy, author of *Effective Listening*, writes: "An accurate response to a speaker's message is a response to his or her *total* communication. It must reflect not only the content of the message, but also the speaker's tone, emotional tenor, and the context of the situation." In other words, we must wait for the entire message in order to truly be actively listening. What happens too often, though, is that students respond prematurely to the first part of someone's communication that makes a tangible point. This can at least be partly remedied by having the students develop a habit of asking, "Are you finished?" or "Is that your whole point?"—as long as they aren't interrupting, of course.

Barriers to Listening

- Paying attention to mannerisms instead of message (how versus what).
- Lack of purpose in listening.
- Paying attention to speaker's looks, clothes, or style.
- Allowing one's mind to wander or be distracted.
- Overly reacting to charged words (barrier words) or phrases.
- An initial lack of interest or care.
- Predisposition or prejudice.
- Lack of prior knowledge and/or context.
- Second language learning.
- Lack of understanding nonverbal cues and signals.
- Speaker's lack of awareness.
- Distracting environment.
- Trying to multitask.
- Peer pressure.
- Poor memory and/or note-taking.
- Poor executive functioning skills.
- Wanting to say something about yourself.
- Wanting to give advice or solve problems.
- Listener is tired, hungry, sick.

One way to deal with barriers to listening is to brainstorm a list of possibilities with your own students. Have each of them identify a listening barrier that could negatively affect his or her listening. This could either be for a specific class period (*That loud scraping sound is bothering me.*) or for longer time frames (*When people are dressed like that, I don't trust what they say.*). Once they have identified something that could negatively affect their listening, they can make a plan to solve the problem. Solutions can be as simple as changing seats or as complex as seriously committing to whole-body listening. This makes an excellent pre-seminar activity.

Jump-Start: Fake It Until You Make It

One of the best ways for students to become better listeners is to simply adapt the posture, the look and feel of a good listener. Students can start with the idea of "fake it 'til you make it" and then specifically focus on active listening from there. Kittie Watson and Larry Barker, authors of *Listen Up Second Edition*, write: "If you want to jump-start your listening improvement program, there is one technique that will give you immediate rewards … It simply involves focusing on looking and sounding like you are listening effectively to others … Even though you may be able to repeat what others have said word-for-word, you still aren't perceived as really understanding or caring unless you look like you are listening. As the saying goes, people don't care how much you know until they know how much you care."

Even when students are faking it, they can still improve their listening skills. Watson and Barker write: "Research has shown that when we consciously try to put our body and mind in a positive listening mode—that our listening effectiveness actually increases." With the initial potential increase, students can mindfully build their listening skills.

Students can definitely benefit by at least trying to listen because they will be perceived as good listeners. Wolvin and Coakley write: "Indeed, others base their evaluation of our listening behavior on how they perceive we listen rather than on how we actually listen." So, initially, the following is what students can do to adopt the posture of listening.

The Postures of Listening

Listening Looks Like:
- Smiling.
- Sitting up.
- Leaning forward.
- Nodding.
- Maintaining eye contact/orientation to speaker.
- Staying still and focused.

Listening Sounds Like:

- Asking questions.
- Summarizing.
- Paraphrasing.
- Providing evidence.
- Voicing interest cues: "Seriously?" "Uh-huh" "Whoa!"
- Attentive silence (as an invitation to others).

Remember, if you come to class with one idea and do all of the talking or poor listening, then you will leave class with only that same one idea. But if you truly listen to others, you might leave class with ten ideas.

The Goal of Better Listening in a Socratic Classroom

So, how do we help students get better at active listening? Like many other learning situations, it's all about direct teaching, practice, role-modeling, and coaching along the way.

Students should first understand the purpose of better listening. As Leonard writes: "Some students seem to misinterpret the task they are given. They seem to believe—and we too often seem to tell them—that their main tasks are to *think* and to *speak*. When students are graded on classroom performance, it is almost always on the basis of what they say. But, if there is to be a true discussion, students will spend most of their time listening actively while others speak, then building on their classmates' contributions. Explaining the students' responsibility in this way can help them to understand the importance of listening carefully."

The main goal of active or empathetic listening is to be open to and embrace new ideas. I often say to my students something like: "Remember, if you come to class with one idea and do all of the talking or poor listening, then you will leave class with only that same one idea. But if you truly listen to others, you might leave class with ten ideas." When all of the students listen effectively, the entire group benefits. Participants can then critically analyze and strengthen ideas and creatively add new ones. The dialogue becomes a spiraling process that advances the participants into new domains of thinking.

Although grading listening can be difficult, students can first be asked to assess or grade themselves. In addition, they can be asked to use reflective exit tickets that ask questions such as: Identify someone who brought up an idea that you liked. What was the idea? By defining active listening as a visual process (whole-body listening), teachers could also grade students with a observational listening checklist. Just explain to the students ahead of time that you will be grading them on the *perceived* listening that they show. Obviously, some students can listen effectively without sitting up, or maintaining eye contacting, but those students could have differentiated expectations.

Disagreement

The goal in a Socratic classroom is to listen to an idea or a "train of thought" to the very end. This requires curiosity, interest, restraint, clarifying questions, evidence, patience, and more. Only once the idea is fully developed, once the "train of thought" is as thorough and complete as the group can make it, should students then attempt to critique, defend, or disagree with it.

Students should be able to present their disagreement in a constructive way. First, it requires that they fully comprehend the position enough to actually disagree with it. Then, in order to remain objective, they should agree or disagree with the evidence and ideas, not the people who presented them. According to Mortimer Adler, if after listening and understanding the idea completely, you still disagree with someone, there are four basic responses or responsibilities. In short, students should only agree with a completed idea and they should disagree responsibly and constructively by taking further action.

Adler's Four Disagreements

You believe the other person:	Adler's Example Disagreement Phrase	Adler's Suggested Action
Is Uninformed	"I think you hold that position because you are uninformed about certain facts or reasons that have a critical bearing on it."	Indicate the necessary information that the other person is lacking, which, if possessed, would result in a change of mind.
Is Misinformed or Mistaken	"I think you hold that position because you are misinformed about matters that are critically relevant."	Indicate the mistakes that the other has made, which, if corrected, would lead the other to abandon the position taken.
Has Drawn the Wrong Conclusion	"I think you are sufficiently well informed and have a firm grasp of the evidence and reasons that support your position, but you have drawn the wrong conclusions from your premises because you have made mistakes in reasoning. You have made fallacious inferences."	Be ready to point out those logical errors which, if corrected, would bring the other person to a different conclusion.
Has Not Reasoned Far Enough	"I think you have proceeded from sound reasoning from adequate grounds for the conclusion you have reached, but I also think that your thinking about the subject is incomplete. You should have gone farther than you did and reached conclusions that somewhat alter or qualify the one you did reach."	Be able to point out these conclusions and how they alter or qualify the positions taken by the person with whom you disagree.

Source: *How to Speak How to Listen* by Mortimer J. Adler

In my experience, there are students who will still disagree without being able to express why. Many of these ultimate disagreements are based on fear. Behind a lot of a student's fearful thinking is: if I disagree with you, maybe *I'm wrong*. Students may disagree because they don't like the person who stated it. They may be uncomfortable with or confused by the idea because they believe it goes against their beliefs or morals, or more vaguely, that it goes against their instincts or intuition. They may be afraid of the idea because of how adopting it might make them look.

A good listening and thinking environment should always include taking risks. Students should be encouraged to be open-minded, to at least "try out" other ideas, even (or especially) if they are different. This may simply take the form of asking questions: "Are you afraid of this idea?" or "Does this idea leave you confused?"

Watch out for allowing students to simply *agree to disagree*. Although this idea is perhaps cordial and polite, it does allow students to avoid the critical thinking and interpersonal skills involved in potentially challenging conversations. If the discussion is particularly heated, the topic may be better suited for a future debate. Otherwise, students can still grapple with the disagreements as long as they have the intention of exploring the ideas toward mutual benefit and respect.

Teachers as Listening Role Models

Even without a significant amount of time dedicated specifically to the direct instruction of listening, teachers can always be good role models. Wolvin and Coakley write: "Teachers are in the position to be our first professional role models of effective listening." As with many things, students often copy what they see and experience, so the first thing we must do as teachers is model good listening habits. This may be more difficult for teachers than they initially believe.

Although many teachers would likely say they are good or even great listeners, many are not when it comes to attending staff meetings, professional development workshops and other adult meetings. In my experience, teachers can be some of the worst listeners. If we are to become quality role models for students, we must become better listeners in all spheres of life: to students, to spouses and family members, to colleagues, to administrators, to trainers, to consultants.

Quality listening creates better listeners. Many teachers begin the school year saying something along the lines of, "I will respect you if you will respect me." The idea is that the teacher hands out respect *first*, hoping or expecting the students to reciprocate. In the same way, as leaders and role models, teachers can start the year demonstrating strong, effective listening skills. In essence: "I will listen to you if you will listen to me."

One of the only ways for a Socratic Seminar group to move into the *norming* stage or the *performing* stage is for the facilitator to get really good at active listening. Only strong listening skills will enable a facilitator to think and consider which clarifying questions to ask, which follow-up questions might produce quality dialogue, and what coaching actions are needed at any given time in the process.

Any teacher who wants to become a better facilitator must work on his or her personal active listening skills. This can be really simple. Ask open-ended questions and let the students do the talking. Actively listen. Listen some more. Be interested. Demonstrate genuine wonder and curiosity. Follow ideas that you become *naturally* curious about (not just things that are curriculum-related or "school important"). Be curious enough to not let students say vague things, especially without citing the text.

Practice listening during lunch, at staff meetings, while doing recess duty, or even while waiting in line at the grocery store. Purposefully make times where you focus on listening. Don't comment on what you hear. Listen to new music. Don't critique. Don't worry about analysis. Just spend some time listening. Go on a walk and count how many different types of sound you hear: cars, birds, water, crunching gravel, etc. Practice. Practice. Practice.

The Speaker's Role in Listening

Oral communication is a two-way process: the speaker projecting sound and conveying ideas; and the listener receiving the sounds and making meaning. Although the burden of oral comprehension falls on the listener to take action if he or she does not understand, the speaker still has responsibilities on the transmission end—to be as focused, clear, succinct, and thorough as possible. This includes small actions such as slowing down, making eye contact, smiling, using hand gestures, and modulating one's voice. And it can include larger actions, such as using videos or presentation materials, staying energetic and enthusiastic, developing confidence, and telling captivating stories.

In seminar, the speaker's role in listening is important to keep everyone engaged. Novice participants tend to speak directly or only to the teacher, creating the illusion for the rest of the participants that the conversation is somewhat private or personal. Watch a discussion carefully, and as soon as the teacher and a single student start conversing, the other students immediately start side conversations. So, one of the most frequent facilitator actions for novice groups is to keep reminding students that they must speak to the whole group. Include a gesture with your hand, so that eventually the action itself will act as a nonverbal signal: "Please talk to the group and not just to me."

My Students Just Won't Listen!

Even after years of facilitating, I still get groups that just don't listen well. When this happens, the first thing I do is to add some procedural comments: "We're interrupting each other right now." Or: "What do we need to do in order to listen better?" My second intervention is to require wait time after every single speaker, usually around five seconds. The next level of intervention is to require that each student who wishes to speak must summarize what the previous speaker said—to that other person's satisfaction. Students hate this and usually course-correct quickly. Another good strategy is to track interruptions and create a two-strike policy or some other procedure to remove disruptive students.

When things get really nutty, call a time-out and leave the circle, give the students a break, get them moving around, use a mini-lesson or otherwise hit the reset button. Try something like: "I'm calling a time-out right now. Okay, everyone, this isn't working. I'd like everyone to get up, grab your things, circle clockwise twice around the tables and then sit in a new spot. We'll try a new question and this time let's all focus on active listening. Okay, here's our new question ..."

Listening to Music in Seminar

Music can be an excellent choice as a "text" for seminar. The issue, of course, is that students must *actively* listen to it in order to create meaning, make notes, and generate questions. To many undiscerning students, a song is either good or bad; they either like it or they don't. Just as they must have strategies for close reading, many students must have a plan for "close listening," especially to get past the like/dislike phase. To be effective, students must be guided toward various features of the music.

With written texts, teachers often guide students toward specific features, such as headings and structure in non-fiction or metaphor, symbol, and foreshadowing in fiction or poetry. Textbooks typically have pull-out boxes or side panels that highlight specific people or events. Other subjects use visual elements or charts for students to focus on. However, music alone (without lyrics) requires students to *Listen For* effectively—something many of them have not practiced. Certainly, students with musical training are able to listen for specific features, but students without musical knowledge must have specific things to listen for.

Aaron Copland, the famous composer, mechanically separates the listening experience into three component parts: the sensuous plane, the expressive plane, and the musical plane. He defines the sensuous plane as "the plane on which we hear music without thinking, without considering it in any way." This is the primary plane of interaction for many students. Music on this level either appeals or not. Students will either like the music or not. Obviously, we want students to move beyond this plane, especially in Socratic Seminar.

About the second plane, Copland writes: "My own belief is that all music has an expressive power, some more and some less, but that all music has a certain meaning behind the notes and that the meaning behind the notes constitutes, after all, what the piece is saying, what the piece is about." Of course, questions then arise: *What is the music expressing? Does it express the same thing to every listener? Does it always express the same thing or does it change?*

Copland suggests only trying to affix a general meaning to a piece since "Music expresses, at different moments, serenity or exuberance, regret or triumph, fury or delight. It expresses each of these moods, and many others, in a numberless variety of subtle shadings and differences. It may even express a state of meaning for which there exists no adequate word in any language."

Expressive Continua Examples

lugubrious	doleful	miserable	depressed	gloomy	sad
unhappy	ecstatic	blissful	joyful	happy	pleased
content	happy				

An initial pre-seminar exercise for music is to have the students find descriptor words for the piece, such as happy, sad, dark, serene, powerful. This in itself may be interesting since the same piece will most likely elicit several different words. Then students can also explore the quality or degree of some of the words. Copland uses an example regarding Bach's *Well-Tempered Clavier*: "Is it pessimistically sad or resignedly sad; is it fatefully sad or smilingly sad?" To help in this process, students can be given words (perhaps even vocabulary words) along a continuum in order to "locate" a feeling for a particular piece. Using a continuum can help students visualize what they're doing and can help compare and contrast different pieces of music. One caution is that this can sometimes accidentally develop into more of an exercise in semantics instead of a discussion of the music.

After finding descriptive words, the students can then generate numerous questions for the seminar itself. Some of these would inquire about the piece, some about music in general, and others about overarching processes. Selecting an opening question from these will depend on the purpose of the seminar. Here are some of the questions I have been wondering about: *Would you have to be sad in order to compose truly sad music? Is there actual sadness in the music? Can music make you sad or do you respond with sadness? If the former, how does it transfer? If the latter, where does the sadness in me come from? Are certain chords, notes, or patterns inherently happy? What makes a song popular (contagious)? What are the differences between men's voices and women's voices? What makes a piece of music great? Would a "great" song always elicit the same response or always a different response? Why do I go through phases of listening to certain types of music? Is music a form of medicine?*

A creative thinking activity could involve thinking about the music in analogous ways. Using other multiple intelligences can help students find ways to connect the music to what they already know. Here are some sample questions: *What color is this piece of music? What shape is it? What posture is it? If this piece were an animal, what animal would it be? What plant would it be? What part of the brain would it be? What sport would it be? What type of food would this piece be?*

Sample Listening Elements for Music

Major/Minor Key	Voice
Accompaniment	Similarities to Other Works
Repetition	Time Signature(s)
Articulation	Sound Effects
Theme and Variation	Instruments
Form	Context of the Song
Melody	Rhythm
Pitch	Harmony
Lyrics	Tone Color

Copland's third listening level is the sheerly musical plane. "Besides the pleasurable sound of music and the expressive feeling that it gives off, music does exist in terms of the notes themselves and of their manipulation." This is the level of actively listening to elements of music, which for Copland are: rhythm, melody, harmony, and tone color (timbre). It is not in the scope of this book to say much more than this for the purposes of Socratic Seminar. Certainly music classes can explore these elements with far greater aptitude, clarity, and depth.

I am not advocating that an English teacher using a song in class must also teach the elements of music. However, if we are trying to get students to develop thinking habits, if we want their skills to transfer across disciplines and beyond the classroom walls, then we can all contribute whenever possible. Copland writes: "The intelligent listener must be prepared to increase his awareness of the musical material and what happens to it. He must hear the melodies, the rhythms, the harmonies, the tone colors in a more conscious fashion. But, above all he must, in order to follow the line of the composer's thought, know something of the principles of musical form. Listening to all these elements is listening on the sheerly musical plane."

The key word for me in Copland's quote is awareness. Besides helping students practice active listening, raising questions about music in seminar can help students build greater awareness of music. Importantly, if the students have enough experiences, then they can develop better habits of thinking about and listening to music.

> **In music we gain a sense of rhythm through the absence of sound. A similar process occurs in communication between two people.**
> **~ Sheldon Roth**

Listening Texts

One way to focus on active listening is to use a text to anchor dialogue about listening itself. In these conversations, students can explore the levels of listening and the various barriers to listening. They can tell stories about what it feels like to be effectively listened to or excluded. Once there is greater awareness around active listening as a practicable skill, students can set goals for themselves and start improving.

There are numerous picture books that are commonly used for reading aloud that make for great listening texts. Make sure to check out various poems that are great for discussions about listening and sounds as well.

Picture Books for Teaching Listening

Buster by Denise Fleming

Armadillo's Orange by Jim Arnosky

I Have a Little Problem, Said the Bear by Heinz Janisch

Howard B. Wigglebottom Learns to Listen by Howard Binkow

Why Should I Listen? by Claire Llewellyn

The Other Way to Listen by Byrd Baylor and Peter Parnall

The Listening Walk by Paul Showers

A Handful of Quiet: Happiness in Four Pebbles by Thich Nhat Hanh

Silence by Lemniscates

Poems for Teaching Listening

"Bells" by Edgar Allen Poe

"The Sound Collector" by Roger McGough

"Honky Tonk in Cleveland, Ohio" by Carl Sandburg

"The Highwayman" by Alfred Noyes

"Fossils" by Ogden Nash

"Beat! Beat! Drums!" by Walt Whitman

"The Rusty Spigot" by Eve Merriam

"Casey at the Bat" by Ernest L. Thayer

"Cynthia in the Snow" by Gwendolyn Brooks

"If" by Rudyard Kipling

"Ars Poetica" by Archibald MacLeish

"Listening" by Jean Valentine

I've included John Godfrey Saxe's famous poem, "The Blind Men and the Elephant," which is ideal for conversations about listening.

The Blind Men and the Elephant
John Godfrey Saxe

It was six men of Indostan
To learning much inclined,
Who went to see the Elephant
(Though all of them were blind),
That each by observation
Might satisfy his mind.

The First approach'd the Elephant,
And happening to fall
Against his broad and sturdy side,
At once began to bawl:
"God bless me! but the Elephant
Is very like a wall!"

The Second, feeling of the tusk,
Cried, -"Ho! what have we here
So very round and smooth and sharp?
To me 'tis mighty clear
This wonder of an Elephant
Is very like a spear!"

The Third approached the animal,
And happening to take
The squirming trunk within his hands,
Thus boldly up and spake:
"I see," quoth he, "the Elephant
Is very like a snake!"

The Fourth reached out his eager hand,
And felt about the knee.
"What most this wondrous beast is like
Is mighty plain," quoth he,
"'Tis clear enough the Elephant
Is very like a tree!"

The Fifth, who chanced to touch the ear,
Said: "E'en the blindest man
Can tell what this resembles most;
Deny the fact who can,
This marvel of an Elephant
Is very like a fan!"

The Sixth no sooner had begun
About the beast to grope,
Then, seizing on the swinging tail
That fell within his scope,
"I see," quoth he, "the Elephant
Is very like a rope!"

And so these men of Indostan
Disputed loud and long,
Each in his own opinion
Exceeding stiff and strong,
Though each was partly in the right,
And all were in the wrong!

MORAL

So oft in theologic wars,
The disputants, I ween,
Rail on in utter ignorance
Of what each other mean,
And prate about an Elephant
Not one of them has seen.

In my opinion, Socratic Seminar is split into three parts. 1. Listen. Listen to other points and opinions. Your final opinion about the text may be changed if you listen. 2. Annotate. Annotations can help you remember what to say about your point, and they are required. 3. Talk. Talk to get your point across. Talking in a small group for nervous speakers is a great way to practice public speaking. To understand a text you need to use all three, mixed with a few things from your Socratic Seminar teacher.

~ JK (grade 6)

Summing Up

1. Of all the skills in Socratic Seminar, active listening is arguably the most important and the least practiced or appreciated.

2. There are five levels of listening for Socratic Seminar:
   - Hearing
   - Assumed Listening
   - Listening For
   - Active Listening
   - Empathetic Listening

3. Students should NOT raise their hands in Socratic Seminar.

4. There are three sets of regulatory cues students can look for and use:
   - Turn-yielding cues
   - Turn-maintaining cues
   - Turn-requesting cues

5. Whole-body Listening helps define how students can listen better.

6. There are many barriers to listening that can be addressed.

7. There are four responses to disagreement.

8. Teachers must be good listener role models.

Your Next Steps

- Teach listening mini-lessons regularly, especially in the beginning of the school year.

- Ask colleagues of all grade levels how they get students to listen better. There are numerous strategies out there and some of them will work well for you and your style.

- Use a turn-and-talk before entering into the formal part of the seminar. This provides students with a brief speaking and listening exercise before every seminar.

- Consider using a "walk-and-talk" where students continue a paired discussion circling around the room or quietly up and down the hall.

- Research and apply the "Alexander Technique" to help students achieve a more balanced state of readiness and poise.

- Make sure to check out sound expert Julian Treasure's excellent TED videos.

- Don't miss deaf percussionist Evelyn Glennie's TED Talk *How to Truly Listen.*

- One of the most comprehensive books on listening is Wolvin and Coakley's *Listening.*

Sample Seminar Plan

The art of teaching is the art of assisting discovery.
~ Mark Van Doren

WHAT FOLLOWS IS a Socratic Seminar plan for *The Pledge of Allegiance*, which I often use for my first official seminar of the school year. This is usually two or three weeks in after I have established basic classroom behavioral and procedural expectations. I often use this text because it is more complex than many students presume and because it is a common text about which few students apply critical or creative thinking.

Although most U.S. students are extremely familiar with *The Pledge of Allegiance*, what many people don't know is that it has changed several times. In addition, the U.S. flag has, of course, changed numerous times over the years, due to the number of states incorporated into the United States. My thought is that if I can show students there's much more to think about in something as familiar as *The Pledge of Allegiance*, then they should be able to appreciate that we can think deeply about anything. After all, many students and teachers say *The Pledge of Allegiance* almost every day, or at least routinely, yet many do not fully comprehend what the Pledge is all about.

Enter Socratic Seminar.

Title:	*The Pledge of Allegiance*
Grade:	6
Time:	Pre-seminar 45 minutes
	Post-seminar 15 minutes

Dialogue Length: 40-60 minutes

Handouts: *The Pledge of Allegiance* and Norms for Socratic Seminar

Main Objectives: Students will engage in the Socratic Seminar process by working together, listening and speaking respectfully, asking questions, citing the text, and following the discussion norms. Each student will participate at least once.

The Text

The Pledge of Allegiance is a complex text and as such, could easily be a great seminar introduction for almost any grade or subject. With words like *allegiance, Republic, indivisible,* and *liberty*, younger students can begin exploring the importance of words and definitions. Middle school students can explore themes such as citizenship, civic responsibility, freedom, and rights. There are controversial issues surrounding the Pledge that would likely appeal to older students, such as: *Should students be required to say The Pledge of Allegiance? Should the Pledge change?* In addition, there are numerous possible connections and extensions for the text:

- A way to explore citizenship themes in social studies.
- Leadership and community principles for homeroom or advisory.
- *The Hippocratic Oath* in science class.
- Exploring the word *indivisible* (Is anything indivisible?), or the arrangements of various numbers of stars on the Flag as a math teacher.
- Investigating other pledges or national anthems.
- In physical education and sports, use it to dialogue about teamwork.
- Creating accompanying music.
- Crafting a personal, classroom, team, or school pledge.
- Exploring the backgrounds of Francis Bellamy and his cousin, Edward Bellamy, author of the utopian novel *Looking Backward*.

The Pledge of Allegiance is already a complex text, but I always search for ways to make texts even more complex. By adding several versions of the

Pledge and two historical versions of the flag, the complexity of the text increases even further, creating more potential talking points.

Pre-Seminar

Day 1 (20 minutes): Two days or class periods before the seminar, I introduce the seminar norms with the students. I read the text aloud once or twice and model for the students my own thinking and wonder by talking aloud as I read: "*The Pledge of Allegiance* ... hmm, I wonder why it is *the* Pledge and not a pledge. I wonder how a pledge is different from a promise ... I wonder what was happening in 1892 when this pledge was first written ..."

I have students annotate directly on a copy or use sticky notes to generate their own questions, comments, and connections. They often notice things like the shift from *my* flag to *the* flag, wonder why the words Flag, Republic, and Nation are capitalized, and often inquire why the Pledge is made to the flag.

I have students do a turn-and-talk to share what they think is their best question and their best connection. Then I have them share some of those with the entire class. I have them listen to each other to add annotations to their papers in a different color. They can add a third color during seminar. Later in the year they will be graded on their annotations using anchor papers, so this stage of adding annotations is important for future success.

Day 2 (25 minutes): A day before the seminar, I reread the text aloud again, this time focusing on the vocabulary and otherwise finishing the preparation of the text. This early in the year, I like to read the text aloud twice, but later I usually have the students do the second read either silently or in pairs.

A few students volunteer for dictionary duty and they provide us with definitions. Although many of the students have been saying the Pledge for years, they do not fully comprehend: *pledge, allegiance, republic, indivisible, liberty,* and *justice.* I don't want the seminar dialogue to get fixated on definitions, so we talk about the words and definitions until the students seem satisfied that they know what they mean. I ask the students to rank the three words that seem most important for us to know more about in order to have good conversation for Socratic Seminar. They put boxes around those words, label them 1, 2, and 3, and we discuss those words a bit more.

If necessary, both pre-seminar days can be compacted into a single class period, or some of the pre-seminar work could be assigned for homework.

Opening Question Process

I have used this text before, but I sometimes choose new versions of the flag, so that I can keep myself fresh and my thinking alert. This time around, I am particularly caught by the patterns of the stars. I make some of my own annotations: *What exactly is a republic? What is a democratic republic? Why do we pledge to the Flag? (And why is it capitalized)? Who designed the star patterns? How many total patterns have appeared on the U.S. flag? Why is Republic capitalized? What happened in 1923 that might have impacted the change? What was going on in 1954 that the words "under God" were added? Should "under God" remain in the Pledge?*

I keep in mind that "Why has *The Pledge of Allegiance* changed?" will make a bad opening question because it requires too much historical knowledge and context. Unless I am deeply into a specific social studies unit, such questions will likely lead to mere opinion-swapping, pure conjecture, or the need for serious research. Instead, I think more about big ideas and reword the potential opening question to: *Why should a pledge of allegiance change?* I save this as a potential follow-up question. I also rewrite it as *Should we change The Pledge of Allegiance again?* and recognize it as a potentially good closing question toward the end of the seminar. I really get stuck wondering: *Why do we pledge to the Flag?*

Because this is my first seminar of the year, I decide to draft a few variations of the question. Knowing my particular students, I finally decide on the opening question: *Why do we pledge allegiance to the Flag instead of the President or the White House?* I decide to phrase it this way because my original inquiry seemed a bit too abstract. Finally, I keep my annotated copy for the day of the seminar, circling a few additional questions.

Facilitator

Day 3: Because this is our first Socratic Seminar, I go over the norms one more time on the day of the seminar. I will keep reminding students of the norms as needed until they develop the habits of mind somewhere down the road. For example, I will redirect students who talk mainly to me so that they address and make eye contact with the entire group.

I will be asking myself several reflective questions after the seminar. Since I will be tracking a number of things, I should have the necessary data. *How many students spoke at least once? How many cited the text? How many students were actively listening? How many students engaged in side conversations? What kinds of contributions did students make? Did my shy students speak? How well did the students build on each other's ideas?*

During the seminar, I will track participation using a conversation map, so that I can engage the students in a Visual Debrief.

Students

Day 3: The students are still very much working on the skill of actively listening to each other and building on what others say, even though we have practiced some of this for basic classroom expectations. As they enter the room, I hand them all the following exit ticket to be filled out during the seminar. This should help them focus on active listening a little bit more. When the students sit down, they take out their copy of the text and the norms sheet to have in front of them. With experienced groups I may also have them use the Ways to Participate in Socratic Seminar handout for added responsibilities and ownership.

As they listen, they can add notes and questions that they hear from others in a new color on their papers. They should now have three different colors showing various notes.

Exit Ticket

Name:

What is one new idea you heard that you would share with your friends or family?

List one thing you learned today:

One thing I am still wondering about is:

Socratic Seminar

I review the norms and have the students turn-and-talk about a norm that might be challenging for them. I remind them that they should all speak at least once. We have not yet talked about seminar jobs, so we skip that for now. However, if we were at that point (in a few more seminars), I would have the students write a short job description at the bottom of their papers.

I start the formal part of the seminar with: "Okay, today's seminar is about to begin. I've chosen a question that we can discuss with the text in front of us. Some others are interesting as well, but those questions lead us outside the text to find answers. We're here to better understand this text, and I am wondering: *Why do we pledge allegiance to the Flag instead of the President or the White House?* I'd like you to turn-and-talk with a neighbor about this question, and then we'll bring it back to the whole group." After about a minute, I give the signal we are about to start and I re-ask the opening question. Now I kick it off, saying, "Who would like to get us started?"

And the fun begins!

Several students instinctively raise their hands, but seeing that I am not calling on anyone, a few blurt out starting answers and stop because they are speaking at the same time. They look at each other and then finally one student presses forward and begins the dialogue. I watch carefully and note who started talking and who pushed forward.

I remind students on several occasions that they should speak to everyone in the group and not just to me. When I do that, I make a circular hand gesture so that later I can just make the gesture to remind students.

I ask several follow-up questions to probe for deeper thinking, often questions like: "Yes, but why pledge to the Flag itself?" and "Can you knowingly pledge allegiance as a young student?" and "Is there really liberty and justice for all? If not, then why are we saying it?"

The dialogue goes well for a while and I have been tracking who speaks and what kind of contributions (SPQR) they make. I notice several students who haven't spoken yet. When the conversation hits a lull, I say, "I have a new question: *Why should a pledge of allegiance change?* Let's do a turn-and-talk and then I'd like to hear from someone who hasn't spoken yet." This action gets all but one student to participate.

As the conversation continues, I notice the last student who hasn't spoken is struggling to figure out how to join. I watch closely and when the student nonverbally seems like he has something, I invite this student to contribute. He repeats what someone else said and I make a note. Everyone has participated at least once, so one of my main goals is already achieved.

If the quality of the dialogue (enthusiasm, citing the text, building ideas) fades, I have a closing question ready: *Should we change The Pledge of Allegiance again?* If we have time, I will ask it in order to "bring the text alive" and to personalize the concept for the students. If we run out of time, I can use that question for a writing assignment. Because this is our first seminar, I typically spend any extra time on coaching and debriefing, so I will likely save it for later.

Post-Seminar

I plan to stop the seminar with twelve minutes remaining. We will debrief with the questions: *What did you notice today? What did we do well today? What do we need to improve for next time?* In addition, the students will have a few minutes to complete their exit tickets. I collect their annotated papers and their exit tickets.

We will do a Visual Debrief either the day after the seminar or a few days before the next one. When we do, we can establish three group goals, such as:

- Speak more equally.
- Stay on topic.
- Ask more questions.

Evaluation and Grading

I remind my students that their grade will be based on two things: individual participation and the exit tickets. I use a simple system in the beginning of the year because I am more focused on coaching the group to work together until I get a baseline sense of how each student participates. After establishing group cohesion, I'll set up specific individual goals and soon we will focus on the quality of their contributions, not just the quantity. I'll grade the exit tickets based on expectations we have established as a class, such as using complete sentences, and restating the questions. Each student participated at least once, so they each receive full participation credit, but next time I can add a simple rubric like this:

4 – Spoke at least once and appeared to listen respectfully.
3 – Spoke at least once.
2 – Listened respectfully, but did not participate.
1 – Did not speak at least once, and did not appear to listen well.
0 – Disrupted the seminar process.

Facilitator Debrief

As usual in the beginning of the year, the students struggled to actively listen to each other and, therefore, to truly build on each other's ideas. Many students "listened with their mouths open," meaning they were basically just waiting for their turns to speak, rather than seeking to understand. I will plan some mini-lessons and closely monitor the active listening in upcoming seminars. One possible intervention is to require the students to rephrase the previous speaker before they may participate, though this will greatly slow dialogue down.

My dialogue map and codes show that three students contributed nearly half of the dialogue, and that several students spoke the minimum of one time. I have not established a baseline for this group, but it is highly likely that I will need to balance the participation in order to maximize the group's potential. The goal of Socratic Seminar is to have a genuine conversation, so automatically forcing shy students to speak or limiting talkative students is not necessarily productive, but more balance will probably allow the group to share and build on the best ideas. I make some notes and prepare for the next seminar.

My Next Steps

- We will do a Visual Debrief and establish individual and group goals for the next seminar.

- I will read and grade the exit tickets and have the students keep their handouts and tickets in seminar folders.

- I will scan through the annotated papers to see who struggled with asking questions and making notes. In particular, I check to see how much was added in different colors. I also note who had an exemplary collection of annotations.

- I will introduce the *Ways to Participate in Socratic Seminar* handout before the next seminar. This will provide more opportunities for students to participate.

- I will teach the concept "listening with your mouth open" to my students and discuss what it means to actively listen.

- I will teach whole-body listening and introduce the five levels of listening.

- The poem "The Blind Men and the Elephant" is a useful text for groups to understand that all of their contributions are needed in order for the group to "see the elephant." I may decide to use that as a seminar text in the coming weeks if the students need additional understandings of why to work as a group.

- I will prepare for the contingency of talking to some of the shy and/or talkative students outside of class.

- Over the next few weeks I will note student interests so that I can select the next few seminar texts from the many I might use.

- I will prepare four or five anchor papers for grading annotations. I will introduce these to students and display them on the walls within a couple of seminars.

13

Problem Solving

At its best, schooling can be about how to make a life, which is quite different from how to make a living.

~ Neil Postman

BEFORE JUMPING INTO various problems and solutions for Socratic Seminar, please keep in mind a few things. The first is that Socratic Seminar uses the *gradual release of responsibility* model, so there will always be a need for coaching and improving as students try out new responsibilities. The second is that Socratic Seminar is also a constructivist approach, so the students will be creating meaning as they go and this is going to be a sloppy process (like nearly any creative process). The third is that seminar is essentially an arena for practicing thinking skills and then practicing them again ... and again.

Essentially, the students are going to make mistakes and lots of them. They will interrupt each other, draw unsupported conclusions, say illogical things, and so on. Although every facilitator has a different comfort zone, I strongly encourage teachers to err on the side of letting the students struggle. They will create the greatest understandings and most enduring memories during the hardest endeavors. With strong cooperation, patience, and reflection, students can successfully engage in *productive* struggle.

> **If you are searching for better chemistry within the group, consider using a sociogram, which is a representation of the network of social patterns within a group.**

Should I assign seats for Socratic Seminar?

First of all, if you already use assigned seating for behavioral issues, then yes, you probably should use them for seminars. This is especially true for larger classes where you will want to strategically think about how to split the class into two groups for an inner and outer circle. Remember that specific positions in the formation such as *next to* and *across from* are usually the most troublesome.

If you normally use assigned seating, consider letting the students decide where they want to sit for seminar. This could pose the first potential problem for the students to solve over the course of the next several seminars. If the first seminar goes smoothly, then the students already made good choices. If the seminar does not go well, debrief with the students about what happened. They may even recommend having assigned seats.

If you are searching for better chemistry within the group, consider using a sociogram, which is a representation of the network of social patterns within a group. Creating these can help with strategically placing students for turn-and-talks and for seminar. A simple post-seminar sociogram is to ask participants to write down the name of two or three students who helped them understand the text better. Tally the results and then in the next seminar, place the four most helpful students in the four cardinal directions in the seminar circle.

Positioning all of these students more strategically is very complex, but a colleague of mine has had great success using the website *Sometics.com*. He asks a few simple questions of the students: Who do you work well with? Not work well with? Who do you want to socialize with? Not socialize with? The website then uses an algorithm to place students in specific formations.

What do I do when students don't participate?

By far, the number one reason I have found is that students simply don't know what to say at any given time. Many conversations move too quickly for some students and they struggle because they do not have enough relevant things to say. The main solution to get students participating is to spend more time in the pre-seminar stage. With more annotations, questions, and potential ideas, students will have more relevant material to share in the dialogue.

To get the students initially warmed up, try Brooke MacKenzie's "One Quick Thing" idea from February 12, 2018, on Edutopia. She had students share "one quick thing" at the beginning of class with three rules: it had to be one thing, it had to be quick, and it could be anything—as long as they were excited about it. MacKenzie found: "As my students began to share one quick thing regularly, I noticed a change in their energy. They burst through the door. They participated actively during the whole period. Even their perceptions of themselves as readers seemed to become more positive."

> **Keep in mind there are two types of silence: active and passive.**

Thomas Newkirk, author of *Embarrassment*, points out that students often opt out or don't participate because of stigma, shame, or embarrassment. There are many reasons for these feelings, ranging from not wanting to be labeled a nerd, to not knowing how to pronounce a word, to possibly sharing an unpopular idea or viewpoint. For most students, class participation is a gain-loss calculation: What can I gain versus what could I lose? For example, a student may want to speak, but not if he or she thinks there will be a socio-emotional cost. If students aren't participating, then they likely fear that the cost of participating is not worth it.

Make a list of everything you can think of that could cause a student to not participate. What could be causing potential stigma, shame, fear, or embarrassment? What barriers could you take down? How could you create a safer space? How could you encourage and reward risk-taking? Keep in mind, if there are students dominating the seminars, they will need to be dealt with simultaneously in order to create space for shy students. If necessary, meet with students outside of class. Have them make anonymous lists of reasons they don't participate, and what would motivate them to take risks.

Take a risk and try something new as a facilitator. I noticed one year that the boys were dominating all of our conversations. Despite my best coaching actions and interventions, I could not get the girls to participate much. I finally took a risk and tried facilitating two separate seminars (moving back and forth between them), one just for the boys and another just for the girls. The boys continued as usual, but the girls blossomed and shared more in a single seminar than they had all year. After a few seminars where the girls got to practice their habits of mind, I brought everyone back together and we were able to continue with more balanced equity.

If the entire group goes quiet, ask a new question or repeat the old one. Use wait time. Use more wait time. Be patient. Keep in mind there are two types of silence: active and passive. If the silence is active, keep waiting. (I once waited a painfully long 47 seconds before a group got going.) If the silence is passive, ask questions: *How can we rephrase this question to make it clearer? How can we get unstuck? Where is the text still confusing? What's another way of looking at this? What do we need to do in order to move forward?*

Consider using a text that explores vulnerability, shyness, shame, or embarrassment. This may not get shy students to initially participate, but perhaps could lead them on the road to courage and risk-taking. Plenty of Brené Brown quotes or excerpts could work to begin dialogue, such as: "Because true belonging only happens when we present our authentic, imperfect selves to the world, our sense of belonging can never be greater than our level of self-acceptance."

Consider allowing nervous or withdrawn students to make up the seminar work in some alternative way. Have them keep a journal, put them in charge of a seminar blog, or have them draw a cartoon that captures the main points of the dialogue. Allow them to turn in papers or replace their participation by recording their thoughts on a video. Keep in mind when grading that a student who doesn't speak, but doesn't cause any problems either, should still deserve some credit for listening.

In addition:

- Track and code participation; look for trends.
- Use turn-and-talks or think-pair-shares.
- Have a shy student ask your opening question.
- For introverts or slow processors, give them the text ahead of time, and/or read the text twice.
- Provide video recordings for students to watch on their own.

- Cold-calling on people hardly ever works (use turn-and-talk instead).
- Say, "I'd like to hear from someone who hasn't spoken yet." Then wait. Create "empty space" for students to speak into. Then wait some more.
- Use an app like Equity Maps to collect, share, and analyze data.

What do I do when students dominate the conversation?

In the role of coach, make sure to intervene and provide reasons why students benefit from actively listening more. I always tell my students that if they walk into class with one idea about the text and then dominate the conversation without listening, they will leave the classroom with the same one idea. By actively listening, they will actually learn new ideas and viewpoints.

Don't be afraid of limiting a student's participation. One technique I like to use involves dice. Depending on the size of the group, I will give the talkative students a die with six, eight, or ten sides. They place the die on the highest number and use it to count down each time they participate. When they use their last number, they can't speak any more. This technique works really well because the students end up self-monitoring and become more selective about what they share.

In addition:

- Always track participation and look for trends.
- In the concentric circle model, consider sending the talkative student to the outer circle to observe and listen more.
- Have those students sit next to you and/or create a hand gesture that can remind students to listen more or participate in other ways.
- Encourage students to put their "extra" thoughts in a notebook or blog. Have them jot everything extra on sticky notes that they can place later somewhere in the room.
- Tell those students they can't talk for 3-5 minutes or until 3-5 people have spoken.
- Give everyone two coins or tokens to "spend" talking, and when they use those two, they can't speak again until all of the coins in the group are spent.

My groups often finish my opening question in just a few minutes. What do I do?

Pursue thinking and justifications more, and use follow-up questions (role of bloodhound). Go back and review the guidelines for a good opening question because a well-formed opening question should last a long time. Perhaps as a general rule, a good opening question, with pursuit and follow-up questions (both the role of *bloodhound*), can last about 7-10 minutes times the grade level. So, about 14-20 minutes in second grade, 35-50 minutes in fifth, and 60-90 minutes in ninth grade.

Here are some reliable follow-up questions:

- What in the text makes you say that? Where is that? Can you read it to the group?
- What is an example of that? What's another example?
- Who can add to this? Can we broaden this idea?
- Could you summarize that in your own words?
- Who agrees/disagrees with that idea? Why?
- Could you paraphrase what he/she just said?
- Can you explain that further? Can we deepen this idea?

My class has more than forty students. How do I get them all participating?

This is challenging, but my advice is to figure out a way where you can split the class into two separate seminars. Maybe another teacher in the building would be willing to lead half the students. Maybe give half of the students some independent work while you facilitate one group and then switch. You could build a research project into the process and send half the students to the library. Smaller groups mean more speaking time for each student, so see if it is somehow possible. If not, use more turn-and-talks or think-pair-shares to give students ample speaking and listening opportunities.

For very large classes, there is a variation of the concentric circle model that divides the students into three-person triads. A "pilot" sits in the inner dialogue circle to talk about the text and is advised by two "copilots." Run an inner/outer circle seminar and then every five minutes or so, provide an opportunity for the triad to talk with each other. The pilot then brings the thoughts and ideas back to the inner circle to continue the dialogue.

The outer circle copilots still operate as process coaches by sharing their observations and providing insights into what is working for the inner group. At regular intervals, rotate the pilots and copilots so that every triad member has a chance to be in the inner circle. Although the dialogue in the inner circle may be somewhat limited by the smaller number of participants, the students do gain structured turn-and-talk time with their triads.

How do I facilitate seminars with a small group of five or six students?

Facilitating extremely small groups can be as difficult as very large groups. Due to a scheduling glitch one semester, I had a Socratic Seminar group of only four students. This proved difficult, especially when someone was absent. Sometimes the seminars just felt like long, extended think-pair-shares. Unless the text was extremely complex, with numerous talking points and nuances, the four students quickly exhausted their ideas. Texts that may have been decent for a larger group simply ran out of steam, despite my best facilitator actions. What I learned was that text selection was vastly more important.

What worked best for our tiny group was surreal art from artists like Salvadore Dali, M. C. Escher, and Michael Parkes. Other artists such as Hieronymus Bosch, Leonora Carrington, Mathieu Saunier (Khan Nova), and Mark Ryden have good pieces that I would consider using in such circumstances.

What happens when students are unprepared or absent?

As a general rule, unprepared students should not be allowed to participate in the seminar itself, especially when they have not read the text. When students are unprepared, I usually have them sit out of the circle and make notes as they listen to the conversation. They turn their notes in as their participation grade.

When students are absent, they can write papers, blog, or make a video as a substitute for not being there. Remember that seminars primarily involve speaking and listening, whereas many other alternatives will involve reading and writing. When students are sick for a few days and then show up on the day of the seminar, I either give an alternative assignment, or if the text is short enough, I have them read and annotate it, and then join us mid-seminar.

Unprepared or absent students can also contribute to the group by later examining the dialogue map and/or conversation data. They can use a See-Think-Wonder routine to analyze patterns, look for trends, and then help set group and/or individual goals. In this way, they can assist with the process, though they may still need to follow through on understanding the text. In addition:

- Use a blog so that students can access seminar materials from home.
- Record the seminar and post the video so students can watch when they are able.
- Create a student job to post notes or summaries on Google Docs or Padlet.
- Create several generic alternative assignments that students have ahead of time.
- Use Skype or Zoom for students to join from a distance.

I have a class of the school's troublemakers. Can I do Socratic Seminar with them?

My students have learning disabilities. Can I still do seminars?

My students are mostly ELLs. Can I do Socratic Seminar with them?

All groups present various challenges, and facilitating Socratic Seminars with certain classes may never be easy. But the general answer in all three cases is yes. Text selection is most important for all three groups.

In the first case, many teachers are surprised to find that Socratic Seminars work very well with so-called troublesome students. The reason is that many at risk or otherwise troublesome students are often bored in school and/or don't have any strong personal connections to the "school game." For these students, text selection is even more imperative. Choose texts that the students can immediately relate to and definitely consider having the students bring in their own texts. Many facilitators find that song lyrics work really well. I also find that texts about school and learning often engage these students because they have different opinions about what "good" education should be.

In the second and third cases difficulties can arise, but students of all ages and abilities can have quality conversations. Each teacher must use his or her professional wisdom to choose the type of text that will allow the students to be most successful. Visual texts are often reliable because students can share what they see in the image as an initial way to participate, thereby balancing participation. Alexis Wiggins writes: "... I have found that the requirements for equal and balanced participation is a great boon to immigrant and ELL students who may otherwise choose to be silent for most of the year."

Keep in mind that no matter what students' struggles are, they all need practice with communication and thinking skills in safe environments. Make sure not to let students off the hook just because they are learning English as a second language or have learning challenges of some sort. There are always solutions to get students involved. For example, Goldsmith found the following worked well with his ELL students:

> Allow students to call on each other for assistance. When students aren't sure of an answer during a class discussion, our reaction is very important. If you say it's OK and move on to another student, they've learned it's OK to be disengaged and so have the other students. You can narrow the question to be more specific, but if that still doesn't work, let the student call on two friends and listen to their answers. After the student listens to both friends, you can follow up with questions such as, "Does that make sense to you?" and "Could you say it in your own words?" This ensures students aren't off the hook when they say, "I don't know." You're sending the message, "Well, now is a great time to learn!"

We finished discussing the text today, but my students don't get it. What happened?

This is a really important question with several embedded problems. The most important is that if the students don't "get it," then you obviously had specific outcomes in mind for the text and the opening question. Ultimately, this means that you had an agenda for the seminar, putting you in an authority position, or top-down power structure.

Socratic Seminar is a constructivist, student-centered approach, so placing yourself in this position is antithetical to the process. The fact that you wanted a specific outcome for the seminar is a problem in itself. It likely means that the text was not complex enough, that it did not contain enough ambiguities and justifiable interpretations. It also likely means that the opening question did not elicit multiple viewpoints and/or opinions.

It's difficult to diagnose the problem without observing what happened, but there are numerous issues that could be at play. For example, if the students misinterpreted the text, then they may have misunderstood a key word or phrase, they may have drawn an illogical conclusion, or overlooked an important element of the text. It's also possible that some of the participants were too afraid to share the ideas that would have led to a breakthrough.

Don't worry. Relax. Make notes and reflect on what happened. Don't tell the students they "didn't get it," but ask them what they thought happened in the seminar. Ask yourself questions about what happened. In addition, here are some of the typical roots of such a problem:

- The students did not have enough dialogue time.
- The text was way too difficult; lack of prerequisite knowledge.
- The group was stuck in the *storming* stage of development.
- The pre-seminar did not sufficiently prepare the text for dialogue.
- The students needed time to synthesize and make sense in post-seminar.
- The students came to a viable answer instead of a conventional answer.

I want to facilitate dialogue about social justice, tolerance or culturally sensitive issues. What should I do?

Due to their highly personal, highly charged nature, these conversations are more difficult than typical seminars that focus on academic texts. It is not within the scope of this book to extend into the many nuances and complications that are involved in facilitating such difficult conversations, but I would be remiss if I didn't make some suggestions. For starters, consider shifting your seminar atmosphere from a "safe space" to a "brave space," as Brian Arao and Kristi Clemens suggest in their article in the book *The Art of Effective Facilitation*. As they advise, this begins with how you might establish group norms: "We strongly encourage facilitators who use the brave space framework to strive for protracted dialogue in defining brave space and setting ground rules, treating this conversation not as a prelude to learning about social justice but as a valuable part of such learning."

To truly and deeply converse about difficult topics, the seminar group must attain extraordinary levels of trust, safety, courage, intimacy, and faith in the process. Participants must feel willing and able to share vulnerabilities, deep scars and traumatic events, historical and genetic baggage, and shameful personal failures. They may need to safely vent abrasive frustration and explosive anger. Such conversations may require swearing, cultural slang, "loaded words," and incendiary language. The group may need to yell, laugh, cry, and sob together before achieving tangible results. This may require groups to be in the *norming* or *performing* stages of group development.

If these conversations were easy, we likely would have solved many of humanity's problems already. Since we haven't, here are some resources I have come across that may help. The *Teaching Tolerance, Teaching for Change and Facing History and Ourselves, Difficult Dialogues National Resource Center,* and *National Coalition for Dialogue and Deliberation* websites have numerous resources for teachers of all levels to begin such conversations. Some books I have found useful:

- *The Art of Effective Facilitation: Reflections from Social Justice Educators* edited by Lisa M. Landreman.
- *Crucial Conversations: Tools for Talking When Stakes Are High* by Kerry Patterson, Joseph Grenny, Ron McMillan and Al Switzler.

- *Fierce Conversations: Achieving Success at Work & in Life, One Conversation at a Time* by Susan Scott.
- *Braving the Wilderness: The Quest for True Belonging and the Courage to Stand Alone* by Brené Brown.
- *Quiet: The Power of Introverts in a World That Can't Stop Talking* by Susan Cain.
- *Embarrassment and the Emotional Underlife of Learning* by Thomas Newkirk.

How do I facilitate Socratic Seminars with students in pre-K to 1st grade?

Not much is really different. As the professional for this age group, choose an appropriate text and start by asking questions that have two alternatives: *Is this story happy or sad? Do you like or dislike this poem?* Use pictures of various facial expressions, like a happy face and a frowning face. Ask questions like: *What are you feeling right now, this one or this one? So, what do you think this character is feeling, this picture or this one?* Have the students explain their answers as much as they can, and encourage multiple students to share. Watch out for anecdotes. Consider limiting the sharing to a few sentences.

Help the students recognize that they are part of a group by encouraging them to actively listen to each other using whole-body listening. A slow but effective way is to have each student repeat what the previous student said before adding to the conversation. Create group affiliations by asking questions like: *Who else agrees with Lenora? Who disagrees with this idea?*

When the students are ready, move to questions with three or four alternatives, and eventually ask open-ended questions.

My students have low reading abilities. What do I do for seminars?

Students with low reading abilities still deserve to wrestle with and think about complex ideas and issues. They are still thinkers and deserve to hone their critical and creative thinking skills. Use texts that are not reading-reliant, such as: photographs, paintings, film clips, or audio books. Focus on the skills of working together and asking questions. Teach them about critical and creative thinking and get them to use their speaking and listening skills to help them become more active thinkers and eventually more active readers. Of course, they still need to develop reading skills!

Text selection is extremely important for these students. Keep in mind that texts with interpretive issues are not necessarily difficult to read. Even if you have high school students reading at a third-grade level, there are plenty of accessible texts with ambiguities that can be effectively used for Socratic Seminar. Two of my personal favorites are short stories: "The Two Brothers" by Leo Tolstoy and "An Ominous Baby" by Stephen Crane.

Facilitating seems like a lot of multitasking, which I'm not good at. What do you suggest?

I'm not confident that I can think quickly on my feet to ask follow-up questions. What do I do?

Don't worry and get started anyway. Start by slowing the seminars down by adding wait time after each speaker to give yourself an opportunity to think (3-5 seconds after each speaker should work). Take your time creating the conversation map or tracking student contributions. Let the students know that you value their input and that you want to listen and record everything.

Keep a laminated list of follow-up questions, the *16 Habits of Mind*, and/or facilitator actions nearby and constantly refer to them during the seminar. Use them as checklists mechanically until you get the hang of when and how to use them more naturally. Keep your tracking codes simple, for example, start by using the S-P-Q-R system and add other codes as you can.

Most importantly, pass the responsibilities over to the students as early as possible. Give the students a copy of *Ways to Participate in Socratic Seminar* and get them participating in new ways. Even if the students aren't good at multi-tasking either, they only need to be responsible for a single job. Tell them what you want and hope to accomplish and recruit them into the purpose.

My supervisors are coming to watch my seminar. What do I tell them to look for?

In general, tell them to look for student engagement, and in particular how well the students are addressing each other respectfully and working together as a team. If you are in the *forming* or *storming* stage of group process, I would recommend also having the administrators look at how well you facilitate and coach the group. Specifically, this means appreciating the actions and non-actions you take in order to get the students to work together using their speaking and listening skills. If you are in the *norming* stage, have the supervisors also focus on how well the students have taken up seminar responsibilities or jobs and how well the group is functioning on its own. If you feel you are in the *performing* stage, have the administrators observe the power dynamics and how you are able to integrate yourself back into the group as an equal participant.

My honors students are highly competitive and won't work together. What do I do?

Definitely use a group grade, keeping in mind that such a grade does not have to affect the actual GPAs of the students. In her classes, teacher and author Alexis Wiggins "discovered quickly that whether the grade counted or not didn't make a difference. I didn't notice a change in participation, homework completion, or quality of discussion … They treated the rubric, the symbolic grade, and the collaborative process as seriously as my previous students had."

Embed the Socratic Seminar in a writing project where the participants must cite and/or quote other students. Use graded reflections and exit tickets where participants must refer to other students. Consider using a seminar and debate model that encourages listening to and examining other viewpoints. Focus on empathetic listening.

I would definitely recommend using an extremely complex and challenging text that will force all the participants to struggle together toward a common purpose. Philosophers like Immanuel Kant, Charles Peirce, Martin Heidegger, Jiddu Krishnamurti, and numerous others have dense writings that should boggle many individual minds, but sufficiently challenge groups to work together in order to make meaning. Plato's "Allegory of the Cave" has worked consistently well for me.

I have used excerpts from Lao Tzu's *Tao Te Ching*, Marvin Minsky's *The Society of Mind*, and one of my favorite books ever, *The Seven Mysteries of Life* by Guy Murchie. Also, try using a nonlinear or nontraditional text like *Finnegan's Wake* by James Joyce, poems by E. E. Cummings, or a story like *"Repent, Harlequin!" Said the Ticktockman* by Harlan Ellison. Try surreal art, abstract song lyrics, or something different like an old map as a text.

The following excerpt by Charles Peirce may not connect well to your curriculum (although seminars can always connect to speaking and listening standards), but such a text should push even the most talented students toward collaboration.

Excerpt from *The Fixation of Belief* by Charles Sanders Peirce.

II.

The object of reasoning is to find out, from the consideration of what we already know, something else which we do not know. Consequently, reasoning is good if it be such as to give a true conclusion from true premisses, and not otherwise. Thus, the question of validity is purely one of fact and not of thinking. A being the facts stated in the premisses and B being that concluded, the question is, whether these facts are really so related that if A were B would generally be. If so, the inference is valid; if not, not. It is not in the least the question whether, when the premisses are accepted by the mind, we feel an impulse to accept the conclusion also. It is true that we do generally reason correctly by nature. But that is an accident; the true conclusion would remain true if we had no impulse to accept it; and the false one would remain false, though we could not resist the tendency to believe in it.

We are, doubtless, in the main logical animals, but we are not perfectly so. Most of us, for example, are naturally more sanguine and hopeful than logic would justify. We seem to be so constituted that in the absence of any facts to go upon we are happy and self-satisfied; so that the effect of experience is continually to contract our hopes and aspirations. Yet a lifetime of the application of this corrective does not usually eradicate our sanguine disposition. Where hope is unchecked by any experience, it is likely that our optimism is extravagant. Logicality in regard to practical matters (if this be understood, not in the old sense, but as consisting in a wise union of security with fruitfulness of reasoning) is the most useful quality an animal can possess, and might, therefore, result from the action of natural selection; but outside of these it is probably of more advantage to the animal to have his mind filled with pleasing and encouraging visions, independently of their truth; and thus, upon unpractical subjects, natural selection might occasion a fallacious tendency of thought.

That which determines us, from given premisses, to draw one inference rather than another, is some habit of mind, whether it be constitutional or acquired. The habit is good or otherwise, according as it produces true conclusions from true premisses or not; and an inference is regarded as valid or not, without reference to the truth or falsity of its conclusion specially, but according as the habit which determines it is such as to produce true conclusions in general or not. The particular habit of mind which governs this or that inference may be formulated in a proposition whose truth depends on the validity of the inferences which the habit determines; and such a formula is called a guiding principle of inference. Suppose, for example, that we observe that a rotating disk of copper quickly comes to rest when placed between the poles of a magnet, and we infer that this will happen with every disk of copper. The guiding principle is, that what is true of one piece of copper is true of another. Such a guiding principle with regard to copper would be much safer than with regard to many other substances — brass, for example.

Summing Up

1. Socratic Seminars use *gradual release of responsibility.*

2. Assigning seats is worth considering, especially with concentric circles. Use a sociogram to consider how to place students.

3. There are many reasons why students might not participate. Overall, use a new question, a turn-and-talk, and the phrase, "I'd like to hear from someone who hasn't spoken yet."

4. Don't be afraid to limit a dominating student's participation.

5. Quality follow-up questions will keep most conversations going.

6. Very large or very small groups, or groups of students with special needs might require different procedures and texts.

7. Conversations on sensitive issues like social justice or tolerance can be more difficult and might require a shift in thinking from "safe spaces" to "brave spaces" in order for participants to share.

8. Highly competitive, advanced students need extremely complex and difficult texts that will force them to work together in order to make meaning.

Your Next Steps

- Always be on the lookout for good texts. They can turn up in the strangest of places.

- Because Socratic Seminars are group endeavors, the texts should often be extra difficult. Ask teachers a level or a grade or two ahead to find out what they are using for their individual students. Those texts can often make good selections for your groups.

- Consider splitting groups up into smaller seminars until they can be more successful in larger groups. Many students will only participate in pairs or small groups (and therefore need practice), before feeling comfortable in larger settings.

- Use tracking as the primary method to solve your problems. When you see something positive that you want to increase or something negative that you want to decrease, then track those things. For example, tracking will allow you to notice who needs to listen more and who needs to talk more.

- Read more about group dynamics and how groups of people naturally function together. Many teams and groups function in predictable ways. Talk to your sports coaches at school about how they manage and encourage their teams.

- Consider the type of text that you are using in order to connect better to your students. Some students will respond better to songs, or artwork, or demonstrations. Almost any text can be connected to a unit of study's essential questions or "Great Ideas."

- Consider building a classroom constitution at the beginning of the year.

- Always ask the students how the seminars can improve.

What questions do you have at this point?

Afterword

BEFORE ENDING, I want to offer three other names for the techniques and processes outlined in this book. This is in case anyone has an issue with the name being related to Socrates, or the fact that the name *Socratic Seminar* appears in numerous other places or publications, or in case you think I'm actually describing something different here. Sometimes when you try something new, you do not want to be tethered to its history.

These three names are from foreign languages, from a book entitled, *They Have a Word For It* by Howard Rheingold. I chose these because they are not just words—they translate into English as entire concepts. Because they are not English words, they liberate you to do your own thing without having to worry about what others think. There's nothing quite as deflating as excitedly telling another teacher that you're trying something new, a Socratic Seminar, only to be met with, "Oh, we tried those two years ago. They don't work well."

The first is an Indonesian word: *rojong* (roy-Yong). According to Rheingold, its simple definition is "mutual cooperation." But he goes on to say *rojong* is used "to connote the relationship among a group of people who are committed to accomplish a task of mutual benefit." What a perfect word this really is, because this is exactly the thing that would separate a Socratic Seminar from a discussion. This group would be about creating mutual benefit *from being a group*, rather than a collection of individuals. So, you could facilitate a *rojong* seminar or perhaps just a *rojong*.

The second is a Javanese word: *tjotjog* (CHOT-chog). In its simple definition from Rheingold it is "harmonious congruence in human affairs." He offers an interesting extension of this, and later defines a part of the word as being, "cooperative efforts [that] mesh together to an almost supernatural degree, through a combination of practice, skill, confidence, mutual regard, and timing." Again, a great alternative name for Socratic Seminar because of the idea of combining as a group to achieve something that we, as individuals, could not. So, schedule a *tjotjog* seminar or a *tjotjog*.

The third possibility on offer is a Chinese word: *shih* (SHE). The simple definition from Rheingold is "an insightful, elegant kind of knowledge."

He has this to add: "A person can possess a wide and deep knowledge of factual material, but unless that person has a kind of insight, judgment, and, above all, good taste in the way that this knowledge is used or presented, that person cannot be said to possess *shih*." This is another good choice because there is a beauty to Socratic Seminar when the group has achieved a stunning Eureka! moment. And together, the participants share an experience they know they have earned through hard work that could not have been achieved independently. Sometimes I think nothing is more beautiful.

So these are three possibilities. You could schedule a *rojong* seminar, a *tjotjog* seminar, or a *shih* seminar, if you would like, instead of calling them Socratic Seminars. The method is what is important, and not what you call it. This book is dedicated to achieving numerous dialogue and thinking goals whether it is through Socratic Seminar, or through a cohesive group effort of another name.

All the best to you in your thinking adventures!

The next book in this series will focus on some of my favorite classroom tools for promoting critical and creative thinking.

Appendices

Appendix A

The Great Ideas - Mortimer J. Adler

Angel
Animal
Aristocracy
Art
Astronomy & Cosmology
Beauty
Being
Cause
Chance
Change
Citizen
Constitution
Courage
Custom & Convention
Definition
Democracy
Desire
Dialectic
Duty
Education
Element
Emotion
Eternity
Evolution
Experience
Family
Fate
Form
God
Good & Evil
Government
Habit
Happiness
History

Honor
Hypothesis
Idea
Immortality
Induction
Infinity
Judgment
Justice
Knowledge
Labor
Language
Law
Liberty
Life & Death
Logic
Love
Man
Mathematics
Matter
Mechanics
Medicine
Memory & Imagination
Metaphysics
Mind
Monarchy
Nature
Necessity & Contingency
Oligarchy
One & Many
Opinion
Opposition
Philosophy
Physics
Pleasure & Pain

Poetry
Principle
Progress
Prophecy
Prudence
Punishment
Quality
Quantity
Reasoning
Relation
Religion
Revolution
Rhetoric
Same & Other
Science
Sense
Sign & Symbol
Sin
Slavery
Soul
Space
State
Temperance
Theology
Time
Truth
Tyranny & Despotism
Universal & Particular
Virtue & Vice
War & Peace
Wealth
Will
Wisdom
World

Appendix B

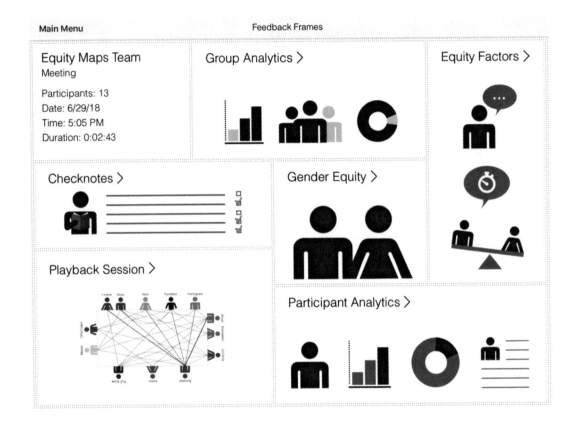

1. Equity Maps App: Feedback Frames

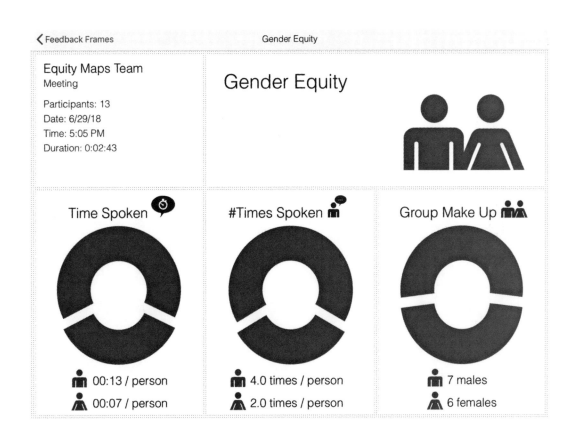

Equity Maps Team
Meeting

Participants: 13
Date: 6/29/18
Time: 5:05 PM
Duration: 0:02:43

Gender Equity

Time Spoken 🕐

👤 00:13 / person
👤 00:07 / person

#Times Spoken 💬

👤 4.0 times / person
👤 2.0 times / person

Group Make Up 👥

👤 7 males
👤 6 females

2. Equity Maps App: Gender Equity

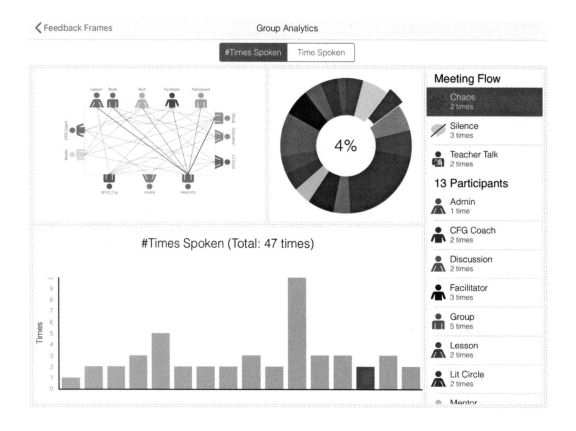

3. Equity Maps App: Group Analytics

4. Equity Maps App: Checknotes

Appendix C

The Pledge of Allegiance
Francis Bellamy

1892

"I pledge allegiance to my Flag and the Republic for which it stands, one Nation indivisible, with liberty and justice for all."

1892 to 1923

"I pledge allegiance to my Flag and to the Republic for which it stands, one Nation, indivisible, with liberty and justice for all."

1924 to 1954

"I pledge allegiance to the Flag of the United States of America and to the Republic for which it stands, one Nation, indivisible, with liberty and justice for all."

1954 to Present

"I pledge allegiance to the Flag of the United States of America, and to the Republic for which it stands, one Nation under God, indivisible, with liberty and justice for all."

Appendix D

The Blind Men and the Elephant

John Godfrey Saxe

Is six important? *when was this written?*

where's Indostan?

It was six men of Indostan
To learning much inclined,
Who went to see the Elephant *(visit?)* *(why is this capitalized?)*
(Though all of them were blind),
(1) That each by observation
Might satisfy his mind.

The First approach'd the Elephant, *(why the spelling?)*
And happening to fall
(2) Against his broad and sturdy side,
At once began to bawl:
"God bless me! but the Elephant
Is very like a wall!"

The Second, feeling of the tusk,
Cried, -"Ho! what have we here
(3) So very round and smooth and sharp?
To me 'tis mighty clear
This wonder of an Elephant
Is very like a spear!"

The Third approached the animal,
And happening to take
(4) The squirming trunk within his hands,
Thus boldly up and spake: *(Past tense of speak)*
"I see," quoth he, "the Elephant *(said)*
Is very like a snake!"

The Fourth reached out his eager hand,
And felt about the knee.
(5) "What most this wondrous beast is like
Is mighty plain," quoth he,
"'Tis clear enough the Elephant
Is very like a tree!"

The Fifth, who chanced to touch the ear,
Said: 'E'en the blindest man *(Spelling?)*
(6) Can tell what this resembles most;
Deny the fact who can,
This marvel of an Elephant
Is very like a fan!"

The Sixth no sooner had begun
About the beast to grope, *(To feel about with hands)*
Then, seizing on the swinging tail *(7)*
That fell within his scope,
"I see," quoth he, "the Elephant
Is very like a rope!"

And so these men of Indostan
Disputed loud and long, *(8)*
Each in his own opinion
Exceeding stiff and strong,
Though each was partly in the right,
And all were in the wrong! *= Incomplete*

MORAL

So oft in theologic wars,
The disputants, I ween, *(9)* *(to think)*
Rail on in utter ignorance *(to utter complaint)*
Of what each other mean,
And prate about an Elephant
Not one of them has seen!

Prate = talk a lot

Similes = similar but not exact same

★ Could there be more than six people?

★ were they actually blind?

★ I wonder how many things an elephant could be...

★ Was the order important?

wall + spear + tree + fan + snake + rope = elephant?

1. Sample Middle School Annotations Anchor Paper: A/A+

The Blind Men and the Elephant
John Godfrey Saxe

[handwritten: what/where is Indostan?]

It was six men of Indostan *[boxed: Indostan]*
To learning much inclined,
Who went to see the Elephant *[handwritten: why caps?]*
(Though all of them were blind),
That each by observation *[handwritten: word choice?]*
Might satisfy his mind.

[handwritten: 1st]
The First approach'd the Elephant,
And happening to fall
Against his broad and sturdy side,
At once began to bawl:
"God bless me! but the Elephant
Is very like a wall!" *[handwritten: How big is this elephant?]*

[handwritten: 2nd]
The Second, feeling of the tusk,
Cried, -"Ho! what have we here
So very round and smooth and sharp?
To me 'tis mighty clear
This wonder of an Elephant
Is very like a spear!"

[handwritten: 3rd]
The Third approached the animal,
And happening to take
The squirming trunk within his hands,
Thus boldly up and spake: *[boxed: spake:]*
"I see," quoth he, "the Elephant *[boxed: quoth]*
Is very like a snake!"

[handwritten: 4th]
The Fourth reached out his eager hand,
And felt about the knee.
"What most this wondrous beast is like
Is mighty plain," quoth he, *[handwritten: It's not plain!]*
"'Tis clear enough the Elephant
Is very like a tree!"

[handwritten: 5th]
The Fifth, who chanced to touch the ear,
Said: "E'en the blindest man
Can tell what this resembles most;
Deny the fact who can,
This marvel of an Elephant
Is very like a fan!"

The Sixth no sooner had begun *[handwritten: 6th]*
About the beast to grope,
Then, seizing on the swinging tail
That fell within his scope,
"I see," quoth he, "the Elephant
Is very like a rope!"

And so these men of Indostan
Disputed loud and long, *[handwritten: Did they have to dispute?]*
Each in his own opinion
Exceeding stiff and strong,
Though each was partly in the right,
And all were in the wrong! *[handwritten: They all had parts of the whole]*

MORAL

So oft in theologic wars,
The disputants, I ween, *[boxed: ween]*
Rail on in utter ignorance *[boxed: Rail]* *[handwritten: what do these words mean?]*
Of what each other mean,
And prate about an Elephant *[boxed: prate]*
Not one of them has seen!

*[handwritten: 1 stanza + 6 stanzas
+1 stanza + Moral = 9]*

[handwritten: What does the moral mean?]

[handwritten: This seems old]

2. Sample Middle School Annotations Anchor Paper: B/B+

The Blind Men and the Elephant

John Godfrey Saxe — *who was he?*

It was six men of Indostan *where?*
To learning much inclined,
Who went to see the Elephant *why?*
(Though all of them were blind),
That each by observation *why?*
Might satisfy his mind.

The First approach'd the Elephant,
And happening to fall
Against his broad and sturdy side,
At once began to bawl: *?*
"God bless me! but the Elephant
Is very like a wall!"

The Second, feeling of the tusk,
Cried, -"Ho! what have we here
So very round and smooth and sharp?
To me 'tis mighty clear
This wonder of an Elephant
Is very like a spear!"

The Third approached the animal,
And happening to take
The squirming trunk within his hands,
Thus boldly up and spake:
? "I see," quoth he, "the Elephant
Is very like a snake!"

The Fourth reached out his eager hand,
And felt about the knee.
"What most this wondrous beast is like
Is mighty plain," quoth he,
"'Tis clear enough the Elephant
Is very like a tree!"

why? The Fifth, who chanced to touch the ear,
Said: "E'en the blindest man
Can tell what this resembles most;
Deny the fact who can,
This marvel of an Elephant
Is very like a fan!"

The Sixth no sooner had begun
About the beast to grope,
Then, seizing on the swinging tail
That fell within his scope,
"I see," quoth he, "the Elephant
Is very like a rope!"

And so these men of Indostan
Disputed loud and long,
Each in his own opinion
Exceeding stiff and strong,
Though each was partly in the right,
And all were in the wrong! *why didn't they work together?*

MORAL

So oft in theologic wars,
The disputants, I ween, *?*
Rail on in utter ignorance
Of what each other mean,
And prate about an Elephant
Not one of them has seen!

some seem accidental but some on purpose

When was this written?

3. Sample Middle School Annotations Anchor Paper: C/C+

The Blind Men and the Elephant
John Godfrey Saxe

It was six men of Indostan *what?*
To learning much inclined,
Who went to see the Elephant
(Though all of them were blind),
That each by observation
Might satisfy his mind.

The First approach'd the Elephant,
And happening to fall
Against his broad and sturdy side,
At once began to bawl:
LOL "God bless me! but the Elephant
Is very like a wall!"

The Second, feeling of the tusk,
Cried, -"Ho! what have we here
So very round and smooth and sharp?
To me 'tis mighty clear
This wonder of an Elephant
Is very like a spear!"

The Third approached the animal,
And happening to take
The squirming trunk within his hands,
Thus boldly up and spake:
? "I see," quoth he, "the Elephant
Is very like a snake!"

The Fourth reached out his eager hand,
And felt about the knee.
"What most this wondrous beast is like
Is mighty plain," quoth he,
"'Tis clear enough the Elephant
Is very like a tree!"

The Fifth, who chanced to touch the ear,
Said: "E'en the blindest man
Can tell what this resembles most;
Deny the fact who can,
This marvel of an Elephant
Is very like a fan!" *A fan?*

The Sixth no sooner had begun
About the beast to grope,
Then, seizing on the swinging tail
That fell within his scope,
"I see," quoth he, "the Elephant
Is very like a rope!"

And so these men of Indostan
Disputed loud and long,
Each in his own opinion
☆ Exceeding stiff and strong,
Though each was partly in the right,
And all were in the wrong!

MORAL

So oft in theologic wars, *I don't get this*
The disputants, I ween,
Rail on in utter ignorance
Of what each other mean,
? And prate about an Elephant
Not one of them has seen!

Why an elephant?

4. Sample Middle School Annotations Anchor Paper: D/F

Appendix E

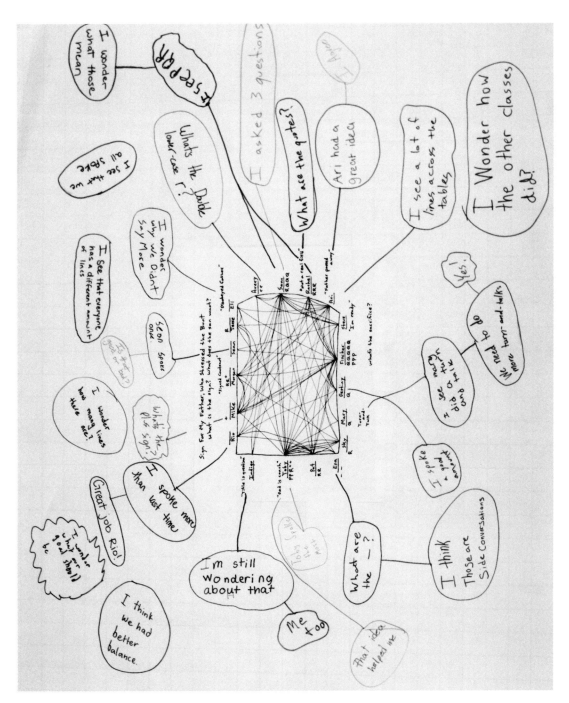

Visual Debrief Map

References and Suggested Readings

Ackerman, Angela, and Becca Puglisi. 2012. *The Emotion Thesaurus: A Writer's Guide to Character Expression.* CyberWitch Press.

Adler, Mortimer J. 1982. *The Paideia Proposal.* New York: MacMillan Publishing Company.

------. 1983a. *How to Speak How to Listen.* New York: Simon & Schuster, Inc.

------. 1983b. *Paideia Problems and Possibilities.* New York: MacMillan Publishing Company.

------. 1984. *The Paideia Program: An Educational Syllabus.* New York: MacMillan Publishing Company.

------. 1992. *The Great Ideas: A Lexicon of Western Thought.* New York: MacMillan Publishing Company.

Adler, Mortimer J., and Charles Van Doran. 1972. *How to Read a Book.* New York: Touchstone.

Alexander, Patricia A., and Lauren M. Singer. Oct. 15, 2017. "A New Study Shows That Students Learn Way More Effectively from Print Textbooks Than Screens." Retrieved March 15, 2018, from *Business Leader.*

Almossawi, Ali. 2013. *An Illustrated Book of Bad Arguments.* New York: The Experiment, LLC.

Arao, Brian, and Kristi Clemens. 2013. "From Safe Spaces to Brave Spaces," in *The Art of Effective Facilitation*, edited by Lisa M. Landreman, pgs. 135-150. Sterling, VA: Stylus Publishing, LLC.

Ball, Wanda H., and Pam Brewer. *Socratic Seminars in the Block.* Larchmont, NY: Eye on Education, Inc.

Bassham, Gregory, William Irwin, Henry Nardone, and James Wallace. 2007. *Critical Thinking: A Student's Introduction.* New York: McGraw-Hill Companies, Inc.

Beers, Kylene, and Robert E. Probst. 2013. *Notice and Note: Strategies for Close Reading.* Portsmouth, NH: Heinemann.

------. 2015. *Reading Nonfiction: Notice & Note Stances, Signposts, and Strategies.* Portsmouth, NH: Heinemann.

------. 2017. *Disrupting Thinking: Why How We Read Matters.* New York: Scholastic Teaching Resources.

Bloom, Benjamin S. 1956. *Taxonomy of Educational Objectives.* New York: David McKay.

De Bono, Edward. 1970. *Lateral Thinking: Creativity Step by Step.* New York: Harper & Row.

------. 1985. *Six Thinking Hats.* New York: Little, Brown and Company.

Brown, Brené. 2017. *Braving the Wilderness: The Quest for True Belonging and the Courage to Stand Alone.* New York: Random House.

Brown, Montague. *The One-Minute Philosopher.* Manchester, NH: Sophia Institute Press.

Cain, Susan. 2012. *Quiet: The Power of Introverts in a World That Can't Stop Talking.* New York: Crown Publishers.

Carter, Rita. 2002. *Exploring Consciousness.* Berkeley and Los Angeles: University of California Press.

Copeland, Matt. 2005. *Socratic Circles: Fostering Critical and Creative Thinking in Middle and High School.* Portland, ME: Stenhouse Publishers.

Copland, Aaron. 1939. *What to Listen For in Music.* New York: Penguin Putnam, Inc.

Covey, Stephen R. 1989. *The Seven Habits of Highly Effective People.* New York: Simon & Schuster, Inc.

Coyle, Daniel. 2018. *The Culture Code: The Secrets of Highly Successful Groups.* New York: Bantam Books.

Daniels, Harvey. 1994. *Literature Circles: Voice and Choice in the Student-Centered Classroom.* York, ME: Stenhouse Publishers.

Droit, Roger-Pol. 2001. *Astonish Yourself: 101 Experiments in the Philosophy of Everyday Life* (trans. Stephen Romer). New York: Penguin Group.

Egolf, Donald B. 2001. *Forming, Storming, Norming, Performing: Successful Communications in Groups and Teams.* Lincoln, NE: Writers Club Press.

Engel, Susan. "The Case for Curiosity." Retrieved July 1, 2018, from ASCD.

Garlikov, Rick. "Teaching Effectively: Helping Students Absorb and Assimilate Material." Retrieved November 17, 2014, from *Garlikov.com*.

------. "The Socratic Method: Teaching by Asking Instead of by Telling." Retrieved January 5, 2018, from *Garlikov.com*.

Goldsmith, William. 2013. "Enhancing Classroom Conversation for All Students." *Phi Delta Kappa.* 94(7), Retrieved July 19, 2015 from EBSCO.

Greenberg, Jan. (ed). 2001. *Heart to Heart: New Poems Inspired by Twentieth-Century American Art.* New York: Harry N. Abrams, Inc.

Gunderson, Lee. 1995. *The Monday Morning Guide to Comprehension.* Toronto, Ontario: Pippin Publishing.

Hale, Michael S. and Elizabeth A. City. 2006. *Leading Student-Centered Discussions.* Thousand Oaks, CA: Corwin Press.

Himmele, Pérsida, and William Himmele. *Total Participation Techniques: Making Every Student an Active Learner.* Alexandria, VA: Association for Supervision and Curriculum Development.

Hintz, Allison, and Anthony T. Smith. 2013. "Mathematizing Read-Alouds in Three Easy Steps." *The Reading Teacher*, 67(2), pgs. 103-108. Retrieved July 15, 2015, from EBSCO.

Johnson, Erik. 2011. "Developing Listening Skills through Peer Interaction. *Music Educators Journal*, 98(2). Retrieved June 23, 2015, from EBSCO.

Koellner-Clark, Karen, L. Lynn Stallings, and Sue A. Hoover. 2002. *Socratic Seminars for Mathematics.* The National Council of Teachers of Mathematics.

Leonard, Herman B. 1991. "With Open Ears: Listening and the Art of Discussion Leading." In C. R. Christensen, D. A. Garvin & A. Sweet (eds.).

Education for Judgment: The Artistry of Discussion Leadership (pp. 137-151). Boston, MA: Harvard Business School Press.

Lewin, Larry. "Teaching Critical Reading with Questioning Strategies." Retrieved January 29, 2018, from ASCD.

Li, Dennis. December 11, 2017. "Why Student Data Should Be Students' Data." Retrieved February 2, 2018, from Edutopia.

Mack, Arien, and Irvin Rock. 1998. *Inattentional Blindness.* Cambridge, MA: A Bradford Book (M.I.T. Press).

MacKenzie, Brooke. February 12, 2018. "One Quick Thing." Retrieved March 2, 2018, from Edutopia.

Minsky, Marvin. 1988. *The Society of Mind.* New York: Simon & Shuster.

Moorman, Chick, and Nancy Weber. 1989. *Teacher Talk: What It Really Means.* Merrill, MI: Institute for Personal Power.

Morgan, Norah, and Juliana Saxton. 2006. *Asking Better Questions.* Markham, Ontario: Pembroke Publishers.

Murchie, Guy. 1999. *The Seven Mysteries of Life: An Exploration of Science and Philosophy.* Boston and New York: A Mariner Book, Houghton Mifflin Company.

Murphy, Kevin J. 1987. *Effective Listening: Hearing What People Say and Making It Work for You.* New York: Bantam Books, Inc.

Newkirk, Thomas. 2017. *Embarrassment and the Emotional Underlife of Learning.* Portsmouth, NH: Heinemann.

Nichols, Maria. 2006. *Comprehension through Conversation: The Power of Purposeful Talk in the Reading Workshop.* Portsmouth, NH: Heinemann.

Opitz, Michael F., and Matthew D. Zbaracki. 2004. *Listen Hear! 25 Effective Listening Comprehension Strategies.* Portsmouth, NH: Heinemann.

Phillips, Christopher. 2001. *Socrates Café: A Fresh Taste of Philosophy.* New York: W. W. Norton & Company, Inc.

Postman, Neil and Charles Weingartner. 1969. *Teaching as a Subversive Activity.* New York: Deli Publishing.

Rael, Joseph E. and Lindsay Sutton. 1993. *Tracks of Dancing Light: A Native American Approach to Understanding Your Name.* Rockport, MA: Element, Inc.

Rheingold, Howard. 2000. *They Have a Word for It: Lighthearted Lexicon of Untranslatable Words & Phrases.* Louisville, KY: Sarabande Books.

Richards, Ivor A. 1942. *How to Read a Page.* New York: W. W. Norton and Company.

Robinson, Ken. 2001. *Out of Our Minds: Learning to Be Creative.* Chichester, England: Capstone Publishing, Ltd.

Russell, David H. and Elizabeth F. Russell. 1959. *Listening Aides through the Grades.* New York: Teachers College Press, Columbia University.

Schuster, Lainie, and Nancy C. Anderson. 2005. *Good Questions for Math Teaching: Why Ask Them and What to Ask.* Sausalito, CA: Math Solutions Publications.

Shaunessy, Elizabeth. 2005. *Questioning Strategies for Teaching the Gifted.* Waco, TX: Prufrock Press, Inc.

Stead, Tony. 2014. "Nurturing the Inquiring Mind through the Nonfiction Read-Aloud." *The Reading Teacher*, 67(7), pgs. 488-495. Retrieved July 15, 2015, from EBSCO.

Strauss, Valerie. December 20, 2017. "The Surprising Thing Google Learned about Its Employees—and What It Means for Today's Students." *The Washington Post.* Retrieved January 5, 2018.

Strong, Michael. 1997. *The Habit of Thought: From Socratic Seminars to Socratic Practice.* Chapel Hill, NC: New View Publications.

Tahan, Malba. 2015. *The Man Who Counted: A Collection of Mathematical Adventures.* New York: W. W. Norton & Company.

Tredway, Lynda. 1995. "Socratic Seminars: Engaging Students in Intellectual Discourse." *Educational Leadership*, 53(1). Retrieved October 23, 2007, from EBSCO online.

Truesdale, Susanne P. March 6, 2013. "Whole-Body Listening Updated." Retrieved from *AdvanceWeb.com.*

Tuckman, Bruce. 1965. "Developmental Sequences in Small Groups." *Psychological Bulletin.* 63, 384-399.

Van Allsburg, Chris. 2011. *The Chronicles of Harris Burdick.* New York: Houghton Mifflin Books for Children.

Wagner, Tony. 2008. *The Global Achievement Gap: Why Even Our Best Schools Don't Teach the New Survival Skills Our Children Need—and What We Can Do About It.* New York: Basic Books.

Watson, Kittie W. and Larry L. Barker. 2014. *Listen Up Second Edition.* Trafford Publishing.

Wiggins, Alexis. 2017. *The Best Class You Never Taught: How Spider Web Discussion Can Turn Students into Learning Leaders.* Alexandria, VA: Association for Supervision and Curriculum Development.

Wiggins, Grant and Jay McTighe. 2005. *Understanding by Design.* Alexandria, VA: Association for Supervision and Curriculum Development.

Wilberding, Erik. 2014. *Teach Like Socrates: Guiding Socratic Dialogues & Discussions in the Classroom.* Waco, TX: Prufrock Press, Inc.

Wolvin, Andrew, and Carolyn G. Coakley. 1996. *Listening* (4th ed). Boston, MA: McGraw-Hill Companies, Inc.

Wong, Harry K. and Rosemary Wong. 1998. *The First Days of School: How to Be an Effective Teacher.* Mountain View, CA: Harry K. Wong Publications. Inc.

Young, Jon, Ellen Haas and Evan McGown. 2008. *Coyote's Guide to Connecting with Nature for Kids of All Ages and Their Mentors.* Shelton, WA: OWLink Media.

Yuhas, Daisy. June 27, 2018. "Piqued: The Case for Curiosity." Retrieved from *HechingerReport.com*

Zeiderman, Howard. 1989. *A Guide for Leading Discussions Using Touchstones,* Vol. I. Annapolis, MD: Touchstones.

Zemelman, Steven, Harvey Daniels and Arthur Hyde. 2012. *Best Practice, Fourth Edition: Bringing Standards to Life in America's Classrooms.* Portsmouth, NH: Heinemann.

Zwiers, Jeff, and Marie Crawford. 2011. *Academic Conversations: Classroom Talk that Fosters Critical Thinking and Content Understandings.* Portland, ME: Stenhouse Publishers.

Zwiers, Jeff, and Sara Hamerla. 2018. *The K-3 Guide to Academic Conversations.* Thousand Oaks, CA: Corwin Press.

Acknowledgments

There are a great many people to thank in a project of this size and it would be impossible to list everyone who had an influence on this book. I first remember having seminar-like discussions back in tenth grade with our English teacher Nan Washburn. I still have fond memories of one discussion in particular about free will versus determinism, and sometimes I wonder how those intellectual discussions influenced this path of my life.

As a professional, it was certainly Michael Strong's book *The Habit of Thought* that helped me solidify my philosophy about teaching and learning. But ideas do not make practice. Without the wonderful Louise Stilphen and the magic and joy of Sparhawk School, I would never have had a chance to take risks and put my ideas into practice. Socratic Seminar evolved into a class of its own, allowing me to use a tremendous variety of texts across many grade levels. Many thanks are due to nearly everyone there, but specific thanks (in no particular order) go to Neil Stilphen, Morgan Smyrl, Susan Adams, Catherine Kulik, Danielle Shylit, Maryclaire Paullis, Eric Getz, Marion Cipolle, Cheryl Fuller, Laura Hogan, Dave Robinson, Kaitlyn MacDonald, and the many amazing students who *Socraticized* texts with me.

The Power of the Socratic Classroom started coming together through the Calderwood Teachers As Writers program through the Boston Athenaeum. A lot has changed from those initial drafts, but the process finally got started after years of dreaming. Many thanks go to Buck Harris who truly got interested in Socratic practice.

There were many people who helped me hone my craft as a teacher and facilitator, but special thanks to Don Sugg, Mike Wolfkiel, Denise Ahlquist, Terry Roberts, Oscar Graybill, Danny Combs, Scott McFarland, and the many authors who have written about inquiry and thinking. This includes the National Paideia Center, the Touchstones Discussion Project, and the Great Books Foundation.

Finally, with Author U and the guidance of The Book Shepherd, Judith Briles, the team was assembled to produce what you have in your hands. There are many people to thank for various parts of the book, including

Dave Nelson and Equity Maps, Rachel Perry, Eric Peterson, Chris Lazartic, John Maling, Peggie Ireland, Octavia Betz, and Barb Wilson. Special thanks are due to Nick Zelinger at NZ Graphics who put up with all of the changes and adjustments. I must also give special thanks to all of the amazing people at Aspen Academy who helped in one form or another.

About the Author

Charles Fischer has taught in public, charter and private schools in a variety of settings, from rural Maine to inner-city Atlanta to suburban Denver. For more than 20 years, he has worked with a wide range of students from Kindergarten to AP English and has been nominated for a Teacher of the Year award four times. He has his Master's degree in Teaching & Learning from the University of Southern Maine, and received his B.A. in English Literature and Creative Writing from Binghamton University.

Charles writes fiction and nonfiction, with forays into poetry. His first novel, *Beyond Infinity,* won a 2014 Independent Publisher Book Award bronze medal (YA fiction).

Follow his blog on his website: CharlesAmesFischer.com

How to Work with Me

As a consultant and speaker, Charles Fischer offers numerous *writing* and *thinking* classes, professional development workshops, Skype or Zoom meetings, and more. His primary expertise is the Socratic Seminar. In addition, he teaches and coaches in critical and creative thinking, active listening, close reading, asking better questions, and many more. Under his guidance, teachers help students achieve more than they ever thought possible. In turn, students read, write, and think more than they ever thought possible.

As an author and speaker, Charles is available for school visits, connecting on Skype or Zoom, and book signings.

CharlesAmesFischer.com
Phone: 303-521-6694
Email: Charles@CharlesAmesFischer.com
Facebook: CharlesFischerAuthor
Connect with me on LinkedIn
Twitter: @aragornfischer

Index